Public Involvement and Community Engagement in Applied Health and Social Care Research

Public Involvement and Community Engagement in Applied Health and Social Care Research: Critical Perspectives and Innovative Practice

EDITED BY

WILLIAM MCGOVERN
Northumbria University, UK

HAYLEY ALDERSON
Newcastle University, UK

BETHANY KATE BAREHAM
Newcastle University, UK

and

MONIQUE LHUSSIER
Northumbria University, UK

emerald
PUBLISHING

United Kingdom – North America – Japan – India – Malaysia – China

Emerald Publishing Limited
Emerald Publishing, Floor 5, Northspring, 21-23 Wellington Street, Leeds LS1 4DL.

First edition 2026

Reprints and permissions service
Contact: www.copyright.com

British Library Cataloguing in Publication Data
A catalogue record for this book is available from the British Library

ISBN: 978-1-83608-681-9 (Print)
ISBN: 978-1-83608-678-9 (Online)
ISBN: 978-1-83608-680-2 (Epub)

This book is dedicated to my partner

Ruth McGovern
And very dear friends
Craig Mann and Patrick Owens
With love and appreciation
William McGovern

Contents

About the Editors

William McGovern is the Faculty Academic Lead for Public Involvement and Engagement in the School of Communities and Engagement at Northumbria University. He is also The Public and Patient Engagement and Involvement co-lead for NIHR, IDEAS-NET: Interdisciplinary Evaluation of Complex Interventions in Health and Social Care. He has edited collections of work on Stigma, Drugs and Identity, Safeguarding Children in Schools, Teaching Sensitive Subjects, and an Anthology of Recovery Poetry.

Hayley Alderson is an NIHR Advanced Fellow/Senior Research Associate at Newcastle University. She has a practice background in substance misuse. To date, her research has been conducted in or has closely aligned with social care settings and seeks to benefit highly vulnerable populations such as families on the edge of care, children in care/care leavers, individuals experiencing domestic violence and abuse, and substance-misusing parents and their children. Her research has a strong focus on translational research, which is driven by a commitment to improving outcomes for vulnerable children and families.

Bethany Kate Bareham, Senior Research Associate at Newcastle University, has a background in health psychology and public health. Her research aims to support vulnerable populations, including older adults and those with alcohol and mental health problems. Patient involvement is central to her approach. She received national recognition for collaborative research.

Monique Lhussier is Professor in Public Health and Well-being at Northumbria University and the Director of the Centre for Health and Social Equity. She is driven by understanding both the experiences of marginalisation and the processes and structures that enable them so that they can be challenged.

About the Contributors

Emma A. Adams is a National Institute for Health and Care Research (NIHR) Doctoral Fellow based at Newcastle University. Her research is based in public health and inequalities with a focus on homelessness, mental health, and substance use, and uses participatory and co-production approaches.

Mark Adley is a Postgraduate Researcher at Newcastle University, funded through the NIHR ARC NENC as part of their research theme on *Inequalities and marginalised communities*. He has a professional background within criminal justice, substance use, and homelessness settings, and his PhD explored multiple exclusions and disadvantages within LGBTQ+ populations in the North East of England.

P. Arun Kumar (he/him) is the Programme Manager for the Enhanced HIV Programme at the National Centre for Infectious Diseases in Singapore. He has previously worked with the National HIV Programme. He works collaboratively with multidisciplinary teams on theoretically informed and community-engaged HIV and sexual health research in Singapore.

Sharon Barnes has been volunteering at The Centre in Maryport, Cumbria for over 15 years and is the Community Engagement Officer. A highly regarded figure in the local community, she has inspired loyalty from a group of dedicated volunteers and is responsible for the day-to-day running of The Centre.

Elaine Bidmead is a Senior Research Fellow for The NIHR Applied Research Collaboration, North East North Cumbria, at the University of Cumbria, where she researches health inequalities with a focus on coastal and rural communities. She is committed to engaging and involving communities and voluntary organisations as partners in research.

David Black is a Patient and Public Involvement Partner and Appointed Hospital Governor. He is interested in how the insights of caregivers, patients, and the public are used in co-production to inform research and positively impact quality improvement programmes in healthcare settings. His research activities include participation, engagement, and involvement across a wide range of health, social care, and social welfare themes. Supporting multiple research studies as a lay representative and co-applicant, he is a co-author of several papers and writes and speaks about patient and public involvement in research.

Greta Brunskill is a Public Partnerships Manager with the NIHR HealthTech Research Centre in Diagnostic and Technology Evaluation based at Newcastle University. She brings experience from NHS and research roles, and more recently a new role with Voluntary Organisations Network North East (VONNE) to support VCSE and research partnerships. She is passionate about meaningful and inclusive involvement in health research.

Steph Capewell is the Founder and Chief Executive of Love, Amelia, a North East charity supporting children and families experiencing poverty and hardship. A qualified social worker, she is dedicated to reducing child poverty through community collaboration, research, advocacy, and innovative solutions that address the root causes of disadvantage.

Randolph C. H. Chan (he/him) is an Associate Professor in the Department of Social Work at the Chinese University of Hong Kong. His research centres on the intersections of minority stress, resilience, and mental health among LGBTQ+ individuals and other socially marginalised populations.

Christina Cooper is an Assistant Professor in community well-being at Northumbria University. Co-leading the See Me North Project, aiming to mobilise community assets to improve outcomes for people experiencing homelessness, her interests lie in marginalisation, intersectional understandings of health, inequality, and social justice, and place-based action driven by participatory approaches.

Matthew Cooper is a Researcher at Newcastle University and Patient Safety Research Collaborative. His work is centred around health psychology and behaviour change, and his research looks at how healthcare practice can be better developed to provide holistic (physical, mental, and social healthcare). He has worked with carers across a range of topics and leads a public involvement group in the development of research questions and priorities for practice. His research is funded by the NIHR Patient Safety Research Collaborative within the Safer Integrated Health & Social Care Environments theme.

Kevin Dong (he/him) is a Health Promotion Officer at Western Sydney Local Health District. His role involves developing, implementing, and evaluating public health projects that raise awareness about blood-borne viruses and sexual health. He is also a dedicated advocate in the community sector, collaborating with various cultural, LGBTIQ+, and advocacy groups.

Charmaine Agius Ferrante, PhD, Assistant Lecturer in Education, Children and Young People, Northumbria University. She is currently the Director of Education in the Department of Social Work, Education and Community Well-being. She is a Senior Teaching Fellow at HEA and the Programme Lead for MA & BA Childhood and Early Years Studies.

Melissa Fothergill is an Assistant Professor in the Department of Psychology at Northumbria University and a Health and Care Professions Council Registered Sport and Exercise Psychologist. She is interested in understanding and breaking down barriers to participation in sports and physical activity across the lifespan.

Seana Friel is Research Fellow at the Tilda Goldberg Centre for Social Work and Social Care, University of Bedfordshire. Seana has made significant contributions to large-scale leaving care studies and was a peer researcher on a project exploring outcomes for Care Leavers with Mental Health and/or Intellectual disabilities.

Pamela Louise Graham is an Assistant Professor in Community Well-being at Northumbria University. She is the Public Involvement and Engagement Lead for Fuse: The Centre for Translational Research in Public Health. She is interested in issues affecting the health and well-being of children, young people and families in educational and community settings.

Kim Hall is an Assistant Professor in the Department of Social Work, Education and Community Well-being at Northumbria University. Her research is grounded in creative co-production methodologies. Kim works with community groups, including kinship care groups, to understand the social inequities that seek to marginalise and stigmatise certain life experiences.

CJ Hamilton is a first-year MPhil Social Intervention and Policy student at the University of Oxford and a Care-experienced Research Assistant at the Tilda Goldberg Centre for Social Work and Social Care, University of Bedfordshire. CJ has professional experience supporting childhood sexual violence and children's social care research, advocacy, and consultancy.

Claire Hart is an Occupational therapist and counsellor with experience in phenomenological research with refugees in the UK. Her research and scholarship are designed to foreground the voices of marginalised populations and explore socio-political influences on occupational opportunities.

Lai Peng Ho is a Senior Principal Medical Social Worker at the National Centre for Infectious Diseases Singapore. She is passionate about advocating for people living with HIV. Her research focusses on psychosocial concerns and well-being of people with HIV.

Emma-Joy Holland is a Research Associate. She is interested in research around health and inequalities, with projects focussed on alcohol and substance use and homelessness. Prior to working at Newcastle University, she worked within the Stroke Research Team at the University of Central Lancashire, where her role involved organising and facilitating Patient and Public Involvement groups relating to this research.

Robin Hyde is an Assistant Professor in Children, Young People's Nursing at Northumbria University. An experienced registered children's nurse and senior academic specialising in advanced and paediatric advanced practice education. His research interests include realist approaches, advanced practice, and the health and well-being of children and young people.

Muhamad Alif Bin Ibrahim (he/him) is a social scientist who completed his PhD in Society & Culture at James Cook University, Singapore. Drawing on psychological and sociological approaches, his research involves LGBTQ+ relationships and families, qualitative research methodologies, coping and resilience, and critical approaches to health and illness.

Katherine Jackson is a Senior Research Associate. She is interested in applying feminist and sociological theories of care to developing interventions that support people struggling with problematic alcohol use. She is also interested in research ethics in practice and improving institutional structures that support the well-being of researchers.

Michael Johansen is an HDRC Research Lead and Research Associate. His background was in education, and he is now conducting research in Public Health. His research implements mixed methodologies, and he has a strong focus on addressing Multiple Complex Needs and their impact on health inequalities.

Thisanut Kaewnukul (he/him) is a Health Promotion Officer at ACON in Sydney, Australia. He specialises in HIV and sexual health initiatives, which include community outreach, workshops, and programme evaluation. He has successfully managed social marketing campaigns, developed creative assets, and analysed digital campaign performance in Thailand and the Asia-Pacific region. He is passionate about fostering partnerships and supporting research to drive impactful, community-focussed outcomes.

Donna Kay is a mother from the North East of England. She is an activist and advocate for the rights of people who use or have used drugs. As 'Women's Lead' at Recovering Justice, she has focussed much of her activism and advocacy on supporting mothers, particularly those who have experience of children's social care involvement and child removal. She is passionate about reducing the stigmatisation of people who use drugs and improving access to health and social care and support.

Linzi Ladlow is a Research Fellow in Family Research at the Centre for Innovation in Fatherhood Research at the University of Lincoln. She uses creative and participatory methods to research with children, young people, and families. She has expertise in young parenthood.

Lydia Lochhead has an extensive professional background and experience working with people and communities who use drugs in criminal justice and drug treatment settings. She is currently working as a Senior Research Assistant for Northumbria University on projects exploring mental well-being, substance use, exploitation, domestic violence, and stigma.

Amy Lynch is Assistant Professor at the West Midlands Applied Research Collaboration at Warwick Business School, University of Warwick. She has experience in developing successful academic research–practice partnerships. Her interests include developing an understanding of leadership and innovation through creative and participatory approaches, including peer research.

Ruth McGovern is a Professor of Public Health and Social Care and NIHR Population Health Career Science Fellow at Population Health Sciences Institute, Newcastle University. Her research has a strong interdisciplinary focus, aiming to promote social justice by improving health and social care for disadvantaged children and families.

Dave McPartlan, is an Honorary Researcher at University of Cumbria. After 35 years of teaching, he undertook his PhD, which focussed on investigating the efficacy of a whole-school mental health strategy through coproduction with young people in school. In his current role, he is further developing this research, focussing on his innovative methodological approach.

Fayrouz Al Haj Moussa is a PhD researcher in Social Work and Community Wellbeing at Northumbria University. She holds a Bachelor's degree in Pharmacy and a Master's degree in Public Health (Nutrition). Building on her interdisciplinary expertise and driven by a strong commitment to address health inequalities among marginalised populations, she is currently conducting research focused on community services that promote the mental health of refugees and asylum seekers.

Cassey Muir is a Research Associate at the Population Health Sciences Institute, Newcastle University and the Public Involvement and Engagement Lead Researcher within the NIHR Children and Families Policy Research Unit, University College London. Her research aims to improve both the health and social needs of vulnerable children and families. She is interested in co-production and intervention development linked to adverse childhood experiences, mental health, resilience, and stigma. She has won awards in public involvement and engagement for her research with children and young people from Fuse, the Centre for Translational Research in Public Health and NIHR School for Public Health Research.

Olivia Mullaney is an HDRC Research Lead and Research Associate. She has an interdisciplinary background in linguistics, neuroscience, and psychology. Her research focusses on addressing health inequalities in North East England through collaborative interventions. She works extensively with marginalised communities, specialising in supporting individuals with specific learning difficulties to promote inclusive health and educational outcomes.

Emily R. Munro is Professor of Social Work Research and Director of the Tilda Goldberg Centre for Social Work and Social Care, University of Bedfordshire. Munro has undertaken an extensive body of research on leaving care, including work that has advanced the use of participatory research methods across the research cycle.

Loc Nguyen (she/they) specialises in the public health sector, focussing on LGBTQ+ health, multicultural health, HIV, and sexual health. Loc has extensive experience in designing and implementing health programmes, services, research, and policies that address stigma and discrimination, as well as their impacts on health outcomes.

Amy O'Donnell is Professor of Applied Health and Social Care Research. She leads a research programme focussed on optimising global health and social care systems to better support people with multiple long-term conditions. She has a particular interest in how theories drawn from implementation and complexity science thinking can inform system change.

Sujith Kumar Prankumar (he/him) is a Senior Research Associate at the Kirby Institute, UNSW Sydney, and is currently based at the Nottingham Law School, Nottingham Trent University. Informed by an interdisciplinary background in sociology, philosophy, law, and religion, his works closely with marginalised communities in Australia, Papua New Guinea, and Singapore on community-engaged research projects focussed on health and well-being.

Sheena E. Ramsay is Professor of Public Health & Epidemiology, Director of Fuse, the Centre for Translational Research in Public Health, and an honorary Consultant in Public Health. Her research focusses on addressing socioeconomic determinants of ill health to improve health and social care for the most disadvantaged populations.

Charlotte Lucy Richardson is a Senior Lecturer at Newcastle University and a pharmacist. As part of her research, she has worked with a range of caregivers and has an interest in understanding how to better support carer health and well-being. She is partly funded by the NIHR ARC NENC to research this area as a Social Research Fellow, and she also works as part of the NIHR Patient Safety Research Collaborative within the safer management of polypharmacy in multiple long-term conditions and Safer integrated health and social care environments themes.

Ian Robson is an innovator in collaborative enquiry and social design, fostering knowledge, and practice change that focusses on marginalised groups. He has recently received the Louise Emanuel Award for his pioneering work to improve the mental health of babies in the UK. He specialises in creating inclusive spaces where research, philosophy, art, and lived experience converge to address complex social issues.

Zeb Sattar is an Assistant Professor in Health Policy. She has an interdisciplinary research background in health and social care, which has enabled her to pursue research on ethnicities and health. More recently, her work focusses on understanding and improving access to health services, as well as representing diverse population groups.

Emma Senior is Education Lead of the Northern Hub for Veterans and Military Families Research at Northumbria University, specialising in meeting military-connected community needs through military family research. She is also an Assistant Professor in Nursing (Adult) and a Specialist Community Public Health Nurse, leading curriculum development and workforce development initiatives and holds expertise in narrative methodologies and co-production.

Felicity Shenton is the PICE Manager for the NIHR Applied Research Collaboration NENC. Her background is in children's human rights, participatory research, peer research, co-production, and service user involvement in education, research and service improvement. Felicity has a long-standing commitment to promoting the voices of those most excluded and alienated.

Claire Smiles is a Research Associate at the Population Health Sciences Institute, Newcastle University. Her research explores the unique challenges women and children from marginalised backgrounds experience. She works collaboratively with lived experience communities, practitioners and stakeholders to co-produce meaningful research that is grounded in real-world experiences.

James Stack, PhD, Lecturer on the Childhood and Early Years Programme at Northumbria University. He is a Teaching Fellow of the Higher Education Academy (FHEA). His background is in developmental psychology, and he is interested in how infants and young children make sense of their social worlds.

Anna Tarrant is a Professor of Sociology at the University of Lincoln in the UK. She is the Director of the Centre for Innovation in Fatherhood and Family Research and a UK Research & Innovation Future Leaders Fellowship called 'Following Young Fathers Further'. She has widely published on marginalised fatherhoods and has advanced innovative qualitative methodologies, including qualitative secondary analysis and longitudinal co-creation.

Mark Telford is an Assistant Professor in Children, Young People's Nursing and a Specialist in Community Public Health Nursing at Northumbria University. With over 30 years of experience, he has held various clinical and academic roles. His research interests include interprofessional working, leadership, digitalisation, safeguarding children, and public health.

Kira Terry is a Public Contributor. She has been involved and engaged with the research led by Dr Cassey Muir as a young advisor. She presented at the Young Carers International Conference and online events held by the NIHR School for Public Health Research. She was involved in the co-production of a social and emotional well-being storybook called *Twinkle, Twinkle Arti* for children who experience parental alcohol and/or drug use. She has also co-written blog posts on her involvement in research. She is passionate about making sure the voices of public contributors, especially children and young people, are listened to and acted upon.

Elizabeth Titchener is a Research Assistant, and she is interested in health psychology and stigma within healthcare settings. She is also interested in using co-production and community engagement to explore multiple complex needs.

Paul Watson is the Assistant Director of the Northern Hub for Veterans and Military Families Research at Northumbria University, specialising in military-connected children and young people. He is also an Assistant Professor in Nursing (Children and Young People) and Specialist in Community Public Health Nursing and leads multiple research projects with expertise in narrative methodologies and co-production.

Laura Way is a Senior Lecturer in Sociology at the University of Roehampton (UK). Her research interests lie in ageing and gender, marginalised identities, and subcultures. An experienced qualitative researcher, she is especially keen on advancing creative and participatory approaches to research. Her recent publications include a co-edited collection with Matt Grimes titled *Punk, Ageing, and Time* (Palgrave Macmillan, 2024).

Kate Whitmarsh works at The Centre, which is a West Cumbrian charity providing social and creative opportunities for people to connect and grow. From finance to fundraising, business planning to project management, she has been shaping The Centre's journey as the Development Officer. Committed to empowering communities, she is a keen advocate for supporting everyone to have a voice.

Horas T. H. Wong (he/him) is a Senior Lecturer at the University of Sydney whose research explores the intersections of sexuality, migration, culture, and health. With a background in social sciences, anthropology, public health, and nursing, he has worked collaboratively with marginalised communities as a peer, nurse, and researcher in Hong Kong and Australia.

Foreword

The introduction to the collection begins with the bold statement, and all that follows is for YOU (the reader). The collection is a thoughtfully curated exploration of the evolving landscape of Public Involvement and Community Engagement (PICE) in research but in a 'brave' space. Over the past few decades, PICE has become a central requirement in research practice, especially in health and social care, which I feel reflects a growing recognition of the value of involving the public and diverse communities in the co-production of research. YOU should engage with this collection if you wish to be more informed and if you wish to ensure your works potential to be more inclusive, equitable, and impactful.

The collection is structured around four broad but connected themes, each addressing critical and innovative aspects of PICE work:

1. **International, Regional, and Local Perspectives of PICE Work**: This section opens with contributions that highlight the complexities of PICE in multicultural and regional contexts. For example, Sujith Kumar Prankumar et al. discuss LGBTQ+ health research across Australia, Singapore, and Hong Kong, emphasising the importance of equitable and culturally safe research partnerships. Elaine Bidmead et al. then explore regional co-production in North East and North Cumbria, focussing on 'fairness' and meaningful engagement. The section concludes with a chapter on transforming public engagement in local authority research, and you should engage with this to know more about the importance of trust and community-centred approaches.
2. **Creativity and Innovation, Perspectives and Opportunities in PICE Work**: This section delves into innovative approaches to PICE, challenging misconceptions about creativity and offering practical examples of how creative methods can enhance research. Ian Robson's chapter, for instance, redefines creativity in PICE work, while Charmaine Agius Ferrante and James Stack describe their use of the World Café approach to engage parents in understanding child transitions. Other chapters explore co-production with young researchers, community asset mapping, and anti-stigma approaches, showcasing how innovative methods can foster inclusion and collaboration.
3. **PICE Work in Marginalised Communities**: This section focusses on the challenges and opportunities of engaging marginalised communities in research. Contributions include discussions on trauma-informed research with people experiencing homelessness, co-production with individuals who have experienced homelessness, and the reproductive health needs of women who use

drugs. Mark Adley's chapter offers a reflective account of navigating multiple marginalisations in queer research, while Katherine Jackson et al. explore the ethics of care in PICE work with individuals experiencing substance use issues. The section concludes with a chapter on co-production in refugee research, highlighting the importance of addressing power dynamics.

4. **Parents–Carers–Adolescents and Children's Perspectives of PICE Work:** The final section of the collection focusses on the involvement of young people, parents, and carers in research. Contributions include discussions on involving young people who experience parental substance use, avoiding research fatigue among carers, and engaging girls in alternative education settings. The Young Dads Collective: Sustaining PICE Through a Qualitative Longitudinal Participatory Research Programme chapter highlights the potential of PICE to empower young fathers, while the final chapter by Emily R. Munro et al. emphasises the importance of relational safety and capacity building in co-producing research with care experienced young adults.

Navigating the Collection

The collection is accessible and easy to navigate, and each chapter offers a complete exploration of a specific aspect of PICE work. However, the collection reveals common concerns and shared insights, particularly around methodology, positionality, and the practical challenges of implementing PICE in diverse contexts. The contributors are engaging, and each provides reflective accounts of their experiences, offering readers the opportunity to consider how these insights might inform their own research practices.

Conclusion

This collection is not prescriptive; it does not tell readers what to do. Instead, it invites reflection and dialogue, encouraging researchers, practitioners, and communities to think critically about their approaches to PICE. By sharing lived experiences and practical examples, the collection creates a 'brave space' for learning and growth, ultimately aiming to enhance the quality and impact of health and social care research through meaningful Public Involvement and Community Engagement.

The authors encourage you to continue engaging with the chapters, reflecting on their implications, and considering how they might inform your own work. The journey through this collection is one of discovery, challenge, and inspiration, offering valuable insights for anyone committed to advancing PICE in research.

So, I go right back to the start of the editorial teams' question in the introduction: Has this made YOU (the reader) think a little deeper and differently?

Claire Ashmore
Programme Manager; Three NIHR Research Schools'
Mental Health Programme

Acknowledgements

We would like to acknowledge the individuals, groups, organisations, activists, and community members who participated or contributed to the chapters: without your input, we would have found it difficult to achieve the depth of detail and insight that we did.

We would also like to thank our colleagues who saw what we were trying to achieve, encouraged us, and supported us: Eileen Kaner, Oonagh McGee, Rachael Hope, Katy Mayer, and Claire Ashmore.

Finally, we would like to acknowledge that this work has been supported financially to be open access by the National Institute for Health and Care Research (NIHR) Applied Research Collaboration (ARC) North East and North Cumbria (NENC), Centre For Health and Social Equity (CHASE) Northumbria University and Newcastle City Council. The views expressed are those of the authors and not necessarily those of the funding authorities.

Introduction to PICE Work and Themes Within the Collection

William McGovern[a], Hayley Alderson[b],
Bethany Kate Bareham[b] and Monique Lhussier[a]

[a]*School of Communities and Education, Northumbria University, UK*
[b]*Institute of Population Health Sciences; Faculty of Medical Sciences,*
Newcastle University, UK

Introduction

This collection, 'Public Involvement and Community Engagement in Applied Health and Social Care Research: Critical Perspectives and Innovative Practice', has been conceptualised and designed to make YOU (the reader) think a little deeper and differently about key concerns associated with the development and delivery of Public Involvement and Community Engagement (PICE) Work. Over the last two decades, PICE work has progressed from being an idea worthy of consideration to a central feature and requirement of research practice. As such, working together with members of the public and different communities based on location, identity, experience, and interest is now recognised as vital to the co-production of high-quality research, research design, and knowledge exchange. PICE in research is now an assessed criteria within every UK, European and Internationally based funding institution and authority. Interest in this area is partly driven by the identification that PICE work is associated with better engagement of the community in processes, relationships, decision-making, intervention development, and implementation to achieve long-term and sustainable outcomes. Additionally, there is recognition that co-producing research with people who both use and provide services offers the potential to reduce stigma, discrimination and inequality. When undertaken successfully, PICE is associated with a multitude of personal, social, societal, and service-level benefits. Many of the organisations and institutes seeking to build research capacity in communities and commission PICE-informed research outline their expectations for academics, practice partners, and researchers to consider when developing, designing, implementing, and disseminating research. These organisations and institutes also scrutinised themselves for their ability to do so. Those institutions that govern professional and regulatory organisations also engage, to an extent, with identifying 'good PICE practice' and aspects of innovation in PICE work. Support and guidance around PICE work are readily available to new and established researchers, and yet, within many contexts, there is often still a lack of understanding about the more critical aspects of PICE, such as representation, rights, co-production, tokenism, ethics, and sustainability. What is also often missing is the voice of communities and organisations who are involved as participants and their representations in relation to how they experience involvement in research and PICE processes.

Scope

This collection has been collated to explore many of the concerns highlighted above. It is based on the understanding that having a practical and theoretically informed insight into critical concerns and innovation in PICE is essential for a whole range of stakeholders be they individuals, the community, organisations, academic researchers, post graduate? Researchers and/or research commissioning institutes. This edited collection incorporates both the experience of undertaking PICE in different contexts from the researchers' and a lived experience perspective, which is crucial if, as a collective endeavour, we are to develop mechanisms for genuine knowledge exchange. In doing so, the collection creates a 'brave' space for sympathetic critical reflection on PICE work. As an editorial team, we have sought contributions from a diverse range of established, mid and early career researchers from a variety of backgrounds, disciplines, and subject areas. Researchers have worked together with practice partners, organisations, activists, and people with lived experience to engage in dialogue about important critical and innovative PICE practice. Public and practice partners would probably have been invited as co-authors, even if we had NOT asked for it; however, as an editorial team (alongside our commissioners and publisher), we proactively sought to encourage their involvement to bring authenticity to the reflections reported here, which would have been difficult without them. What you will also find, if you engage with the chapters is that early, mid, and established researchers/academics often have the same concerns and that continuous reflective and reflexive practice is key to good quality PICE.

Structure and Content of the Collection

To help you navigate the collection, we have organised the contributions under four very broad and yet connected themes. In Section 1, as the name implies, we are concerned with *International, Regional, and Local Perspectives of PICE Work*. Illustrative PICE topics are discussed here in relation to key PICE concerns in multi-national, regional and UK Local Authority settings. We open the collection with a contribution from Sujith Kumar Prankumar et al. 'International Community-involved LGBTQ+ Health Research: Multidisciplinary Reflections and Strategies'. In this chapter, Sujith Kumar Prankumar et al. discuss the complexity of multicultural LGBTQ+ health and migration research in Australia, Singapore, and Hong Kong while highlighting the importance of equitable and culturally safe research partnerships. This is followed by a contribution from Elaine Bidmead et al., titled: 'Co-production of a Regional Approach to Community Engagement in Health and Care Research in the North East and North Cumbria'. In this chapter,

Elaine Bidmead et al. explore concerns with involvement and 'fairness' as they outline and reflect on their regional co-production work and commitment to grow more meaningful opportunities and benefits across the Voluntary Community and Social Enterprise sector. We conclude the section with a contribution titled 'From Tokenism to Trust: Transforming Public Engagement in Local Authority Research and Practice through Health Determinants Research Collaborations'. In this chapter, Michael Johansen et al. discuss the concepts of 'power and trust' and their importance in relation to establishing a sustained research infrastructure which places communities at the heart of inequalities research.

Section 2 of the collection *Creativity and Innovation, Perspectives and Opportunities in PICE Work* begins with a contribution from Ian Robson and is titled 'Engaging with the Theory and Practice of Creative PICE Work'. Ian Robson has recently been awarded the Association of Infant Mental Health UK Louise Emanuel Award for his contribution to practice, research and policy in this area. In this opening chapter, Ian Robson situates PICE work in the complexities of modern public services and seeks to address misconceptions about creativity – its reduction to superficial decoration or its mystification as an elite talent –and offers a more grounded and inclusive understanding. In Chapter 5, 'The World Café Approach: Partnering Parents Towards a Deeper Understanding of Child Transitions', Charmaine Agius Ferrante and James Stack describe and reflect upon their 'innovative' use and rich real-life examples of baby social sessions, which enabled them to understand more about attachment formation and baby transitions by bringing researchers, parents, and practitioners together in the research process. The following chapter, 'Co-producing Better Mental Health Research with Young Researchers in Educational Establishments', is provided by Dave McPartlan. In this chapter, Dave McPartlan reflects on his own personal research journey from teacher–student–researcher and how he sought to 'flatten school and adult hierarchies' by adapting and amalgamating Action Research and Participatory Action Research approaches. The next chapter is provided by Kim Hall et al. titled: 'Community Asset Mapping: An Ethical, Strength-based Approach to Co-production and Inclusion'. In this chapter, Kim Hall et al. critically appraise their own practices as they sought to co-produce and implement their research. In doing so, they also report positively on aspects of innovation and their research in relation to the ways in which they promoted an anti-stigma approach within their methods and engagement. We complete this section of the collection with a contribution from Paul Watson et al. titled: 'Applying a Public Health Lens to Co-production with the Military Connected Community'. In this chapter, Paul Watson et al. reflect on their insights from a number of studies and consider their method of systematically layering Beattie's model of Health Promotion in Veteran research. In doing so, they consider the use of the model for bridging the gap between rhetoric and reality while examining the potential power of collaborative, value-based approaches in transforming health and social care services for the military-connected population.

Section 3 of this collection is titled, *PICE Work in Marginalised Communities.* We open this section of the collection with a chapter from Emma A. Adams and Sheena E. Ramsay: 'Embedding Trauma-informed Principles Within Involvement and Co-production Activities with People Experiencing Homelessness'. Within this chapter, Emma A. Adams and Sheena E. Ramsay, drawing on multiple studies, discuss key practice-related and theoretical issues related to trauma and homelessness before exploring the application and strategies for undertaking research with a trauma-informed lens. Building on concerns in this 'space', Monique Lhussier and Christina Cooper also consider their co-production workshops and the involvement of their 'lived experience group' in relation to homelessness research: 'Co-production From the Perspectives of People Who Have Experienced Homelessness'. In this chapter, Monique Lhussier and Christina Cooper provide us with quotations from participants as illustrative examples of experience and reflect on concerns with inclusive practice before presenting their five key lessons that can be taken forward for working groups with multiple and/or complex needs. In Chapter 11, we have a contribution which explores the 'Collaborating to Explore the Reproductive Health and Social Care Needs of Women Who Use Drugs: A Doctoral Research Study' from Claire Smiles and Donna Kay. In this chapter, Claire Smiles and Donna Kay critically reflect on their respective roles as doctoral students/activists and candidly report on where they had shared research experience and agreement about approaching research collaboration in this sensitive subject and topic area. In the second half of this section, we have a contribution from Mark Adley: 'A Queer Engagement: Navigating the Twists and Turns of Public Involvement and Multiple Marginalisation'. In this highly reflective and candid account of research practice, Mark Adley explores critical concerns regarding how collaborations with people on the margins, who occupy queer or oblique positions in social space, can offer meaningful contributions to research and bring fresh perspectives to established methodologies and methods. The penultimate contribution in this section is provided by Katherine Jackson et al. titled: '"Tinkering with Care" in Public Involvement and Community Engagement with People with Experience of Problematic Alcohol and/or Drug Use'. In this highly thought-provoking account of practice, Katherine Jackson et al. explore the importance of 'caring' and draw broadly on '*Feminist Ethics of Care Theory*' to illustrate that our capacity to 'tinker' to generate good care in different PICE situations is shaped by the social contexts of the research. In the final chapter of this section, we have a contribution from Fayrouz Al Haj Moussa and Claire Hart titled: 'Co-production in Refugee Research: Navigating Power Dynamics'. This chapter explores the ways in which co-production has enormous potential to create meaningful and situated shared knowledge which enhances the presence of refugees. But it also comes with a warning that unless researchers challenge their own need for power and address the structural power that surrounds them, they risk exacerbating existing power imbalances.

Section 4 of the collection is titled, *Parents–Carers–Adolescent and Children's Perspectives of PICE Work*. We open this section with a contribution from Cassey Muir and Kira Terry titled: 'Involving Children and Young People Who Experience Parental Substance Use in Research'. In this chapter, Cassey Muir and Kira Terry explore some of the tensions associated with co-production and involving children in intervention development. In doing so, they argue that researchers need to be unafraid to have difficult conversations with children, and there needs to be an equitable shift from viewing young people as vulnerable due to their experience of adversity or parental substance use to fairness, inclusion and justice where young people are recognised as capable of being change agents. In moving the emphasis from the experiences of children and onto the experiences of carers, the next chapter is provided by Charlotte Lucy Richardson et al. titled: 'Am I a Carer? Avoiding Research Fatigue and Labelling in Health and Social Care Research'. In this chapter, Charlotte Lucy Richardson et al. explore a range of practical strategies for meaningful engagement with carers from their work, including using reflective, experienced-based language to recruit participants, considering carers' logistical needs and ensuring individual carer voices are heard throughout the research process. We then return to the experiences of children for Pamela Louise Graham and Melissa Fothergill contribution: 'Let's Hear It From the Girls: Shining a Light on the Value of PICE in Alternative Educational Provision'. Pamela Louise Graham and Melissa Fothergill's work draws on lessons learnt from a project that set out to explore girls' experiences of mental health and well-being support in alternative educational provision; this chapter highlights the value of engaging with girls in these settings. Key considerations relating to relationships, anonymity, power dynamics, and the practitioner's ability to engage in sensitive conversations with young people are highlighted and discussed. The chapter concludes with recommendations relating to PICE work, interprofessional working and ethically informed practice with young people. Our second to last chapter is provided by Anna Tarrant, Linzi Ladlow and Laura Way and titled: 'The Young Dads Collective: Sustaining PICE Through a Qualitative Longitudinal and Participatory Research Programme'. In this chapter, the potential and challenges of bringing together diverse communities around a shared set of interests in father inclusion are exemplified and considered. The chapter also highlights the significance of the PICE model in fostering trust, ownership, and agency among young fathers who are often underrepresented or overlooked in traditional research, practice, and policy frameworks, demonstrating how they can be effectively supported to become not only subjects of study but active agents of change within their communities. The final chapter of the collection is provided by Emily R. Munro et al. and titled 'Co-producing Research with Care Experienced Young Adults and Social Work Professionals'. In this chapter, Emily R. Munro et al. highlight the need for attentiveness to relational safety, capacity-building, and reflective practices. They also demonstrate the role that values play in building authentic relationships and disrupting traditional power hierarchies while considering practical considerations, including training, adequate time and resources, and the use of a range of communications channels are also important. The chapter includes a reflexive, insightful, and honest contribution from one of the peer researchers (also an author) involved in the study/ies and it concluded with a call for further formal evaluation of co-production models, the Networked Learning Community (NLC) model in particular, and their long-term effects on both research outcomes and the development of participants' skills and confidence.

Navigating the Collection

Each chapter can be read as a complete and individually succinct piece of work in its own right, and each chapter is also formatted to present an illustrative research practice example and then a sympathetic critical appraisal of a concern or innovation which occurred in that setting. As you read, and we hope you do this extensively, you will find common themes and concerns that are discussed across the collection in relation to concerns like positionality, tokenism, and co-production in research conceptualisation, design, and implementation. You will also find variations in relation to the content and contexts in which the research and PICE were conducted. As we developed the rationale for the collection, we simply asked our contributors to contextualise their setting and research, identify a concern or innovation to reflect upon, and then discuss the implications of it. Each chapter concludes with a short summary, reflection, and open discussion of the key implications for future research. What we try to do here is open up the lived personal and professional experience of people involved in research to allow you, the reader, to consider your own approaches, values, knowledge, positionality, and practice in relation to your own research and what you read here. What you choose to do from here, in this space, is very much up to you as a reader. You will have gathered that this book is not about telling you 'what' to do or 'how' to do it, as this would amount to writing some kind of recipe book for PICE. Instead, what we hope to have provided is an engaging and engaged safe reflective space to foster authentic, meaningful, and potentially transformative relationships between lived experience and the process of undertaking research. Our hope is that, as the PICE movement gains momentum and becomes mainstream practice, it embraces complexity and uses research to platform situational and hyperlocal knowledge in a way that challenges traditional epistemologies for a fairer world.

Section 1

International, Regional, and Local Perspectives of PICE Work

Chapter 1

International Community-involved LGBTQ+ Health Research: Multidisciplinary Reflections and Strategies

Sujith Kumar Prankumar[a], Loc Nguyen[b], Thisanut Kaewnukul[c], Lai Peng Ho[d], Randolph C. H. Chan[e], Kevin Dong[f], Muhamad Alif Bin Ibrahim[g], P. Arun Kumar[h] and Horas T. H. Wong[i]

[a]Nottingham Law School, Nottingham Trent University, United Kingdom
[b]LGBTIQ+ Project, Western Sydney Local Health District, Australia
[c]Asian Gay, Bi+, Queer Men's Project, ACON Health, Australia
[d]Department of Care & Counselling, Tan Tock Seng Hospital, Singapore
[e]Department of Social Work, The Chinese University of Hong Kong, Hong Kong
[f]HIV & Related Programs, Western Sydney Local Health District, Australia
[g]School of Social and Health Sciences, James Cook University, Singapore
[h]Enhanced HIV Programme, National Centre for Infectious Diseases, Singapore
[i]Sydney Nursing School, Faculty of Medicine and Health, University of Sydney, Australia

Abstract

This chapter examines the experiences, challenges, and strategies involved in conducting meaningful community-engaged research with Lesbian, Gay, Bisexual, Transgender, queer/questioning and other sexuality and gender

Public Involvement and Community Engagement in Applied Health and Social Care Research: Critical Perspectives and Innovative Practice, 3–15

diverse identities (LGBTQ+) communities across three Asia-Pacific contexts: Australia, Hong Kong, and Singapore. It draws on the multidisciplinary expertise and lived experiences of collaborators working in health,
social sciences, and community leadership. Addressing the complexities of
multicultural LGBTQ+ health and migration research, the chapter explores
structural, interpersonal, and conceptual challenges while critically inter-
rogating Western-centric frameworks of gender, sexuality, and culture. Key
strategies for fostering equitable, culturally safe research partnerships are
presented, emphasising the importance of centring the voices and priorities
of marginalised LGBTQ+ communities by actively involving them throughout the research process, from conception to dissemination. The chapter is
grounded in insights from a participatory focus group facilitated by young,
culturally diverse LGBTQ+ leaders. Through critical reflections, it identifies
opportunities and barriers to advancing community-centred research that
can support community well-being and shape inclusive policy and practice.

Keywords: LGBTQ+; Asia-Pacific; community engagement; health
research; cultural diversity

Introduction

Community engagement has become an essential feature of health and social care
research and a core feature of community engagement is the inclusion of persons
with 'lived experience' in the research. In the UK, National Institute for Health
and Care Research (2021/2024) defines 'lived experience' research as research 'carried out "with" or "by" members of the public rather than "to", "about" or "for"
them'. Such research disrupts subject-object binaries by, among other strategies,
challenging the notion of 'researcher-as-expert' through centring and validating
lived experience and community expertise (Sanjakdar, 2022, p. 3). Community
engagement seeks to enhance research impact by ensuring that research concerning marginalised communities is ethically conducted, responsive to local needs,
and contributes towards both advancing scientific knowledge and developing
interventions that directly benefit these communities (Taffere et al., 2024).

The increasing application of community engagement in health research has
brought attention to concerns with 'lived experience', including what types of
'lived experience' are prioritised, how and why certain community representatives are selected, and whose voices are conferred credibility (i.e., who is accorded
epistemic authority and expertise). Quite often, sacrifices and trade-offs need to
be managed and made to strike a balance between welcoming diverse perspectives
and satisfying institutional timelines and bureaucratic demands (Mason, 2021).
For example, a bias towards selecting individuals who are more confident, highly
educated and experienced (in communicating in academic and sector-specific
language), and who are community leaders, can streamline decision-making but
can also 'easily exclude [less confident] voices [that come from more marginalised

positions]' (Pratt, 2021). A strategy to only include individuals with no engagement experience or professional expertise in the research topic can result in the exclusion of diverse voices and risk essentialising certain types of experiences as authentic (McIntosh & Wright, 2019). Decisions about who is included can create new hierarchies that fundamentally shape research, policy, and programme priorities in ways that may further alienate marginalised communities.

Trade-offs are often made when deciding when and how community members are engaged. Are they research participants, co-designers, advisors, authors, analysts, or investigators, and are they included in the early stages of project conceptualisation and grant review (Rittenbach et al., 2019)? What training and compensation are provided (e.g., Blair et al., 2022)? How are ethics committees engaged? While ethics committees ostensibly protect marginalised and vulnerable community members, they may instead often institutionalise practices that 'co-opt research and ... impose or restrict research agendas' (Roffee & Waling, 2017, p. 14). Community members involved in research often risk being tokenised or are accorded epistemic deference, and, consequently, research based on subjective 'lived experience' has been dismissed as an illegitimate source of knowledge or held as unquestionable and infallible (Casey, 2023). Commenting on the dangers of deference for certain 'authentic' voices based on an uncritical investment in parochial notions of identity, Táíwò (2022, p. 82) noted, 'the same tactics of deference that insulate us from criticism and disagreement insulate us from connection and transformation. They prevent us from engaging empathetically and authentically with the struggles of other people – a prerequisite of coalitional politics'.

Over the past decade, LGBTQ+ communities internationally have been the subject of growing research and policy attention. Yet, despite the increasing focus on intersectionality (e.g., of race, class, sexuality, disability, and gender), research on sexuality and gender diverse communities often continue to treat LGBTQ+ communities as a monolithic group (Ferguson, 2021; Pilling et al., 2017; Sadika et al., 2020; Simpfenderfer et al., 2024). The homogenisation of LGBTQ+ communities centres a Western worldview of sexuality and gender that privileges binary notions of gender and race, which results in, among other things, an oversimplification of diverse experiences, a failure to understand the unique experiences and needs of specific groups, and the reinforcement of negative stereotypes (Vidal-Ortiz et al., 2018). Consequently, overlooking in-group differences can result in a misdirection of resources and further marginalise underrepresented groups (see Adley's chapter in this collection).

This chapter draws on our multidisciplinary lived, professional, and academic experiences working with LGBTQ+ communities on health research across three Asia-Pacific contexts: Australia, Hong Kong, and Singapore. We offer critical reflections on the experiences, challenges, and strategies involved in conducting meaningful community-engaged research across these unique contexts. We first briefly outline the context of our work, and then offer two challenges that present opportunities or barriers with regard to community engagement (i.e., the politics of neutrality and identity; and power dynamics and ethical considerations with research), before discussing strategies that we have implemented in our work that have supported effective community engagement.

LGBTQ+ Research in Australia, Singapore, and Hong Kong

While the three contexts share similarities – they are developed economies with highly educated populations and increasingly visible LGBTQ+ communities, and are former British colonies that have been subject to anti-gay laws – there are important distinctions that materially affect the conduct of LGBTQ+ research.

Australia is a multicultural society with full legal recognition of same-sex marriage since 2017, strong anti-discrimination legislation, a vibrant LGBTQ+ social infrastructure in urban areas, an open media environment, and a generally accepting social climate. In Hong Kong, homosexuality is not explicitly criminalised, and there is some recognition of same-sex partnerships. Significant court cases have incrementally advanced LGBTQ+ rights. This includes a 2023 High Court ruling in favour of same-sex marriage recognition (Leung, 2023), which reflects glowing popular support for marriage equality – now at 60% (Lau et al., 2023). In Singapore, male same-sex sexual activity was decriminalised in 2022 with the repeal of Section 377A of the penal code. However, media restrictions on LGBTQ+ content remain. A constitutional ban on same-sex marriage was introduced with the repeal of 377A, and support for marriage equality, while growing, remains low at 32% (Ipsos, 2024).

These social and political sensitivities have had material impacts on the research environment pertaining to LGBTQ+ topics. LGBTQ+ research in Australia is supported by initiatives and funding from government and academic institutions, resulting in extensive conceptual and empirical research being conducted across a wide variety of topics across the life course, using myriad methods. In the Australian context, community co-design is increasingly mandated in state-funded research. In contrast, LGBTQ+ research in Singapore and Hong Kong remains considerably more constrained, and is often dependent on partnerships with international institutions, philanthropic organisations, and nongovernmental organisations. Scholarship in these latter contexts appears predominantly positivist and empirical, which might reflect national research policy expectations about what constitutes 'good' research, i.e., research with a quantitatively measurable impact.

We are a group of research collaborators with significant experience working with LGBTQ+ and other socially marginalised populations in Australia, Hong Kong, and Singapore. Some of us are full-time social researchers employed at universities, while others are nurses, social workers, health promotion officers, policy officers, programme managers, community advocates, and students, with a few of us fulfilling multiple roles. Within our group, we have engaged in several community-engaged quantitative and qualitative projects at the intersection of race, sexual and mental health, and sexual citizenship. In much of our work, we work closely with community members and organisations, although the sociopolitical realities in our respective contexts shape the design and scope of our studies.

Method

The content of this chapter was informed by our international collaborative research activity and then developed from an online focus group discussion. The discussion, which lasted 85 minutes, was facilitated in English by two authors with the support of the senior authors (SKP and HW). The facilitators, both sexuality and gender diverse young community leaders of migrant backgrounds, iteratively and collaboratively developed the interview guide from a list of collaborator-contributed questions. The shortlisted questions were grouped in five domains: Safe and Ethical Research Practices; Language and Terminology; Intersectionality, Bias, and Cultural Humility; Conceptualisations of Gender, Sexuality, and Cultural Diversity; and Community Engagement and Representation. The discussion was recorded and transcribed verbatim, with the chat logs and transcripts analysed thematically by the first author (SKP). The study did not undergo an institutional ethics procedure, as all of the focus group members are also authors who gave their permission to participate.

Politics of Neutrality and Identity

Understanding positionality is important for health and social care research, and a common feature of research conducted across the various contexts was the necessity to maintain an appearance of neutrality. Participants working in Singapore attributed this to state policies that emphasise neutrality in relation to social issues to 'keep the peace' within society, in acknowledgement of a vocal community of conservative religious activists and in view of the state's endorsement of the heterosexual family unit as the basis of society, with the result that LGBTQ+ populations are barely mentioned in sex education, the media and health promotion (see Ramdas, 2021; Yulius et al., 2018, p. 187). Beyond maintaining silence, neutrality was also associated with the expected and calculated inclusion of voices hostile to LGBTQ+ equality for the sake of 'balance'. The emphasis on neutrality continues to maintain and even exacerbate health inequities in Singapore, as a participant noted:

> One of the Singapore government's reasons for keeping 377A on the books for a long time was to be 'neutral' to 'both sides'... even if one side causes harm. This push for 'respectful neutrality', to give legitimacy to homophobic views alongside LGBTQ+ perspectives... hinders progress. Real change often requires challenging power structures, even at personal cost. True neutrality can reinforce systemic violence, benefiting those in power while harming marginalised communities. For example, LGBTQ+ lives are barely mentioned in sex education or public sexual health communication because of this need to be 'neutral' and 'keep the peace', because of the fear of coming across as supporting a certain marginalised community...

These dynamics – of maintaining neutrality in an effort to not attract criticism, unwanted attention or social stigma – also feature in the Australian and Hong Kong contexts (e.g., Barrow, 2020; Kin & Denise, 2019; Riseman, 2019). In these settings, participants' focus on appearing neutral was reflected in their decisions about which aspects of their identities they disclosed publicly. Their decision as to whether to publicly identify as sexuality or gender diverse, or to keep such information private, was a careful balance between a desire for transparency with community members and concerns about potential political, occupational and funding repercussions. They were anxious that such disclosures could lead to criticism, stigma and discrimination from their respective institutions, the state and the public, and that their research would be deemed 'biased' or 'one-sided', and therefore untrustworthy. Their hesitation to disclose their positionalities was recognised as a barrier to establishing community trust, particularly in studies exploring personal topics such as sexuality and sexual behaviour. As a result, these participants expressed needing to spend more time in building effective and trusting relationships with study populations. Some participants, however, noted that being able to identify themselves as 'insider researchers' – particularly in the Australian context – enabled them to embody a transformative praxis (Thambinathan & Kinsella, 2021) that bolstered rather than challenged their credibility.

The management of neutrality also affected the language used in research. Participants contrasted the diverse and rapidly evolving ways that communities described themselves against the 'elite' language used in research studies that privileged Western binary ways of understanding identity. They grappled with the challenge of navigating between Western and local language regimes, not solely to ensure cultural and context-specific relevance, but more fundamentally to reconcile the tension between critiquing and aspiring to decolonise dominant discourses, and needing to comply with institutional norms necessary for securing funding, advancing careers and achieving research goals that align with both participant well-being and institutional expectations. For example, deciding on the terminology to be used during the recruitment stages of their studies was experienced as challenging and time-consuming. The use of the terms 'queer' or 'LGBTQ+' among multicultural populations, the growing pressure to declare one's pronouns (itself premised on Western epistemologies of gender), and assumptions around culture and ethnicity – such as the use of the term culturally and linguistically diverse (CALD) in Australian recruitment material to describe anyone not Anglo Australian; the instruction to identify as either Chinese, Indian, Malay and 'other' in surveys in Singapore; and the presumption of ethnic homogeneity in Hong Kong – were all acknowledged as privileging dominant ways of understanding ethnicity (i.e., equating ethnic Chineseness with being Singaporean and whiteness with being Australian). The imposition of Western frameworks of sexuality and gender diversity were seen as both actively and implicitly functioning to erase community diversity.

Further, participants reflected on how the reliance on broad terms informed by Western epistemologies of identity shaped the research focus and data, and then led to the over-recruitment of cisgender gay men from dominant cultural backgrounds to participate in research studies. This, in turn, privileged certain ways of understanding gender and sexuality while marginalising the perspectives of ethnic minorities and gender diverse individuals. These minoritised voices often felt pressured to articulate themselves in ways that did not fully align with their own experiences and languages, making it difficult for them to see themselves reflected in the research. For instance, although participants appreciated the inclusive intent behind the demand for pronouns, they noted that the prescriptive ways such questions were presented often pressured them to 'out' themselves or provide false information. For several participants, the pressure on respondents to be transparent in particular ways, alien to their cultural heritage, often felt unsafe for those whose heritage languages did not orally differentiate between pronouns and which had therefore afforded them the capacity to express themselves neutrally, without lying. One participant said:

> I did some research exploring terms like 'Queer' with Chinese communities, and many people did not relate with the terms and had different understandings of them compared to the Western understandings. Many [of them also] felt that they had to come out when speaking in English because English uses pronouns, but in Chinese, all pronouns sound the same. ("ta": 他 – he/him, 她 – she/her, 它 – it)

Power Dynamics and Research Ethics

In addition to navigating identity concerns/constructs and demands for neutrality, participants reflected on the power dynamics that are often present in community-engaged research. These included balancing academic and career goals with community engagement, navigating dynamics within LGBTQ+ communities, and managing demands from institutional ethics committees who might not appreciate diversity and difference within marginalised communities.

Firstly, with growing expectations to meet challenging institutional key performance indicators (KPIs) for career advancement and to attract research funding, participants felt pressured to collect data and publish as efficiently as possible to continue attracting more funding to benefit marginalised communities. For example, one participant described a situation in which their colleague's attempt to share research findings with LGBTQ+ communities in Singapore was blocked by the study's principal investigator. The principal investigator insisted on prioritising publication in academic journals, fearing that others might use their findings if they were released publicly prior to publication. The participant considered this an example of a power imbalance, whereby 'the principal investigator or the senior investigator controls when and how such information is given back to the relevant communities to help the communities in various ways'.

Secondly, participants observed power differentials within LGBTQ+ communities. These differentials were noted along various dimensions, including gender, class, ethnicity, nationality, and educational status.

Power differentials are also apparent in political dynamics within LGBTQ+ communities, whereby some established groups control access and therefore community discourse, making it difficult for alternative voices to influence more inclusive and culturally relevant research and advocacy. Participants discussed how power struggles between LGBTQ+ leaders and groups complicated community engagement. They recounted having experienced debates about who – and whose experiences – should be included on the study team. The conflation of 'co-design' with 'equal' was challenged, as those with most power often controlled the process, as one participant said:

> There are some queer groups who have longstanding relationships with people in power (the media and government), and therefore they want to protect that. It can be quite difficult to negotiate relationships if... you don't follow that particular way that this power broker wants you to do it ... There's quite a bit of infighting, and everybody has a different way of doing things, so it's difficult to figure out the most appropriate way of engaging the community when we're doing research.

Thirdly, participants recalled having frustrating interactions with review committees that often insisted that researchers include problematic terminology (such as outdated or culturally insensitive wording, deficit-based language, and binary notions of gender) that can reinforce stereotypes and retraumatise participants, and who frequently imposed a positivist paradigm and quantitative expectations of evidence on qualitative projects (e.g., generalisability and validity). They felt that health and social research ethics committees, as gatekeepers who were often unfamiliar with qualitative methods since they usually worked within positivist and biomedical frameworks, prioritised compliance and the mitigation of institutional risk over the expressed needs and expectations of community members. In order to receive ethics approval, the participants felt researchers may be compelled to frame the notion of 'risk' to align with the ethics review committees' expectations. As a result, ethics applications encourage the consideration of 'risk' at the individual level (e.g., psychological risk, which is mitigated superficially through the provision of information regarding support services) rather than at the community level (e.g., through engaging in meaningful, trauma-informed co-design).

Beyond noting ethics committees' influence on study design, participants discussed how the use of specific terms (e.g., categories of gender, sexuality, ethnicity, mental health, discrimination, and deficit-based language), as recommended by ethics committees, complicated recruitment efforts. They expressed concern that prospective participants sometimes felt they did not qualify for studies that were, in fact, intended to include them. Essentially, the ethics committees' recommendations often restricted participation to individuals who could easily identify with these terms, which were typically aligned with Western, mainstream conceptions of gender, sexuality, and ethnicity.

Participants working in the Australian context also commented on increasing expectations from funders regarding community engagement. While they appreciated the intent, they felt that the requirement was often met in superficial or 'tokenistic' ways. Participants felt that government agencies and funders cared more about the extent to which KPIs were met, rather than meaningful community engagement. An Australia-based participant with a background in public health expressed concern about the colonial and extractive behaviour regarding knowledge production and sponsorship:

> Health policy (in LGBTQ+ research) is dominated by white, cisgender gay men who are often very vocal. It's almost like they feel like they speak on behalf of the community and feel like they've done the work, but often it's quite tokenistic. When I sit in meetings and hear about the way they do community consultations, I feel quite concerned that they would take credit for that piece of work to build their profile. They might not necessarily understand what they're talking about, but they will always claim that they've done the consultation and engagement, to meet their KPI. I'm like, wow, these people don't really know their work, but they can talk the talk. Sometimes, 'co-design' is box ticking, or used to confirm what the researchers wanted to do anyway, so they ignore the ideas that challenge their initial plans.

Despite their concerns about the lack of meaningful minority ethnic and gender diverse representation at the project management and commissioning levels, participants were encouraged by the slowly increasing number of LGBTQ+ people from culturally diverse backgrounds who are beginning to lead research projects, and by efforts of ethics committees to become more familiar with qualitative, community-engaged research.

Responding to Power and Identity Politics in Health Research

Participants' responses highlighted three linked strategies that can enhance community-engaged research: developing genuine community partnerships, investing in community-driven marketing and communications efforts, and adapting research tools to reflect the ways local communities understand themselves. These will be discussed in turn.

Develop Genuine Community Partnerships

Engaging communities early and throughout the research process, incorporating diverse manifestations of lived experience and expertise, co-developing the study's design – including research questions, methods, instruments, and dissemination plans – before finalisation, and prioritising training and knowledge transfer are essential to building reciprocal trust.

The development of genuine and effective partnerships is associated with greater transparency and accountability and mitigates feelings of exploitation. For example, on the question of data justice: to what extent can community groups give feedback on the study's findings, and to what degree do they own the data they collect or provide? To achieve this, researchers should actively involve community groups in the dissemination of findings, ensuring they have opportunities to provide feedback and feel validated in their contributions. It is also critical for researchers to honour commitments made during the research process by maintaining communication with participants, sharing outcomes, and creating pathways for ongoing collaboration. This includes ensuring community members know where their data are going, how it will be used, and leaving the door open for future engagement or research opportunities. By doing so, researchers can foster trust, mitigate feelings of exploitation and promote data justice, thereby ensuring communities feel ownership and agency over the stories they share. To further foster transparency, accountability, and equitable partnerships, researchers could think about how they disclose their own positionalities, offering clarity to stakeholders about how their personal backgrounds, biases, and social positions influence the research process.

Invest in Community-driven Marketing and Communications Efforts

Efforts to address the underrepresentation of marginalised populations in research should include targeted marketing, recruitment, and engagement strategies. These may involve using imagery that reflects diverse communities to ensure participants feel represented, contracting with community organisations to manage recruitment, and hiring facilitators with relevant lived experience to build trust between participants and research teams. There are four key benefits of this outsourcing approach: firstly, partnering with community organisations enhances the political and public credibility of both the research team and the community organisation. Secondly, it improves participant recruitment efforts by aligning them with scientific and programme needs and priorities. Thirdly, it provides the organisation with a steady income stream that can be applied towards supporting community initiatives. Fourthly, it creates opportunities for skills development within the community organisation.

However, while targeted strategies can be effective, they need to be implemented carefully to avoid stigma. For example, overly narrow approaches in health education can inadvertently signal that certain groups are inherently at higher risk, creating discomfort or resistance. The value of using inclusive, non-stigmatising language to encourage open engagement must be stressed. Fostering trust and dialogue, rather than immediately and solely focussing on sensitive topics like race, sexuality, or Human Immunodeficiency Virus (HIV), can lead to more meaningful and productive relationships.

Adapt Research Tools to Reflect the Ways Local Communities Understand Themselves

The language and structure of research tools can either foster inclusion or alienate marginalised populations. Ensuring flexibility in methods (e.g., art-based approaches, interviews, and surveys), terminology (e.g., using gender-affirming language and avoiding assumptions about pronouns), and delivery (e.g., offering online or in-person options) is essential to respectfully engaging diverse communities. For example, researchers could consider organising paid community focus groups to review and refine research tools, ensuring they are trauma-informed, inclusive, clear, and reflective of lived experiences. Feedback from these focus groups can guide adjustments to language and content, such as adding qualitative questions that invite participants to share personal experiences. The inclusion of a qualitative question about community belonging and access to services could provide unexpected and valuable insights into themes like inclusion, exclusion, trauma, race, and lateral violence, deepening the understanding of participants' lived realities, individually and collectively.

Conclusion

Research into and with LGBTQ+ communities often requires heightened sensitivities due to social and legal marginalisation. Community-engaged research, built on mutual respect and trust, is essential for producing respectful, accurate, rigorous, and actionable research that can directly benefit such populations. Our chapter here has been informed by our empirical work and a sympathetic critical appraisal of it across Australia, Hong Kong, and Singapore. While community engagement can often be a long and challenging process, such research, which is culturally sensitive and positions community members as active collaborators and co-creators of knowledge, can more effectively reflect the community's complex realities and needs, protect their safety and dignity, promote their health and well-being, and strengthen communities. Those who wish to follow our work and learn from our experiences need to consider the context of our work, positionality and the constant need to be reflexive and reflective at every point in their own research journey. Taking steps to adapt research tools to reflect the ways local communities understand themselves, while investing in community-driven recruitment and dissemination efforts, is key to driving more authentic and genuine forms of community engagement.

References

Barrow, A. (2020). Sexual orientation, gender identity, and equality in Hong Kong: Rights, resistance, and possibilities for reform. *Asian Journal of Comparative Law, 15*(1), 126–155. https://doi.org/10.1017/asjcl.2020.2

Blair, C., Best, P., Burns, P., Campbell, A., Davidson, G., Duffy, J., Johnston, A., Kelly, B., Killick, C., MacDermott, D., Maddock, A., McCartan, C. J., McFadden, P., McGlade, A., Montgomery, L., Patton, S., Schubotz, D., Taylor, B., Templeton, F., Webb, P., White, C., & Yap, J. (2022). "Getting involved in research": A co-created, co-delivered and co-analysed course for those with lived experience of health and social care services. *Research Involvement and Engagement, 8*(1), 20. https://doi.org/10.1186/s40900-022-00353-x

Casey, P. J. (2023). Lived experience: Defined and critiqued. *Critical Horizons, 24*(3), 282–297. https://doi.org/10.1080/14409917.2023.2241058

Ferguson, A. (2021). Intersectional approaches to queer psychology. In K. L. Nadal & M. R. Scharrón-del Río (Eds.), *Queer psychology: Intersectional perspectives* (pp. 15–32). Springer. https://doi.org/10.1007/978-3-030-74146-4_2

Ipsos.(2024). *IPSOS LGBT+ pride report 2024*. Ipsos. Retrieved November 5, 2024, from https://www.ipsos.com/en-sg/growing-acceptance-lgbtq-rights-singapore-generational-divides-remain

Kin, C. Y. A., & Denise, T.-S. T. (2019). Regulating sexual morality: The stigmatisation of LGB youth in Hong Kong. In P. Aggleton, R. Cover, D. Leahy, D. Marshall, & M. L. Rasmussen (Eds.), *Youth sexuality and sexual citizenship* (pp. 86–99). Routledge.

Lau, H., Loper, K., & Suen, Y. (2023). *Support in Hong Kong for same-sex couples' rights grew over ten years (2013–2023): 60 percent now support same-sex marriage*. Social Science Research Network. Retrieved November 5, 2024, from https://papers.ssrn.com/abstract=4452861

Leung, K. (2023). Hong Kong's top court rules in favor of recognizing same-sex partnerships in a landmark case. *AP News*. Retrieved November 5, 2024, from https://apnews.com/article/hong-kong-same-sex-marriage-e32da67e8d4b364cb156a2e2ec526850

Mason, W. (2021). Radically slow? Reflections on time, temporality, and pace in engaged scholarship. In B. C. Clift, J. Gore, S. Gustafsson, S. Bekker, I. C. Batlle, & J. Hatchard (Eds.), *Temporality in qualitative inquiry: Theories, methods and practices* (pp. 142–157). Routledge.

McIntosh, I., & Wright, S. (2019). Exploring what the notion of "lived experience" offers for social policy analysis. *Journal of Social Policy, 48*(3), 449–467. https://doi.org/10.1017/S0047279418000570

National Institute for Health and Care Research. (2021). *Briefing note two: What is public involvement in research? Definitions of involvement, engagement and participation. Briefing notes for researchers – public involvement in NHS, health and social care research*. Retrieved November 5, 2024, from https://www.nihr.ac.uk/briefing-notes-researchers-public-involvement-nhs-health-and-social-care-research

Pilling, M., Howison, M., Frederick, T., Ross, L., Bellamy, C. D., Davidson, L., McKenzie, K., & Kidd, S. A. (2017). Fragmented inclusion: Community participation and lesbian, gay, bisexual, trans, and queer people with diagnoses of schizophrenia and bipolar disorder. *American Journal of Orthopsychiatry, 87*(5), 606–613. https://doi.org/10.1037/ort0000215

Pratt, B. (2021). Achieving inclusive research priority-setting: What do people with lived experience and the public think is essential? *BMC Medical Ethics, 22*(1), 117. https://doi.org/10.1186/s12910-021-00685-5

Ramdas, K. (2021). Negotiating LGBTQ rights in Singapore: The margin as a place of refusal. *Urban Studies, 58*(7), 1448–1462. https://doi.org/10.1177/0042098020962936

Riseman, N. (2019, November 22). Australia's history of LGBTI politics and rights. *Oxford Research Encyclopedia of Politics*. https://oxfordre.com/politics/view/10.1093/acrefore/9780190228637.001.0001/acrefore-9780190228637-e-1260.

Rittenbach, K., Horne, C. G., O'Riordan, T., Bichel, A., Mitchell, N., Fernandez Parra, A. M., & MacMaster, F. P. (2019). Engaging people with lived experience in the grant review process. *BMC Medical Ethics, 20*, 95. https://doi.org/10.1186/s12910-019-0436-0

Roffee, J. A., & Waling, A. (2017). Resolving ethical challenges when researching with minority and vulnerable populations: LGBTIQ victims of violence, harassment and bullying. *Research Ethics, 13*(1), 4–22. https://doi.org/10.1177/1747016116658693

Sadika, B., Wiebe, E., Morrison, M. A., & Morrison, T. G. (2020). Intersectional micro-aggressions and social support for LGBTQ persons of color: A systematic review of the Canadian-based empirical literature. *Journal of GLBT Family Studies, 16*(2), 111–147. https://doi.org/10.1080/1550428X.2020.1724125

Sanjakdar, F. (2022). Re-searching margins: An introduction. In F. Sanjakdar, G. Fletcher, A. Keddie, & B. Whitburn (Eds.), *Re-searching margins: Ethics, social justice, and education* (pp. 1–24). Routledge. https://doi.org/10.4324/9780429346286

Simpfenderfer, A. D., Jackson, R., Aguilar, D., Dolan, C. V., & Garvey, J. C. (2024). Using queer framings and positionalities to unsettle statistical assumptions of generalizability and representativeness. *Educational Studies, 60*(1), 19–40. https://doi.org/10.1080/00131946.2024.2303096

Taffere, G. R., Abebe, H. T., Zerihun, Z., Mallen, C., Price, H. P., & Mulugeta, A. (2024). Systematic review of community engagement approach in research: Describing partnership approaches, challenges and benefits. *Journal of Public Health, 32*(2), 185–205. https://doi.org/10.1007/s10389-022-01799-9

Táíwò, O. O. (2022). *Elite capture: How the powerful took over identity politics.* Pluto Press.

Thambinathan, V., & Kinsella, E. A. (2021). Decolonizing methodologies in qualitative research: Creating spaces for transformative praxis. *International Journal of Qualitative Methods, 20*, 1–9. https://doi.org/10.1177/16094069211014766

Vidal-Ortiz, S., Robinson, B. A., & Khan, C. (2018). *Race and sexuality.* Polity Press.

Yulius, H., Tang, S., & Offord, B. (2018). The globalization of LGBT identity and same-sex marriage as a catalyst of neoinstitutional values: Singapore and Indonesia in focus. In B. Winter, M. Forest, & R. Sénac (Eds.), *Global perspectives on same-sex marriage: A neo-institutional approach* (pp. 171–196). Palgrave Macmillan.

Chapter 2

Co-production of a Regional Approach to Community Engagement in Health and Care Research in the North East and North Cumbria

Elaine Bidmead[a,b], Felicity Shenton[b], Greta Brunskill[c], Kate Whitmarsh[d], Sharon Barnes[d] and Steph Capewell[e]

[a]*Institute of Health, University of Cumbria, UK*
[b]*NIHR Applied Rresearch Collaboration (ARC) North East North Cumbria (NENC), UK*
[c]*NIHR HealthTech Research Centre in Diagnostic and Technology Evaluation, Faculty of Medical Sciences, Newcastle University, UK*
[d]*The Centre West Cumbria, UK*
[e]*Love, Amelia, UK*

Abstract

This chapter focusses on developments in the North East and North Cumbria (NENC) that strove to create more opportunities for seldom heard groups and communities to be active partners in health and care research. We focus specifically on co-production with the voluntary and community sectors, summarising the context that influenced a collective drive to do things differently. Two local voluntary, community, and social enterprise (VCSE) organisations share their insights and experiences. We outline a series of regional developments that aimed to address key issues associated with involving communities and VCSE organisations in research and focus on improving relationships and growing more meaningful opportunities

Public Involvement and Community Engagement in Applied Health and Social Care Research: Critical Perspectives and Innovative Practice, 17–29

that benefit people, communities and the VCSE sector, as well as improving the quality of research. Finally, we share some of our key learning and messages for others looking to support and develop new ways of working with communities and VCSE organisations to develop meaningful, reciprocal, and sustainable partnerships in research.

Keywords: Co-production; community engagement; public involvement and community engagement (PICE); inclusive research; voluntary; community and social enterprise sector (VCSE)

Introduction

Research is essential to delivering high quality health, social care, and public health services and interventions (Boaz et al., 2015), but there are concerns about unequal representation in research studies, and arguments that the knowledge produced by research is partial because it often excludes diverse groups who are seldom heard (Kennedy-Martin et al., 2015; Reynolds et al., 2021). This matters because the impacts of interventions may vary in different groups of people (e.g., based on their age, ethnicity, and/or gender) and geographies (such as coastal/ rural/urban, north/south, and socio-economic advantage/disadvantage; Bower et al., 2020). It is therefore essential that research is equitable, inclusive, and representative of different people and places. Researchers and research institutions also need to consider issues around fairness, as Bower et al. (2020, p. 2) note, 'fairness dictates that publicly funded research' and the benefits of participating in such research 'should be accessible to all'. For research that addresses health and care inequalities to have the best possible chance of making a difference to the people and communities most affected, we must ensure that it is informed by and includes their voices. In this context, public involvement and community engagement (PICE) can play a key role by ensuring the needs and experiences of people and communities remain at the heart of health and care research (Staniszewska et al., 2018).

From its inception in 2006, the National Institute for Health and Care Research (NIHR) has developed policies to support and promote public involvement in research. It has recently broadened these to include community engagement. Many UK research funders have increasingly encouraged, and now require, PICE in funding applications. The UK Public Involvement Standards Development Partnership (2019) designed standards to improve the quality and consistency of public involvement in research. The six standards represent the foundations of good PICE in health and care research and include 'working together' with communities to build sustainable, mutually respectful and productive relationships, and creating 'inclusive opportunities' to enable diverse PICE in research.

In 2021, the NIHR reported on 'lessons learnt from the Reaching out Programme' (NIHR, 2021), which focussed specifically on working with communities not typically involved in research. It aimed to support research infrastructures across England to develop new relationships and more effective approaches to building relationships with communities. Such relationships were seen as the 'building blocks to involvement in research and ensuring that research reflects the needs of communities' (NIHR, 2021). The programme made recommendations to support the inclusion of diverse groups in health research and highlighted the importance of creating and nurturing relationships with them. Ensuring involvement is mutually beneficial to both participants and researchers was also recommended, with recognition that it takes time and effort to make this happen.

Recently, the NIHR has renewed its commitment to public partnerships (NIHR, 2024a), restating its 'ambition to make public partnerships diverse, inclusive and impactful'. Together with the UK Standards for Public Involvement, these are the cornerstones of PICE. What the NIHR refer to as 'public partnerships' embodies a vision for research that reflects what matters to people and communities, and their lived experience of health and care issues.

Increasingly, the VCSE sector is recognised as key to engaging more diverse communities in research due to their long-standing and trusted relationships with communities, including with some of the most marginalised people. In this chapter, we describe and engage in a sympathetic critical appraisal of our own practice and developments in the NENC that have aimed to create more opportunities for seldom heard groups and communities to be active partners in health and care research. Focussing on our work with the VCSE sector, we start by summarising the background and context that influenced a collective drive to do things differently before sharing the insights and experiences of two local VCSE organisations' involvement in research. We then outline a series of developments that aimed to address key issues associated with collaborating with communities and VCSE organisations in research. Finally, we share some of our key learning and messages for others looking to support and develop new ways of working with communities and VCSE organisations in research.

Background

Since 2017, the development of PICE in the NENC has been supported by the 'Creating Connections Network'. Coordinated by the region's NIHR research support service (RSS) Hub, the Network involves PICE leads from across NIHR infrastructures and aims to share good practice, support learning and enable collaborative projects and innovation (Creating Connections, 2024). It works closely with research institutions, practitioners and VCSE partners to deliver PICE in the region. Network activity is underpinned by a commitment to ensuring that the voices of people and communities are instrumental in achieving transformational health and care research. Further, network members are committed to creating opportunities for people and communities to engage in all aspects of the research cycle (Pearson et al., 2024), not just as participants in research studies. This includes involvement in identifying research priorities, shaping research questions, designing research methodologies, conducting research, supporting data analysis, and co-producing and sharing research findings (University of

Oxford, Medical Sciences Division, n.d.). It is through this network that connections between key partners and sectors have been established and sustained over time, enabling collaborative efforts to develop new and innovative approaches to support more diverse PICE.

The NIHR Research Design Service NENC (now RSS) was an active partner in the Reaching Out Programme (NIHR, 2021). Through this work, they engaged with seldom-involved communities from Black, Asian and minority ethnic backgrounds, mental health service users, pregnant women, rural communities, working people, and vulnerable children in our region. This led to the co-production of a Community Engagement Toolkit with VCSE partners (NIHR RDS, 2022), which provides 10 principles to guide researchers in their approach to working with communities and community organisations. This toolkit and the learning from the reaching out programme formed the foundation for further innovation to engage and involve more communities in research in the NENC, which we describe later.

Context

The NENC covers a large geographical area; its local integrated care system is the largest in the country in terms of both geographical footprint and population. This presents challenges to ensuring the geographical spread of public and community involvement in research, concerns which are supported by analyses of geographical inequalities in recruitment to research studies (Bower et al., 2020). Consequently, significant numbers of communities are seldom involved in research, whether these be communities of identity, interest, or place (Banks et al., 2013). We have found that engaging these communities can be supported by developing connections with the VCSE organisations that support them and with whom they have existing, long-standing relationships built on continuity and trust. This has long been recognised by researchers who have routinely connected with VCSE organisations to recruit research participants. More recently, however, the value of developing connections with these organisations to involve communities of people as partners throughout the whole research process is being recognised.

Conducting PICE in partnership with the VCSE sector benefits from establishing and maintaining ongoing, respectful and reciprocal relationships (NIHR RDS, 2022). Within the NENC there are examples of strong links between individual researchers, research organisations, and VCSE organisations, which have supported research involvement and engagement activities with diverse communities. We are aware of examples of good practice in the region including PICE work with young people and ethnically minoritised groups, and a strong track record of supporting co-production and peer research approaches. However, we are also aware of a small number of VCSE organisations that are often overwhelmed with requests to facilitate research involvement and participation, as well as many others that are never approached. Importantly, the former organisations can feel burdened and pressured as requests for their time are uncoordinated, frequently duplicate other requests, and are usually made with unreasonably short notice. VCSE organisations have also shared poor experiences of being involved in research, including a lack of remuneration and training, and impact from the research rarely being communicated to those that participated. This can damage the relationship between the VCSE organisation and their beneficiaries, many of whom participate in research because the VCSE organisation has introduced them to it and/or out of a sense of helping to change things for others. Through engaging, some will have been asked to share personal information about traumatic experiences which may have triggered psychological responses (see chapters by Cooper, Lhussier, Adams, and Ramsey in this collection). If public contributors never hear about research outcomes they may be left wondering if what they said made a difference and questioning whether their involvement was worth it. As the intermediary between the individual and the researcher, the VCSE organisation may be perceived responsible for the conduct of the researchers leading to feelings of betrayal towards the organisation. Individuals may then withdraw from supportive services because of this perceived association, resulting in negative consequences for themselves and the organisation.

We invited co-authors from two VCSE organisations to share their perspectives on involvement in research, including insights on how PICE can be challenging, and even a negative experience, for their organisations, and how this might be improved in the future.

VCSE Reflections From Experiences of Research Involvement

'The Centre' is a West Cumbrian charity providing social and creative opportunities for people to connect and grow, based at a community building in Maryport. Their reflections on involvement in research are not untypical.

> We believe that everyone has something to offer and that together we can build brighter and better outcomes for everyone in our community. Giving people a voice and opportunities to express their opinions is an important part of our work and so we want to support research wherever and whenever we can. With a tiny team, limited budget and an ever-increasing demand on services, we have to be selective about what we take on beyond business-critical activity. With every additional task, we must carefully weigh up what direct benefits there will be to our organisation or the community, because at the end of the day, we know we'll have to cut something to make time to facilitate each request. It's a constant juggle and it takes all our resources just to keep the doors open.

> As with everything we have had good and bad experiences. Some researchers have 'dropped in', carried out their research and then vanished, not only leaving participants (and us) without feedback or findings – but ultimately a sense of diminished confidence and trust.

We've found that most people want to be useful and that they have a genuine selfless desire to help others – but we don't think this should be taken for granted. Lived experience clearly has a value and the best experiences we've had are those where the researchers have demonstrated an understanding of this. Researchers who have thought about why people should give up their time and can clearly explain the benefits are far more effective than those who get what they need and run.

When researchers reimburse both community members and VCSE organisations for their time, either in money or 'in kind', it supports a more accessible approach by establishing a reciprocal dynamic to the relationship. Even a minimum of reimbursing 'out of pocket' expenses can make a difference as to whether an individual or an organisation is able to participate – it is often the individuals and organisations who can least afford to participate whose voices are missing from research to begin with.

Language can also be an issue. Participants need to fully understand what they are being asked and how their answers will be used, as well as understanding why they are being consulted. Usually with research, the studies want to capture voices that are not always heard – but there's a reason that they've not been heard before and this needs to be considered. It may be confidence holding them back, it may be a lack of understanding and not wanting to ask for clarification, it may be that they don't see the point of speaking up when they've never been listened to before, or it may be that the last time they gave up some time to take part in research, they didn't get an update or conclusion ... trust is hard to gain and very easily lost. The whole process must consider the needs of both sides – it's that two-way street analogy again ...

We believe that involvement in research needs to be genuine, respectful and useful. There needs to be longer term engagement with VCSE organisations and their communities to be meaningful to all involved, and to avoid it becoming a tick-box exercise. To build trust, researchers must get to know the community before coming in. They need to learn our language!

Due to the current climate, we are single mindedly focused on using our scarce resources to deliver our charitable objectives, build trust and engagement in the community, and keep our doors open. Sadly, we would currently have no choice but to turn down approaches from researchers if the research cannot help us deliver those aims.

Love, Amelia is a baby bank charity that provides practical support to families with children aged 0–16 years who are experiencing poverty and other multifaceted hardships. They also reflect on their experience with researchers.

Operating throughout the North East, we aim to reduce the impact of poverty and inequalities by providing essential items and equipment that children need to be safe, happy, and able to thrive. Our commitment to involving individuals with lived experience ensures that our work is not just **for** the community, but **with** the community, delivering outcomes that matter.

At Love, Amelia, we have found engaging in research offers significant opportunities and benefits, but it also presents some challenges. The families we work with are often among the most marginalised in society, and we strongly believe that giving a voice to those who use our service is crucial to designing and delivering support that is meaningful and impactful. Engaging with families and collaborating through research allows them to express their needs and preferences, shaping a service that truly reflects and responds to their lived realities. This collaborative approach has helped us improve our delivery model and create a more inclusive service that better meets the needs of families in our community.

However, our experience of engaging in research has not been without challenges. Some researchers, in the past, have not worked as collaboratively as we would have hoped, failing to share findings or to set realistic expectations about what our services can deliver. This lack of transparency and partnership can be disheartening for small charities like ours, where resources are stretched.

To ensure that research is beneficial to all parties, it is critical that the collaboration between researchers and VCSE organisations is genuine, with clear expectations, open communication, and mutual respect. Both sides need to be mindful of capacity limitations and ensure that findings are shared transparently with all involved. Only then can research act as a true driver of meaningful change at multiple levels, ensuring that the voices of those most impacted are not just heard but acted upon.

It is important to acknowledge the existence of systemic barriers to meaningful engagement with communities and the VCSE organisations that support them. The processes and systems associated with much health and care research do not create conditions that nurture meaningful, reciprocal relationships between the potential VCSE sector and research partners. The process of applying for research funding can pose significant challenges, particularly in terms of the time and investment needed to develop meaningful partnerships and the often short timeframes for making an application for research funding. There are limited resources to support pre-application activity, which can compound the risk for all partners of investing a lot of time and effort in the pre-application phase when the research may not be funded. This investment of time can be particularly challenging for the VCSE sector, which rarely has any staff time or roles dedicated to research activities, and may already be operating at stretched capacity, as illustrated in the accounts above. Furthermore, it is common for individuals and/or organisations outside of academia to be ineligible as co-applicants, which prevents appropriate resource allocation for their roles in the research. These factors can present real challenges in developing partnerships for research. To ensure the inclusion of new and different voices, the research funding process needs to recognise the value of working with VCSE organisations to reach and involve diverse communities by enabling (rather than hindering) relationships and partnership working.

Co-developing a Partnership Approach to Community Engagement

In 2021, a working group comprised of public partners, VCSE organisations, and members of the Creating Connections network took part in a workshop series exploring the potential of commissioning partnerships with the VCSE to support PICE activity, supported by a grant from the NIHR School for primary care research. From this work, the idea of a coordinator role based in the VCSE sector to support greater connections between VCSE organisations and their beneficiary communities, as well as health and care research, was conceived.

Through joint funding from NENC NIHR infrastructures, a two-year pilot of a VCSE research partnerships coordinator was begun in July 2022. The vision for the role was to support partnerships between research and VCSE organisations, with the longer-term aim of growing the involvement of diverse communities in all aspects of the research process. Through a further grant from the NIHR Centre for Engagement and Dissemination (CED), an additional series of workshops with VCSE partners enabled the co-development of a work plan for the new Coordinator. This process involved exploring and re-visiting priorities, negotiating shared agreement about how to move forward and defining what success from the pilot would look like. Importantly, funding for this developmental work was hosted by Voluntary Organisations' Network North East (VONNE), the regional support infrastructure for the North East VCSE sector, rather than a traditional PICE or research institution.

The coordinator undertook a wide range of activities to support researchers and VCSE organisations. This included sharing research opportunities through VONNE's networks, which include representation across the NENC region and diverse communities of interest. They provided a single point of contact for making VCSE/research connections and, where interests aligned, made direct introductions between researchers and VCSE organisations, providing advice to support early partnership discussions based on establishing reciprocal, sustainable partnerships. They also developed and delivered opportunities for training, skills, and knowledge sharing, including events for researchers and VCSE organisations to encourage adoption of the NIHR Community Engagement Toolkit to support more positive and reciprocal partnerships.

Partway through the pilot, additional funding was secured to further develop this work through an NIHR CED call for proposals 'to understand and strengthen regional infrastructure for involvement, engagement, and participation'. Work is now underway to build on the Community Engagement Toolkit (NIHR RDS, 2022) through the co-production of practical resources to enable both VCSE and research partners to develop more positive reciprocal relationships. The toolkit embodies the values and principles that underpin the approach that we are putting into practice in the NENC and is therefore central to this work. We also continue to roll out training to grow researcher awareness and knowledge about the VCSE sector, as well as VCSE awareness and knowledge about health and care research to establish a better shared understanding from which partnership conversations and relationships can develop.

The Coordinator and a representative from 'Love Amelia' reflect on the pilot role.

Greta Brunskill, VCSE Research Partnerships Coordinator at VONNE July 2022–August 2024

> From the outset, there was interest and appetite for greater opportunities to work together from the VCSE sector and researchers I met. Lots of people commented on how much my role was needed with researchers and VCSE organisations sharing that their connections had come about informally or through chance meetings. Some VCSE organisations also shared that they were interested in research but did not know where to start. The need for support was also evident in the 90 plus requests for help over the two-year pilot.

> At the heart of the role was making connections and introducing partners with shared interests. Where I was able to support this kind of 'match' and early conversations to explore hopes and expectations of a potential partnership, it felt the original intention of the role really came alive. Another positive part of the role was developing opportunities for skill and knowledge sharing to help address gaps in knowledge, and ultimately help VCSE and research partners start their conversations from a better place. Through a serendipitous link with researchers at the NIHR ARC NENC, who also had a remit to support non-academics, we collaborated to deliver an introductory workshop on research and evaluation for VCSEs which was successfully piloted with positive feedback. With VONNE colleagues I was also involved in developing a session called 'What is the VCSE sector?' for research

and health partners, which was also well received. There were also some great examples of communities and VCSE organisations gaining wider value from being involved in research, such as having the opportunity for a health information session, or an organisation gaining access to research evidence that supported their development.

On the challenging side was balancing growing interest and enthusiasm for research in VCSE organisations that had many, many other priorities whilst also managing their expectations. The number of requests for support from research teams looking for community/VCSE partners in the earliest stages of an idea (i.e. to be included in their research funding applications) was very small, with most looking to publicise invitations for PICE contributors or research participants for an established study. My sense is that although there are researchers invested in this kind of partnership working with the VCSE sector, there are still many more who are yet to embrace it. A further challenge was around capturing impact of the role when it can take time for things to have a tangible outcome; different approaches to capturing impact from the initial two-year pilot are being explored.

With the successes and challenges of this initial pilot in mind, I think there is huge potential to further grow connections between the rich and varied VCSE and research communities in the NENC, and for us all to benefit from more impactful research driven and shaped by an inclusive array of community voices. To really get the most from PICE activity, I think taking the research **to** people is so important and working with VCSE organisations helps researchers to meet with people **where they are** in ways that can be so powerful in breaking down potential barriers and creating meaningful involvement. For me, some key next steps will be to further embed VCSE research partnerships support in structures and processes so that researchers are aware and can utilise this at the earliest stages of developing applications for research funding, together with continuing to develop positive ways (such as skill sharing) to build lasting relationships between the sectors beyond specific projects.

Steph Capewell, Chief Executive at Love, Amelia:

Working in partnership and accessing resources and support through VONNE has provided a valuable opportunity to learn from past experiences and improve the collaborative research process, ensuring more effective and mutually beneficial outcomes. The VCSE Partnerships Coordinator has been instrumental in fostering meaningful connections between our charity and researchers whose values and interests align with ours. She has provided an essential bridge, ensuring that communication is clear, and expectations are realistic on both sides. For small charities like ours, where time and capacity are limited, it has been invaluable to have someone advocate on our behalf, highlighting the importance of mutual respect and understanding in research collaborations. The VCSE Partnerships Coordinator has been a strong voice for Love, Amelia and the wider sector, ensuring that our time, resources, and limitations are recognised and respected.

Innovations and Lessons Learned

If health and care research is to be fairer and more representative, we believe that using a co-production approach (NIHR, 2024b) to developing ideas about how to grow more sustainable, reciprocal partnerships between researchers and VCSE organisations is fundamental. We have learnt that it is possible to build on existing networks and infrastructures (e.g., creating connections, VONNE) to bring together the perspectives of VCSE and research sectors to co-produce solutions. Joint funding for the new role was essential in consolidating a partnership with shared interests and priorities in growing greater community connections and diversity in PICE activity. It was also important to locate the resource within the VCSE sector (not in universities or NHS trusts), as this allowed greater flexibility and supported creativity and innovation. It also built on the existing trust and respect in VONNE that was held by VCSE organisations and allowed a more in-depth understanding of the sector to inform the development of the work, making the partnership more equitable. Co-production of the work programme in partnership with VCSE and research organisations helped ensure it was grounded in their experiences and the support *they* felt was needed from the outset. Offering VCSE participants costs for time, travel and subsistence, and holding events in accessible, familiar community spaces ensured that they were able to participate in the co-production process.

Conclusion

Working with VCSE organisations that have trusted and long-standing connections with communities is one important way to reach and involve those who are rarely involved in health and care research. From our collective work and learning over the last five years, we strongly advocate that partnerships need to be reciprocal and meet the needs of the community and VCSE organisations as well as the research. We have also identified the need to continue to address gaps and misunderstandings between the research and VCSE sectors to support better partnership working, including what the VCSE sector is and is not, and the differences between research, evaluation, and service monitoring.

Investment in relationships with VCSE organisations and the community members they serve is essential; these relationships take time and work best where researchers can demonstrate interest and commitment before making significant asks. Working flexibly and creatively in these partnerships can be highly valuable, including when thinking of ways to make the research process and outputs useful to VCSEs and communities. Reciprocity is important and can come in many forms such as skills sharing by researchers to help VCSEs write bids or develop service evaluations. Fundamentally, researchers need to nurture and sustain relationships with VCSE organisations and communities, and more broadly, the VCSE and community's relationship with research. Sharing feedback on how public contributions have been used and the eventual research findings are essential to valuing involvement and maintaining a positive connection with research.

Just as partnerships with VCSEs need careful thought and collaboration, so does innovation that seeks to address historical challenges between the research and VCSE sectors. Innovation needs to be built on solid foundations and trusting, reciprocal relationships; it cannot be imposed on communities or VCSE organisations. Short-term or poorly conceived initiatives can damage and negate relationships.

We have highlighted how current research funding systems pose barriers to VCSE and research partnership working, and we challenge health and care research funders committed to involving diverse communities in research to develop funding calls and processes that encourage and enable partnership working between sectors. This is important not only in ensuring good and inclusive PICE in research, but in supporting diversity of research participants (the people who *take part* in research) by helping to ensure research is designed and delivered in ways that will reach and engage the wide and diverse public.

References

Banks, S., Armstrong, A., Carter, K., Graham, H., Hayward, P., Henry, A., Holland, T., Holmes, C., Lee, A., McNulty, A., Moore, N., Nayling, N., Stokoe, A., & Strachan A. (2013). Everyday ethics in community-based participatory research. *Contemporary Social Science*, 8(3), 263–277. https://doi.org/10.1080/21582041.2013.769618

Boaz, A., Hanney, S., Jones, T., & Soper, B. (2015). Does the engagement of clinicians and organisations in research improve healthcare performance: A three-stage review. *BMJ Open*, 5(12), e009415. https://doi.org/10.1136/bmjopen-2015-009415

Bower, P., Grigoroglou, C., Anselmi, L., Kontopantelis, E., Sutton, M., Ashworth, M., Evans, P., Lock, S., Smye, S., & Abel, K. (2020). Is health research undertaken where the burden of disease is greatest? Observational study of geographical inequalities in recruitment to research in England 2013–2018. *BMC Medicine*, 18(1), 133. https://doi.org/10.1186/s12916-020-01555-4

Creating Connections. (2024). *About creating connections.* https://blogs.ncl.ac.uk/creating-connections/about-creating-connections/

Kennedy-Martin, T., Curtis, S., Faries, D., Robinson, S., & Johnston, J. (2015). A literature review on the representativeness of randomized controlled trial samples and implications for the external validity of trial results. *Current Controlled Trials in Cardiovascular Medicine*, 16(1), 495–495. https://doi.org/10.1186/s13063-015-1023-4

NIHR. (2021). *NIHR reaching out – A practical guide to being inclusive in public involvement in health research.* https://arc-nenc.nihr.ac.uk/wp-content/uploads/2021/04/NIHR-Reaching-Out_-A-practical-guide-to-being-inclusive-in-public-involvement-in-health-research-Lessons-learnt-from-the-Reaching-Out-programme-April-2021.pdf

NIHR. (2024a). *Renewing the NIHR's commitment to public partnerships.* https://www.nihr.ac.uk/news/renewing-nihrs-commitment-public-partnerships

NIHR. (2024b). *Guidance on co-producing a research project.* https://www.learningfor involvement.org.uk/content/resource/nihr-guidance-on-co-producing-a-research-project/

NIHR Research Design Service. (2022). *Community engagement toolkit.* https://arc-nenc.nihr.ac.uk/resources/nihr-community-engagement-toolkit/

Pearson, H., Bell, C., Cox, K., Kayum, C., Knox, L., Gibson, F., Myall, M., Darlington, A. S., Potter, E., & Bird, N. (2024). Integration of patient and public involvement in a doctoral research study using the research cycle. *Research Involvement and Engagement, 10*(1), 87–19. https://doi.org/10.1186/s40900-024-00620-z

Reynolds, J., Ogden, M., & Beresford, R. (2021). Conceptualising and constructing 'diversity' through experiences of public and patient involvement in health research. *Research Involvement and Engagement, 7,* 53. https://doi.org/10.1186/s40900-021-00296-9

Staniszewska, S., Denegri, S., Mathews, R., & Minogue, V. (2018). Reviewing progress in public involvement in NIHR research: Developing and implementing a new vision for the future. *BMJ Open, 8*(7), e017124. https://doi.org/10.1136/bmjopen-2017-017124

UK Public Involvement Standards Development Partnership. (2019). *UK standards for public involvement.* https://sites.google.com/nihr.ac.uk/pi-standards/home

University of Oxford, Medical Sciences Division. (n.d.). *The research cycle.* Retrieved January 2025, from https://www.medsci.ox.ac.uk/research/patient-and-public-involvement/section-3-ppi-and-the-research-pathway

Chapter 3

From Tokenism to Trust: Transforming Public Engagement in Local Authority Research and Practice Through Health Determinants Research Collaborations

Michael Johansen[a], Olivia Mullaney[a] and Hayley Alderson[b]

[a]*Public Health and Wellbeing, Population Health Sciences Institute, Newcastle University, UK*
[b]*NIHR Health Determinants Research Collaboration (HDRC), Gateshead Council, UK*

Abstract

The transfer of public health responsibilities to local authorities has placed greater emphasis on the need for evidence-based decision-making to address health inequalities. Integral to this process is the involvement of the public and communities in research, ensuring that decisions are informed and equitable. While local authorities possess existing structures for community engagement, the establishment of NIHR Health Determinants Research Collaborations (HDRCs) presents a fresh opportunity to address power imbalances potentially inherent in traditional engagement practices. This chapter explores how HDRCs can establish sustainable research infrastructure to embed public involvement and community engagement (PICE) within local authority systems and foster long-term change which places communities at the heart of health inequalities research.

Keywords: Public health; local authority; public involvement; research; health inequalities

Public Involvement and Community Engagement in Applied Health and Social Care Research:
Critical Perspectives and Innovative Practice, 31–42

1. Introduction

Health inequalities disproportionately affect the poorest and most marginalised communities, making it essential that their voices are not only heard but actively engaged in research aimed at addressing these challenges (Parbery-Clark et al., 2023). Since 2013, the transfer of public health responsibilities to local authorities has intensified the emphasis on evidence-based decision-making and public involvement in shaping health policies (LGA, 2022). Although evidence has always been central to council priorities, its use has often been constrained by politics, financial limitations, and the need for rapid decision-making, resulting in its underutilisation (Boaz et al., 2019; Cheetham et al., 2022; Kneale et al., 2017). In response, local authorities are formalising their research structures, building internal capacity, and fostering a research culture that prioritises collaboration with residents (Homer et al., 2022). This represents a crucial shift from conducting research *on* communities to working *with* them, fundamentally transforming public involvement.

Despite these changes, achieving meaningful public engagement remains challenging due to local authorities experiencing substantial and sustained periods of austerity (Gray & Barford, 2018). However, the establishment of in-house research capacity, supported by external research partnerships, offers hope for building more consistent, and impactful PICE.

The National Institute for Health and Care Research (NIHR) has launched 30 HDRCs across the UK. These HDRCs, in partnership with regional universities, aim to embed a research-driven culture in local authorities, enhancing their capacity and infrastructure to tackle health inequalities through evidence-based decision-making (NIHR, 2023a). PICE are central to this initiative, reinforcing the importance of collaboration. As public bodies, councils must remain accountable to their communities. Genuine public involvement ensures that decisions reflect residents' needs and that public funds are spent wisely. However, with the growing demand for public involvement in research, there is a risk of tokenism: engaging communities merely to meet funding or regulatory requirements rather than fostering meaningful collaboration. Moving from tokenism to trust requires ongoing transparency, reflection, learning, and a sustained commitment to engagement (Jackson et al., 2020).

HDRC Infrastructure

HDRCs were established as part of an NIHR initiative. Our team operates across all council departments, and a key goal is to drive health-focussed research and build long-term research infrastructure. We have extensive staff and resources, including a multi-disciplinary team comprising research leads, a knowledge broker, a data scientist, a training lead, and a PICE lead. Most of our independent researchers hold PhDs and come from multi-disciplinary academic backgrounds.

The HDRC's roles are integral to strengthening relationships with the community, Voluntary, Community, and Social Enterprise (VCSE) organisations, stakeholders, and underrepresented groups to collaborate on our research efforts. We work extensively with a PICE board that includes community members and marginalised groups who review and shape our research priorities. Our work is underpinned by equity, and we ensure that public contributors are fairly compensated for their time, demonstrating our commitment to meaningful involvement. This approach to PICE work marks a positive and significant shift within the council, aiming to deepen engagement with residents and aligning our research more closely with community needs.

2. Challenges and Reflections on Funded Research

2.1. PICE As a Funding Requirement

As evidence-based practice gains momentum in local authorities, opportunities for original research grow, and so do the challenges of integrating PICE meaningfully. While PICE is widely recognised as essential for robust research (Liabo et al., 2020), concerns about tokenism arise when power imbalances remain unaddressed or when engagement serves primarily to satisfy funding criteria (Ocloo & Matthews, 2016).

Grant applications now often require evidence that PICE has shaped the research proposal (Wilson et al., 2015). This requirement introduces financial and practical challenges, as PICE involvement incurs costs – such as remuneration, room hire, travel, and VCSE support – that local authorities may struggle to justify without secured funding. Although some small bursaries exist, substantial PICE funding usually becomes available only after grant approval (Jackson et al., 2020). This creates a paradox: while PICE is necessary to secure research funding, the lack of upfront funding often restricts its implementation, compromising both the quality and authenticity of the engagement.

This paradox became evident during a recent funding application, in which we collaborated with local authority and university colleagues to explore the integration of domestic abuse awareness into relationships and sex education (RSE) in schools. While the HDRC could draw on professionals such as practitioners and academics to ensure research feasibility, the success of this public health initiative depended on early engagement with VCSE groups. These groups were critical for shaping the project's direction, navigating the sensitive topic, and ensuring the research was both relevant and welcomed by children and young people. However, the funders required evidence of engagement before approving the grant, and the HDRC lacked immediate resources to facilitate this. The HDRC leveraged its partnership with the university, which provided the remuneration for PICE activities, enabling the project to proceed without delay. This early involvement aligned the research with the lived experiences of those affected, demonstrating the value of meaningful PICE. This example underscores the importance of proactive, early stage PICE funding and the value of established partnerships in overcoming potential barriers. Without this early stage engagement, the quality and authenticity of the project would have been diminished, reducing both its impact and likelihood of funding success.

However, it is important to recognise that incorporating PICE into research requires strategic planning across multiple stages. Involving and sharing decision-making power with communities carries financial implications at both individual and organisational levels. At the individual level, PICE members must be remunerated for their time, with reimbursement costs increasing based on the level of involvement required. At the service level, funding may need to be reallocated to accommodate PICE costs – a significant challenge for local authorities during periods of austerity. Nevertheless, the long-term benefits of empowering communities and improving health equity far outweigh these costs (Ocloo & Matthews, 2016).

Our team seeks to address these challenges by forming ongoing partnerships with universities, pooling resources, and generating networks that strengthen grant applications. By establishing community-informed foundations, we aim to balance financial risks while ensuring that PICE remains meaningful and impactful.

Those who use PICE should proactively avoid and prevent tokenism by ensuring it is a genuinely integrated process, underpinned by a shared commitment to meaningful engagement among all stakeholders (Brett et al., 2014). Our team has facilitated this by engaging in early stage community involvement to ensure research outcomes align with real-world needs. This collaborative approach leverages local authority insights and academic expertise, building trust and demonstrating the value of PICE in creating impactful, sustainable policy interventions (Staniszewska et al., 2018).

One of the main challenges we experience is that certain funding streams are exclusive to higher education institutions. Without HDRC's collaborative relationships, these funding opportunities would remain inaccessible, limiting research progress within local authorities. Collaborating with universities has provided valuable learning opportunities by pooling resources and expertise, reducing financial risks, and ensuring that PICE remains credible and ethical throughout the funding process. Through these partnerships, universities can provide remuneration where local authorities lack internal funding for PICE, but this highlights a need for local authorities to develop their own PICE funding strategies to prevent over-reliance on external support. For this collaborative model to succeed, local authorities, and community representatives must co-create scalable project frameworks that include clear PICE budgeting, particularly when engaging marginalised populations.

NIHR guidelines (NIHR, 2023b) provide a useful starting point for establishing baseline remuneration rates. It is important to recognise that disadvantaged individuals may encounter additional barriers to involvement such as childcare needs or income loss, making standard remuneration inadequate. Context-specific assessments and solutions are necessary to navigate these financial, logistical, and ethical challenges if we are to move towards ensuring inclusive and effective engagement. Sustainable and proactive funding models are essential to making PICE a fundamental part of the research process, not an afterthought (De Simoni et al., 2023). By prioritising these changes, local authorities can move beyond tokenism, ensuring that PICE empowers communities and drives equitable, impactful research outcomes.

2.2. Building Trust and Managing Community Engagement

2.2.1. Public Mistrust of Councils

Public mistrust of councils has been identified as a significant barrier to effective engagement. In 2022, trust in local authorities stood at just 54% (APSE, 2022), reflecting a broader decline in confidence across UK government institutions, contributing to a 'crisis of trust' (Hardin, 2008; Llewellyn et al., 2013; O'Neill, 2002). For council-affiliated researchers, this mistrust complicates efforts to engage communities, as negative experiences with council services – such as housing or social care – often deter participation.

As a research team, we have encountered situations where residents have shared their frustrations with our researchers, stemming from difficulties navigating health and social care systems. It is not unusual for community members to feel frustrated, ignored, or marginalised, and such encounters underscore the challenges of conducting public engagement from within the council, where political decisions and systemic inefficiencies can fuel public animosity (Bagozzi et al., 2022). To build trust, the HDRC prioritises transparency and the creation of safe spaces for community feedback, ensuring residents see how their input influences outcomes (NIHR, 2023a). By fostering consistent and meaningful participation through iterative processes, the HDRC aims to shift perceptions and rebuild trust in the council's role. Overcoming public mistrust is essential for successful PICE; without it, even the most well-intentioned efforts risk being perceived as tokenistic.

2.2.2. Participation Fatigue and 'Taken' Voices

Our HDRC often uses qualitative methods, such as interviews and focus groups, to embed residents' voices in council work. However, involving marginalised and underrepresented communities repeatedly can lead to participation fatigue, creating a risk of over-relying on the same groups (Attree et al., 2011; Baines et al., 2022). This has been echoed by participants within our local community who have expressed frustration, feeling their voices were used in previous research without seeing tangible benefits or recognition, either through feedback or remuneration.

As part of our work, we engaged typically underrepresented groups, including gay and bisexual men, transgender individuals, ethnic minorities, and youth under 19 years. However, representatives of these groups reported to us as having participated in a similar consultation previously, but felt their input was merely used to meet diversity requirements. Additionally, participants noted a lack of follow-up, with no feedback on how their contributions impacted services. The repeated engagement by different council directorates left them feeling overused and undervalued.

To rebuild trust, HDRC researchers co-designed focus group activities with community members to ensure cultural relevance and sensitivity. We implemented a clear remuneration policy, following NIHR guidelines (NIHR, 2023b), and established a feedback process in which council representatives returned to the community to demonstrate how their input shaped service delivery.

This approach aims to repair relationships and ensure participants feel genuinely valued. Sharing this case study with staff promotes a shift in public involvement practices and demonstrates how embedding research values into engagement can make every interaction meaningful.

These efforts align with the HDRC's broader goal of transforming council culture. While systemic change takes time, incremental improvements in engagement can have a significant impact. As a researcher, you may encounter representatives of marginalised communities who express scepticism, rooted in prior negative experiences with other teams. Having clear, unambiguous goals, outlining the scope of involvement, and following through on commitments will help you build trust and leave the door open for future collaborations.

2.2.3. Overburdening of the PICE Network

A significant concern related to participation fatigue is the overreliance on individuals with lived experience. While co-creating services with those affected offers invaluable insights by grounding public services in their realities (Strokosch & Osborne, 2020), this approach can become unsustainable without careful management. The council's duty of care extends not only to the public but also to its employees and wider PICE network. Overburdening individuals with lived experience risks compromising their well-being and reducing meaningful engagement to tokenism. Effectively managing contributions is crucial to avoid criticism about exploiting these individuals, whose perspectives are critical yet often overstretched, particularly in sensitive research areas that may cause emotional strain (see Adams and Ramsey's chapter on Trauma in this collection).

Multi-disciplinary support within research teams is essential. For example, in a recent focus group with individuals in recovery, participants were asked to share their experiences of deaths related to drugs, alcohol, and suicide – deeply personal and emotionally heavy topics. To mitigate potential harm, the sessions were co-designed and co-delivered with trusted VCSE organisations, ensuring support was provided both before and after the focus groups.

Insights gathered throughout this PICE work were essential for shaping the council's strategic approach. This example highlights the delicate balance between gathering input and safeguarding the well-being of vulnerable groups. It underscores the importance of ensuring every engagement is necessary, conducted sensitively, and offers clear benefits beyond meeting procedural requirements. Additionally, it emphasises the ethical responsibility of protecting participants throughout the PICE process.

2.3. Navigating Power Dynamics in Engaging Seldom Heard Populations

Engaging seldom-heard groups requires addressing power dynamics effectively. Arnstein's (1969) ladder of citizen participation provides a framework for understanding and addressing these dynamics, urging researchers to move beyond tokenism and redistribute power to communities. The ladder illustrates varying degrees of citizen power, from manipulation at the lowest level to full citizen control at the highest, emphasising the importance of equitable involvement (Arnstein, 1969). The HDRC, uniquely positioned between the university and the council, bridges these hierarchies and advocates for public empowerment, ensuring a balanced approach.

Historically, power in research has often been concentrated in the hands of researchers (Mitchell et al., 2023). PICE offers a pathway for a more equitable approach, shifting power to the public and making them central to research design and implementation (Bidwell & Schweizer, 2020). This shift is crucial in public health research, as the public's perspectives must guide the research process to ensure its relevance and impact, and their needs directly shape the outcomes.

Navigating power dynamics in research, particularly when engaging seldom heard groups, requires a commitment to equity (McAreavey & Das, 2013). This involves reflexivity, transparency, and adaptability to prioritise public voices (Mitchell et al., 2023). Arnstein's ladder underscores the importance of this commitment, with the HDRC emphasising early PICE activities to review and shape research proposals to reflect community input and needs.

The complexities of engaging seldom-heard groups often intersect with the role of gatekeepers, which must be handled with care. During the project seeking the integration of domestic abuse awareness into RSE in schools (mentioned in Section 2.1), the critical role of gatekeepers became apparent. Despite efforts by HDRC colleagues to maintain transparency through regular meetings, the gatekeeper chose to conduct engagement activities independently, providing the research team with summaries afterwards. While this approach limited direct engagement between researchers and the public, it reflected the gatekeepers' desire to manage the community's involvement in a way they deemed protective of community interests.

This situation underscores the dual role of gatekeepers: they facilitate access to seldom-heard groups and help prioritise their needs, but their decisions can also present challenges for researchers. Without direct interaction, researchers may lack the depth of understanding needed to respond fully to public feedback (Clark, 2010; Kay, 2019; McAreavey & Das, 2013).

To ensure the gatekeeper's role supports equitable power redistribution, clearer frameworks are necessary. These frameworks should include training and guidelines for gatekeepers to foster collaborative, transparent processes. Building trusting relationships and co-creating strategies can help researchers balance these dynamics, ensuring that power is genuinely shared and that public engagement remains central within the research process (Singh & Wassenaar, 2016).

The HDRC, with its unique position and ongoing advocacy for robust PICE practices, is well-placed to establish these frameworks and ensure future projects realise PICE's full potential. This ongoing commitment helps ensure research authentically empowers communities and reflects their needs, making a lasting impact.

2.4. Addressing Structural and Cultural Barriers

2.4.1. Managing Representation and Addressing Inequalities

A core aspect of cultural change within PICE is effectively managing representation to ensure diverse and/or seldom-heard communities are meaningfully
included. However, managing representation alone is not enough; overcoming cultural resistance and systemic barriers is equally important. By expanding public involvement and including underrepresented voices, the council can
more equitably and effectively address the root causes of health inequality. For
instance, our council's sexual health needs assessment brought together diverse
groups to co-design the council's sexual health offer, ensuring the solutions were
inclusive and reflective of varied community needs.

Cultural transformation within local authorities requires commitment, cultural sensitivity, and competence; it also takes time and demands negotiation, sustained effort, and collaboration within and across council departments. Our team
within the HDRC plays a pivotal role in this transformation. However, progress
necessitates an ongoing critical appraisal of our practices and the dismantling of
institutional barriers. These include budget constraints, bureaucratic inertia, and
conflicting priorities across council sectors. Securing long-term buy-in from all
areas of local government involves proactive stakeholder engagement, ongoing
staff training opportunities on PICE values, and alignment with regional and
national priorities to gain policy support.

This ongoing challenge demands resilience and a commitment to seeing
through the slow but essential work of creating systems where PICE is a genuine
priority to improve health equity. Rather than focussing solely on consultation,
researchers must examine their overall PICE strategy and explore opportunities
to embed collaborative practices more deeply in their work. More recently, we
have initiated training workshops on all aspects of research delivery – from shaping an idea to disseminating findings – to facilitate cross-directorate collaboration
and build a unified approach to PICE that strengthens health equity in the region.

Incorporating peer researchers and community champions is one way to
address the inherent power imbalances of conducting research within political
institutions. By empowering individuals from communities most impacted by
health disparities, HDRCs can ensure that research reflects lived experiences and
addresses real-world challenges. This approach not only amplifies marginalised
voices but also helps dismantle systemic inequities, fostering a more democratic
research process that directly engages the communities we aim to serve.

However, this approach also raises another challenge: while inclusivity in
PICE cannot be overstated, over-reliance on a small number of voices risks perpetuating exclusion and undermining PICE's goals. Our HDRC has implemented
strategies such as partnerships with VCSEs to diversify participation, ensuring
that networks are representative, inclusive, and respectful of contributors' time
and expertise.

Regardless of the approach, mobilising knowledge effectively requires PICE
to be collaborative, co-created, co-designed, and co-produced. These practices
must go beyond procedural requirements to deliver meaningful change.

2.4.2. Impact of Austerity on Health Equity

Austerity has shifted the focus of many public services from proactive and preventive to reactive and restrictive measures, worsening health inequalities. Budget cuts and limited resources have hindered councils' ability to prioritise PICE and develop long-term, inclusive strategies for community engagement. For example, funding reductions for preventative services, such as smoking cessation (Anderson et al., 2018), have made it increasingly difficult to engage proactively with communities.

However, in times of financial constraint, PICE becomes even more critical. Engaging marginalised groups in designing services ensures their needs are properly considered, especially when resources are stretched. The HDRC provides additional resources to strengthen public engagement efforts and enhance the council's evidence base. By embedding PICE into service delivery and design, these efforts help mitigate the impact of austerity on health outcomes and the social determinants of health. By amplifying community voices and leveraging HDRC's resources, councils can take steps towards minimising health disparities, even when faced with financial and structural barriers.

3. Conclusion

The HDRC's work is already beginning to influence local policy by embedding research findings into decision-making processes. This is not merely an academic exercise but a tangible effort to shape policies that better respond to community needs. The HDRC's work signifies a call to action for researchers, policymakers, and community members within local government. It offers a transformative opportunity to deepen and expand PICE, positioning PICE not as a procedural obligation but as a necessary and powerful framework for co-designing services that genuinely reflect the needs and priorities of residents (Jackson et al., 2020). By fostering authentic and sustained engagement, HDRCs can build partnerships that promote more sustainable, equitable, and healthier outcomes for our communities.

Trust is central to this transformation. When communities witness clear and measurable outcomes from their involvement, engagement deepens, and a stronger, more resilient relationship between the council and the public emerges. This trust is especially crucial for reducing health inequalities, as it helps ensure the voices of those most impacted by systemic disparities are heard, validated, and acted upon. By building trust through transparent and iterative engagement processes, the HDRC is helping the public take control of their communities and address the wider determinants of health that affect their lives.

Achieving this vision requires an ongoing, collective commitment to embedding inclusive practices, fostering shared responsibility, and ensuring equitable representation in every aspect of research and decision-making. The HDRC is integral in facilitating this shift, working closely with the council and community members to ensure PICE evolves into a model built on trust, collaboration, and meaningful impact. Through this work, HDRC is enhancing the council's capacity to deliver evidence-based policies while cementing PICE as a central element of our long-term strategy to address health inequalities.

In doing so, our HDRC is moving the council beyond traditional, top-down models of engagement, embedding a culture of partnership and co-production where communities actively shape decisions that affect them. This cultural shift prioritises collaboration and shared ownership, encouraging communities to participate fully in addressing local challenges. This transformation is not just about improving processes; it is about fostering a legacy of trust and empowerment that goes beyond tokenism. By empowering the public to take an active role in addressing the wider determinants of health, the HDRC is building a foundation for sustainable, community-led change, ultimately shifting the relationship *from tokenism to trust.*

References

Anderson, W. J., Cheeseman, H., & Butterworth, G. (2017). Political priorities and public health services in English local authorities: The case of tobacco control and smoking cessation services. *Journal of Public Health*, 40(3), e269–e274. https://doi.org/10.1093/pubmed/fdx143

APSE. (2022). *Trust and confidence in councils: What the public think – APSE*. Apse.org.uk. Retrieved September 30, 2024, from https://www.apse.org.uk/index.cfm/apse/research/current-research-programme/trust-and-confidence-in-councils-what-the-public-think/

Arnstein, S. R. (1969). A ladder of citizen participation. *Journal of the American Institute of Planners*, 35(4), 216–224. https://doi.org/10.1080/01944366908977225

Attree, P., French, B., Milton, B., Povall, S., Whitehead, M., & Popay, J. (2011). The experience of community engagement for individuals: A rapid review of evidence. *Health & Social Care in the Community*, 19(3), 250–260. https://doi.org/10.1111/j.1365-2524.2010.00976.x

Bagozzi, R. P., Mari, S., Oklevik, O., & Xie, C. (2022). Responses of the public towards the government in times of crisis. *British Journal of Social Psychology*, 62(1), 359–392. https://doi.org/10.1111/bjso.12566

Baines, R., Bradwell, H., Edwards, K., Stevens, S., Prime, S., Tredinnick-Rowe, J., Sibley, M., & Chatterjee, A. (2022). Meaningful patient and public involvement in digital health innovation, implementation and evaluation: A systematic review. *Health Expectations*, 25(4), 1232–1245. https://doi.org/10.1111/hex.13506

Bidwell, D., & Schweizer, P. (2020). Public values and goals for public participation. *Environmental Policy and Governance, 31*(4), 257–269. https://onlinelibrary.wiley.com/doi/10.1002/eet.1913

Boaz, A., Davies, H., Fraser, A., & Nutley, S. (2019). *What works now?: Evidence-based policy and practice revisited*. Policy Press.

Brett, J., Staniszewska, S., Mockford, C., Herron-Marx, S., Hughes, J., Tysall, C., & Suleman, R. (2014). A systematic review of the impact of patient and public involvement on service users, researchers and communities. *Patient*, 7(4), 387–395. https://doi.org/10.1007/s40271-014-0065-0

Cheetham, M., Redgate, S., van der Graaf, P., Humble, C., Hunter, D., & Adamson, A. (2022). 'What I really want is academics who want to partner and who care about the outcome': Findings from a mixed-methods study of evidence use in local government in England. *Evidence & Policy, 19*(1), 74–94. https://doi.org/10.1332/1744264 21x16535820632215

Clark, T. (2010). Gaining and maintaining access. *Qualitative Social Work: Research and Practice, 10*(4), 485–502. https://doi.org/10.1177/1473325009358228

De Simoni, A., Jackson, T., Humphrey, W. I., Preston, J., Mah, H., Wood, H.E., Kinley, E., Rienda, L. G., & Porteous, C. (2023). Patient and public involvement in research: The need for budgeting PPI staff costs in funding applications. *Research Involvement and Engagement, 9*(1), 16. https://doi.org/10.1186/s40900-023-00424-7

Gray, M., & Barford, A. (2018). The depths of the cuts: The uneven geography of local government austerity. *Cambridge Journal of Regions, Economy and Society, 11*, 541–563.

Hardin, R. (2008). *Trust*. Polity Press.

Homer, C., Woodall, J., Freeman, C., South, J., Cooke, J., Holliday, J., Hartley, A., & Mullen, S. (2022). Changing the culture: A qualitative study exploring research capacity in local government. *BMC Public Health, 22*(1), 1341. https://doi.org/10.1186/s12889-022-13758-w

Jackson, T., Pinnock, H., Liew, S.M., Horne, E., Ehrlich, E., Fulton, O., Worth, A., Sheikh, A., & De Simoni, A. (2020). Patient and public involvement in research: From tokenistic box ticking to valued team members. *BMC Medicine, 18*(1), 79. https://doi.org/10.1186/s12916-020-01544-7

Kay, L. (2019). Guardians of research: Negotiating the strata of gatekeepers in research with vulnerable participants. *Practice, 1*(1), 37–52.

Kneale, D., Rojas-García, A., Raine, R., & Thomas, J. (2017). The use of evidence in English local public health decision-making: A systematic scoping review. *Implementation Science, 12*(1), 53. https://doi.org/10.1186/s13012-017-0577-9

LGA. (2022). *Public health in local government: Celebrating 10 years of transformation*. Local Government Association. https://www.local.gov.uk/publications/public-health-local-government-celebrating-10-years-transformation

Liabo, K., Boddy, K., Bortoli, S., Irvine, J., Boult, H., Fredlund, M., Joseph, N., Bjornstad, G., & Morris, C. (2020). Public involvement in health research: What does 'good' look like in practice?. *Research Involvement and Engagement, 6*(1), 11. https://doi.org/10.1186/s40900-020-0183-x

Llewellyn, S., Brookes, S., & Mahon, A. (2013). *Trust and confidence in government and public services*. Routledge.

McAreavey, R., & Das, C. (2013). A Delicate Balancing Act: Negotiating with gatekeepers for ethical research when researching minority communities. *International Journal of Qualitative Methods, 12*(1), 113–131. https://doi.org/10.1177/160940691301200102

Mitchell, C., Fryer, K., Guess, N., Aminu, H., Jackson, B., Gordon, A., Reynolds, J. P., Huang, Q., Jayasooriya, S., Mawson, R. L., Lawy, T., Linton, E., & Brown, J. (2023). Underserved 'Deep End' populations: A critical analysis addressing the power imbalance in research. *British Journal of General Practice, 73*(732), 326–329. https://doi.org/10.3399/bjgp23x733461

NIHR. (2023a). *NIHR invests a further £55m to tackle health inequalities through local government research*. Nihr.ac.uk. Retrieved September 29, 2024, from https://www.nihr.ac.uk/about-us/news/nihr-invests-further-ps55m-tackle-health-inequalities-through-local-government

NIHR. (2023b). *Payment for public involvement in health and care research: A guide for organisations on employment status and tax*. Nihr.ac.uk. Retrieved September 30, 2024, from https://www.nihr.ac.uk/payment-public-involvement-health-and-care-research-guide-organisations-employment-status-and-tax

O'Neill, O. (2002). *A question of trust: The BBC Reith lectures 2002*. Cambridge University Press.

Ocloo, J., & Matthews, R. (2016). From tokenism to empowerment: Progressing patient and public involvement in healthcare improvement. *BMJ Quality & Safety, 25*(8), 626–632. https://doi.org/10.1136/bmjqs-2015-004839

Parbery-Clark, C., Nicholls, R., McSweeney, L., Sowden, S., & Lally, J. (2023). Coproduction of a resource sharing public views of health inequalities: An example of inclusive public and patient involvement and engagement. *Health Expectations*, *27*(1), e13860. https://doi.org/10.1111/hex.13860

Singh, S., & Wassenaar, D. (2016). Contextualising the role of the gatekeeper in social science research. *South African Journal of Bioethics and Law*, *9*(1), 42–46. https://doi.org/10.7196/sajbl.2016.v9i1.465

Staniszewska, S., Denegri, S., Matthews, R., & Minogue, V. (2018). Reviewing progress in public involvement in NIHR research: Developing and implementing a new vision for the future. *BMJ Open*, *8*(7), e017124. https://doi.org/10.1136/bmjopen-2017-017124

Strokosch, K., & Osborne, S. P. (2020). Co-experience, co-production and co-governance: An ecosystem approach to the analysis of value creation. *Policy & Politics*, *48*(3), 425–442. https://doi.org/10.1332/030557320x15857337955214

Wilson, P., Mathie, E., Keenan, J., McNeilly, E., Goodman, C., Howe, A., Poland, F., Staniszewska, S., Kendall, S., Munday, D., Cowe, M., & Peckham, S. (2015). ReseArch with patient and public involvement: A realist evaluation – The RAPPORT study. *Health Services and Delivery Research*, *3*(38), 1–176. https://doi.org/10.3310/hsdr03380

Section 2

Creativity and Innovation, Perspectives and Opportunities in PICE Work

Chapter 4

Engaging with the Theory and Practice of Creative PICE Work

Ian Robson

School of Education and Communities, Northumbria University, UK

Abstract

This chapter explores the concept of creative public involvement and community engagement (PICE), arguing that creativity is a vital and transformative element in effective engagement and involvement practices. Rather than offering a prescriptive template, the chapter examines the productive nature of creativity and its potential to invigorate PICE activities, aligning them with socially just values. It addresses common misconceptions about creativity – its reduction to superficial decoration or its mystification as an elite talent – and offers a more grounded and inclusive understanding. Drawing on insights from philosophy, art, and social practice, the chapter identifies creativity as a process rooted in intention, sensory and embodied experience, encounters, emergence, and improvisation. The chapter situates creative PICE within the complexities of modern public services, where diverse populations, systemic inequalities, and cross-organisational challenges demand imaginative and collaborative solutions. It argues for creative PICE as an active process of becoming, co-production, and materialising change, using examples and practical approaches to engage communities meaningfully. The chapter concludes with practical guidance for developing creative PICE, emphasising the importance of relationships, openness, and curiosity.

Keywords: Creativity; philosophy; practice; inclusion; culture; innovation

Public Involvement and Community Engagement in Applied Health and Social Care Research: Critical Perspectives and Innovative Practice, 45–55

doi:10.1108/978-1-83608-678-920251004

Introduction

Understanding and considering the characteristics and practicalities of creative public involvement and community engagement (PICE) is an important starting point for those developing research and those who are the recipients of it. This chapter is based on a proposition that good PICE work is creative. However, rather than presenting a manual or template for creative PICE, the chapter explores the productive nature of creativity, then talks about how our PICE activity can be creative. It is an invitation for all of us to reflect on our relationship with PICE – and how our positions, intentions, goals, and methods may be transformed through engaging with the nature of creativity. It is also an opportunity to revitalise our PICE activity and to align it with values. In the following chapter, I set out a case for creative PICE and why being 'creative' is an essential quality of effective involvement and engagement work. I then discuss some of the popular misconceptions about creativity, and more importantly, the characteristics that all forms of creativity tend to share. Finally, I focus on practical advice for developing creative PICE in their projects and organisations. The chapter invites you to revisit your PICE positionality in relation to creativity, policy, and practice in the light of these things.

Why Do We Need Creative PICE?

My proposition is that *good* PICE is *creative* PICE. I define creative PICE as

> any activity in which people use their senses, skills and resources in a purposeful activity which is interactive, imaginative and contributes to change in health, social care, or education.

Before considering the nature of creativity or the practicalities of enhancing creativity within PICE activities, some context helps us appreciate why creativity is essential and not optional. In short, improving public services by utilising creative methods and involving communities in research to create better outcomes is complex and requires imagination. This is especially true today. The development of public services in domains such as health, education, and welfare, especially in the Global North, has been rapid since the end of World War Two (see Lowe, 2004). Not only have health, education, and social care services expanded in scope, but populations have become more diverse. Literature (Meadows & Wright, 2017) has underlined how outcomes in any one social, educational or health issue link to many different variables in the complex and dynamic system of society. Amongst other things, technological developments have enabled new methods and created demand for new interventions. In ageing populations, people are living longer, increasing, for example, the need for complex health provision. As a result, public services need a much better understanding of lived experience and local situations. They must work across organisational boundaries (Sullivan & Skelcher, 2017), including with traditional service users, whilst recognising that many solutions exist beyond the control of public services. These types of consideration need to be recognised in the context that meaningful and authentic collaborations between local communities and other stakeholders (Cotterell & Buffel, 2023) can enhance the quality and relevance of strategies designed to both reduce inequality and promote the uptake of public services. If you are interested in exploring some of the tensions that exist between local communities and the importance of trust, you should also read Johansen et al. (Chapter 4) in this collection.

Since the 1970s, one response amongst others to this challenge has been the replacement of bureaucratic models with managerial (Pollitt & Bouckaert, 2017) ones, focussed on the establishment of markets and their associated competition, metrics, performance management, and so-called customer focus. However, treating patients, pupils, and clients as 'customers' has not developed health, education, or social care systems that work with the social, cultural, physical (and other) resources linked to complex issues (Martin-Kerry et al., 2023). Research evidence has highlighted the need to understand and influence, for example, the social determinants of health (Marmot & Wilkinson, 2005). All too aware of this, today, public services are keen to reference catchphrases such as 'partnership', 'co-production', or activity that is 'asset-based'. PICE is framed by these ideas (e.g., Involve.org.uk, 2024; NHS England, 2022) and seen as an activity that will support it. The lack of consensus amongst empirical researchers/academics, funding authorities, and the public around what co-production is and what it involves is positive in relation to creating a space for ongoing 'learning' debates and conversations to occur and inform practice.

Having a PICE strategy or activities provides no guarantee that meaningful insights into lived experience, utilisation of wider resources in communities, or new thinking or practices will result. This activity needs nurturing, dialogue, animation, experimentation, and imagination. In other words, it needs to be creative.

About Creativity

Even if we agree that 'creativity' is a necessary characteristic of contemporary public services, and especially PICE, the term 'creativity' is ambiguous enough to be used, and misused, in many ways. Things claiming to be creative appear to us in different forms. When reduced, flattened, and commodified, creativity can appear prescriptive, decorative and dare we say tokenistic. In this mode, certain things are creative – a familiar list of activities, when added to PICE, ensure it is creative. 'If we do (x), we are being creative'. This commodified mode of creativity reduces and formulates it, seeming to make being creative 'easier' and predictable. However, in this flattened form, creative PICE can take on a decorative role, where decoration is a superficial 'dressing up' of substance. Elements such as illustrations, performances, and documentary images all can have their place in PICE, but they can also be meaningless if used as decoration for some other 'substance'.

In PICE, an equal danger is that creativity can appear to be vague and abstract. Like the 'emperor's new clothes', it can be presented as an opaque, spiritual, mysterious thing, something that only certain people can do. We may look at completed works of art, writing or performance and either ignore or find it impossible to imagine the process that led to that final form – reinforcing the sense that it is something deeply strange to us. I argue that working with strangeness and difference can be very productive within PICE, but strangeness and difference need not separate us. Indeed, it can be an invitation to encounter, appreciate, question, and learn.

Both approaches (i.e., decoration and mystery) avoid a serious engagement with creativity. The superficiality of decoration trivialises creativity, and creativity as something exclusive and mysterious has the same effect. Both are safe and require nothing from us other than to be a passive audience. This is what Marcuse (1964/2002) argued in his text, *One dimensional man* – that in late modern society, those with power refashion 'creativity' as a tool for individual consumerism and fulfilment, whilst at the same time use it to divert dissent. Creativity as consumerism or distraction, for Marcuse, has the same effect – it pacifies meaningful social change.

Before considering a more authentic and socially just presentation of 'creativity', it is useful to remind ourselves that the contrast between decoration and mystery is not just an abstract issue. For organisations that commission, manage, and (sometimes) implement PICE activities, it is not always clear what 'creative' means because it remains unexamined. It is this lack of clarity that is worth addressing should we wish to develop PICE that is creative. Otherwise, we may reduce creative PICE to decoration or mystery and miss opportunities for genuine transformational engagement. Considering a serious commitment to creative PICE starts with a sympathetic critical appraisal of 'self', positionality, preference, asking 'why do we undertake PICE?'. Whilst initial responses to that question may seem predictable (e.g., to improve services), it is useful to dig deeper into the ethos, values, and purposes that have historically developed our organisations. Careful reflection on our organisational cultures will often find tensions that need resolving, so we can be clear what creative PICE is and what it can do. On the one hand, public service organisations often have been shaped by the values and ethics of patient benefit (e.g., in healthcare), empowerment and emancipation (e.g., in education), or social justice (e.g., in social work). On the other hand, those same public services have been radically re-shaped by forms of new public management (Lapsley & Miller, 2024) and neoliberalism (also see Addison et al., 2022) that have prioritised competition, efficiency, and contracts. This is the messy reality of organisations that commission, manage and implement PICE activities, and this reality needs to be reflected upon so the 'why' of PICE is clear for them. The role of 'creativity' in PICE looks different depending on whether it is decorating transactional relationships (where managerialism rules) or enabling meaningful co-production (where PICE is guided by socially just values). Before leaping into creative PICE, this is our starting point. From this point on, let us assume that creative PICE supports the latter.

Towards an Appreciation of Creativity for PICE

Once organisations choose to base PICE on a mission of social justice, other more helpful understandings of creativity can be explored. Unsurprisingly, there is no single definition of creativity, but contemporary texts emphasise the production of something 'novel, good or relevant' (Sternberg & Kaufman, 2018, p. xiii). Creativity has been linked with authenticity (Gardner, 2006), risk-taking (Amabile, 2018), the ability to generate multiple ideas (Guilford, 1967), flexibility (Sternberg, 2018) and divergent thinking (Williams et al., 2016). For the sake of brevity, Fig. 4.1 re-presents the contributions of select influential philosophers and artists – Gadamer (1986), Deleuze and Guattari (1994, 2013), Joseph Beuys (Borer & Schirmer, 1997), and Louise Bourgeois (Storr, 2016), who can inspire and direct our understanding about the nature of creativity. The summaries in Fig. 4.1 draw on their actual writing, essays, and practice, which you may find helpful to read further.

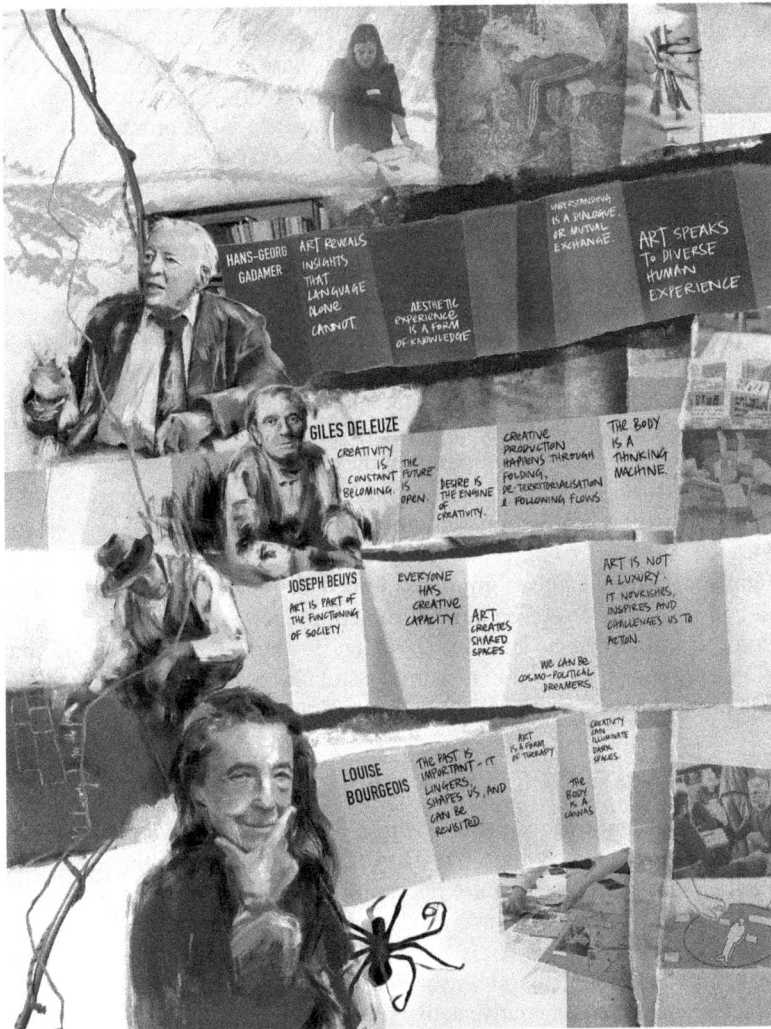

Fig. 4.1. Creativity as Encounter, Improvisation-with and Becoming.

If we spend time with these and other philosophical and artistic voices, it is possible to draw out themes around the nature of creativity. Some key themes are of relevance to PICE.

- Firstly, creativity is related to *intention* (Anscombe, 1957/2000). We are present, listening, receptive, and open to stimuli. We are in a time/place and are alive to a moment, or sensation. Creativity is active. In the capitalist Global North, we are passive subjects, consuming images designed to hold our attention and reacting to prompts. In contrast, creativity starts with noticing and presence.
- When we are in this mode, something moves us. We notice something in our bodies and as we orientate to it, it opens to us – a sound, smell, sight. This second theme is that creativity is sensory and embodied (see Dewey, 1934/2005). Our bodies respond in vital ways; we notice sensations on our skin, and our heart beats faster. Whilst we use language to revise and present what we experience, creativity starts *in the body* (Barrett & Bolt, 2012).
- The fact that we are present, and our bodies are moved, is prompted by a third characteristic of creativity, which is the encounter (Gadamer, 1960/2013). The encounter is the thing that causes us to notice and respond. The encounter adds something new to our experience and is difficult to predict and control. We can be surprised by a feeling of grief, or we can experience curiosity, irritation, awe, or any number of sensations. In the encounter, different things come together, and we contribute to the patterns or momentums created. How we focus and interact changes the situation, whether that be how we frame a photograph, pose a curious question, or select what else we can bring. In being active, we do not simply react, but we bring something to the encounter – like a question.
- From this, creativity is an emergent activity, that is, new things begin to happen as we interact. Each stroke of paint on the canvas opens a further set of potential paint strokes, so to speak. We do not start at the end, as creativity requires that we trust the process and stay in it, remaining open to what is emerging (Deleuze, 1987/2013; Gibb et al., 2021).
- Finally, creativity involves improvisation. It demands that we be experimental and imaginative – to be part of something new is the opposite of slavish reproduction. When we embrace the 'what if?' and step outside of our habits and assumptions, we explore new things and new connections can be explored (Manning & Massumi, 2014).

Developing Creative PICE Practice

It would be dangerous to provide a single, fixed template for creative PICE as defined in this chapter. My approach has been to identity key characteristics of creativity, especially those that are relevant to the task of working with communities of place, identity, or concern to produce better educational, health, welfare, or other public goods (Geuss, 2009). I associate creativity with a sense of intention, as an embodied and sensory process, as an encounter, as an emergent phenomenon and an imaginative activity.

It would also be arrogant of me to suggest practical advice on developing creative PICE had I not worked on this project myself as participant, practitioner, strategic leader, and researcher. In addition to evidence, I draw on my lessons learnt and insights gained in over 30 years of consultation, participation and co-design work with organisations and communities. For example, my work with care-experienced and disabled people has taught me about the importance of establishing authentic and meaningful connections, and the role creativity can have in that context. My work in local authorities and NHS Trusts has taught me about the need for growing senior support for creative practice. Finally, my work with area-based initiatives in the early years, public health and regeneration has taught me about the amazing resources and skills that exist in communities of identity, interest, or place. In my practice, I have always endeavoured to begin creative PICE from a place of relationship, mutual agreement, and recognition.

Holding serious conversations about the purpose of PICE and creative PICE specifically is an ideal starting point. Senior support for the principles and characteristics of creative PICE is a prerequisite for sustainable practice. Here is an opportunity to align organisational, funder, and philosophical commitments and understandings so that a culture of creative PICE can build. It may be quicker to 'buy some art materials', but that would be to trivialise and prescribe the nature of creative PICE, and to ignore building strong foundations for it. This is not to say that slow creativity 'for its own sake' is not valuable in the context of well-being, relationship, and skill building, but that the choice to invest in creative PICE should have purpose and ownership.

Giles Deleuze (e.g., 1987/2013) draws our attention to the production of what is new, and how things are becoming, at various speeds, something new. In his work, Deleuze introduced the concept of the assemblage (see Buchannan, 2021), in which diverse elements work together to produce effects. If we take his concept, we can be inspired to build creative PICE practice in new ways. We can ask: 'What things can work together to produce new insights and forms of practice?'. We think creatively about the sort of assemblage we need and begin to do those things that create new assemblages. We look for the flows, energy, alliances, and connections that can animate our ideas within and outside of our organisations. We can learn to spot the opportunities at the edge of our processes, practices and structures that are exciting and have momentum, and ask 'What can these things do?' (Robson, 2024). If we work with senior colleagues who support creative PICE, we can create new spaces for meaningful activity. To play our part, we help build an assemblage for creative PICE. This assemblage will contain people, projects, and practices who mutually inform one another's 'becoming' (Deleuze, 1987/2013).

Much PICE activity is required by funder requirements or internal quality assurance processes, but creative PICE can also orientate us to a more proactive approach. If we accept (see Fig. 4.1) that creativity involves an active becoming, and an (inter) active form of dialogue, it follows that we start any process of creative PICE with questions, propositions, and encounters. Creative PICE needs a sense of curious purpose and openness, and early connection with experts by experience, members of communities of place, identity, or issue can ensure that we share a sense of purpose and interest. Questions are shaped as we connect our purposes and the activities that make us come alive. Propositions (i.e., claims or statements that can be considered or demonstrated, see Manning & Massumi, 2014) can bring energy to creative enquiry as we work with others to explore them. Encounters or events (e.g., watching a short film together or going for a walk in a neighbourhood) can act as a catalyst and common frame of reference. Before we think about 'methods', creative PICE requires connection, curiosity, and openness.

Creative PICE can be almost anything, which can be both liberating and paralysing, but there can be practical starting points. Early conversations about 'how can we explore this?' can progress when those involved consider what they have to hand (Heidegger, 1927/2010, p. 82). This can include existing skills, hobbies, resources, and so on. There can be an assemblage of actions a creative PICE team can work with, from guided walks, knitting, collecting objects, photography, to folding paper. The diversity of activities is all the more important if we think about engaging with diverse people. Selecting initial activities and materials can be supported by considering the extent to which they are meaningful to those who will use them, to the extent they are accessible to participants, and the extent to which they support enquiry. For that latter concern, it is useful to think about the affordances (Davis, 2020) of activities and materials. A ball of string, a set of postcards, an experience diary or a neighbourhood walk each have different affordances – affordances being possibilities for action. An affordance is constituted in the relation between the properties of an object (or activity) and the capabilities of individuals (Heras-Escribano, 2019). We ask: What is it like handling (x), what can we do with (y), what is interesting about (z)? Can we use something to demonstrate or explore? We may select and order photographs, we can use string to trace a journey, we can work with digital sound recordings to elicit memories, and so much more. In creative PICE, we can see materials and activities as *agentic* (Bolt, 2007; Fox & Alldred, 2016) enquiry partners, ways to materialise thinking, so we can all work on it. We are used to starting with narrative, but the nature of our embodied, sensory, and emotional being means that enquiry often starts with the body, and senses, and methods can help us start tentatively. This is an inclusive mode of practice, as 'decorative' creativity does not begin with that inclusive openness to 'the other' (see Fig. 4.2).

Creative PICE has the potential to work with memories, feelings, and bodily senses to produce a fuller, multidimensional understanding of the experience of bodies, places, and discourses. It is equally important that the embodied, sensory, diverse processes, and insights that creative PICE can create are carefully documented, and not reduced to a set of bullet points. Rich data sets that can be co-constructed in creative PICE need nuanced and diverse documentation practices, which can inform diverse audiences. Designing documentation into creative PICE is important for participants as they expand and reflect on a question, experience, or test a prototype. Photography, shared blogs, postcards, review sessions, and more can refine the direction of enquiry, expand moments of learning, and critically test speculation.

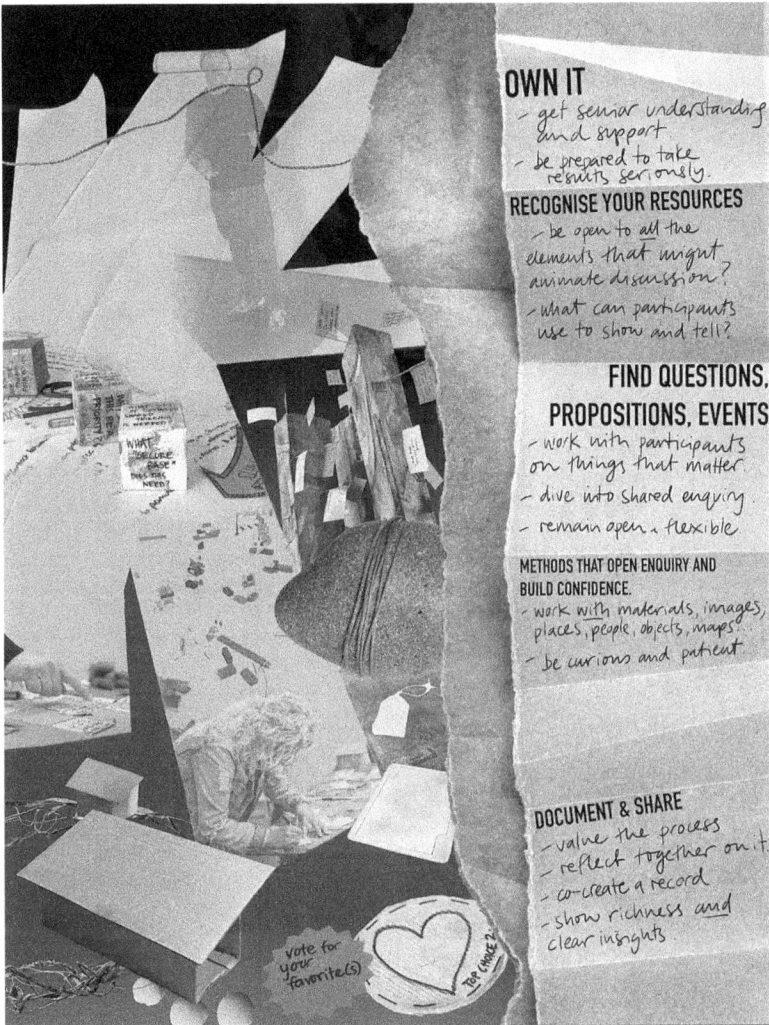

OWN IT
- get senior understanding and support
- be prepared to take results seriously.

RECOGNISE YOUR RESOURCES
- be open to all the elements that might animate discussion?
- what can participants use to show and tell?

FIND QUESTIONS, PROPOSITIONS, EVENTS
- work with participants on things that matter.
- dive into shared enquiry.
- remain open + flexible

METHODS THAT OPEN ENQUIRY AND BUILD CONFIDENCE.
- work with materials, images, places, people, objects, maps
- be curious and patient

DOCUMENT & SHARE
- value the process
- reflect together on it.
- co-create a record
- show richness and clear insights

vote for your favorite(s)

TOP CHOICE?

Fig. 4.2   Developing and Practising Creative PICE.

Conclusion

Intentionally building a culture of creative PICE (and creative organisations) takes boldness, time, and passion. Like other forms of research, it involves a commitment to consider positionality, preference, approach, and critical reflection on what creativity is and what will work best with groups. However, the benefits are huge – we can construct powerful agendas for change, step outside of our habits and assumptions, appreciate experiences, places, care pathways, everyday practices and community resources in new and inclusive ways. Creative PICE need not be decorative or mysterious, but it can start with what is to hand (Heidegger,

1927/2010), and a commitment to explore with people, places, materials, and experiences. Creative PICE can generate meaningful, rich data, and if carefully documented and encountered, can help us to conceive, define, describe, and co-design better futures.

References

Addison, M., McGovern, W., & McGovern. R. (Eds.) (2022). Stigma under the skin. In *Drugs, stigma and identity*. Palgrave Macmillan.

Amabile, T. M. (2018). *Creativity in context: Update to the social psychology of creativity* (1st ed.). Routledge.

Anscombe, G. E. M. (1957/2000). *Intention*. Harvard University Press.

Barrett, E., & Bolt, B. (2012). *Carnal knowledge: Towards a 'new materialism' through the arts*. I.B. Tauris.

Bolt, B. (2007). Material thinking and the agency of matter. *Studies in Material Thinking*, *1*(1), 1–4. https://materialthinking.aut.ac.nz/papers/37.html

Borer, A., & Schirmer, L. (1997). *The essential Joseph Beuys*. Thames and Hudson.

Buchannan, I. (2021). *Assemblage theory and method*. Bloomsbury.

Cotterell, N., & Buffel, T. (2023). 'Holders of knowledge are communities, not academic institutions': Lessons from involving minoritised older people as co-researchers in a study of loneliness in later life. *Qualitative Research in Psychology*, *20*(3), 441–470.

Davis, J. L. (2020). *How artifacts afford: The power and politics of everyday things*. The MIT Press.

Deleuze, G., & Guattari, F. (1987/2013). *A thousand plateaus: Capitalism and schizophrenia (Bloomsbury revelations)*. Bloomsbury.

Deleuze, G., & Guattari, F. (1994). *What is philosophy?* (G. Burchill & H. Tomlinson, Trans.). Version Books.

Deleuse, G., & Guattari, F. (2013). Anti-Oedipus: Capatalism and schizophrenia (Bloomsbury Revelations Series). Bloomsbury.

Dewey, J. (1934/2005). *Art as experience*. Perigee Books.

Fox, N., & Alldred, P. (2016). *Sociology and the new materialism: Theory, research, action*. Sage.

Gadamer, H.-G. (1986/1998). *The relevance of the beautiful and other essays* (R. Bernasconi, Ed.). Cambridge University Press.

Gadamer, H.-G. (1960/2013). *Truth and method (Bloomsbury revelations)*. Bloomsbury.

Gardner, H. (2006). *Multiple intelligences: New horizons in theory and practice* (updated ed.). Basic Books.

Geuss, R. (2009). *Public goods, private goods (Princeton monographs in philosophy)*. Princeton University Press.

Gibb, S., Hendry, R. F., & Lancaster, T. (Eds.) (2021). *The Routledge handbook of emergence (Routledge handbooks)*. Routledge.

Heidegger, M. (1927/2010). *Being and time: A revised edition of the Stambaugh translation (SUNY series in contemporary continental philosophy)*. Routledge.

Heras-Escribano, M. (2019). *The philosophy of affordances*. Palgrave-Macmillan.

Involve.org.uk. (2024). https://www.involve.org.uk/about

Lapsley, I., & Miller, P. (Eds.) (2024). *The resilience of new public management*. Oxford University Press.

Lowe, R. (2004). *The welfare state in Britain since 1945* (3rd ed.). Palgrave.

Manning, E., & Massumi, B. (2014). *Thought in the act: Passages in the ecology of experience*. University of Minnesota Press.

Marcuse, H. (1964/2002). *One-dimensional man: Studies in the ideology of advanced industrial society (Routledge classics)*. Routledge.

Marmot, M., & Wilkinson, R. G. (2005). *Social determinants of health* (2nd ed.). Oxford University Press.

Martin-Kerry, J., McLean, J. Hopkins, T., Morgan, A., Dunn, L. Walton, R., Golder, S., Allison, T., Cooper, D., Wohland, P., & Prady, S. L. (2023). Characterizing asset-based studies in public health: Development of a framework. *Health Promotion International, 38*(2), 1–12.

Meadows, D., & Wright, D. (2017). *Thinking in systems*. Chelsea Green Publishing.

NHS England. (2022). *Accelerated access collaborative patient and public involvement strategy, 2021–2026*. Retrieved November 14, 2024, from https://www.england.nhs.uk/aac/publication/accelerated-access-collaborative-patient-and-public-involvement-strategy/

Pollitt, C., & Bouckaert, G. (2017). *Public management reform: A comparative analysis – Into the age of austerity* (4th ed.). Oxford University Press.

Robson, I. (2024). Complicity in the catastrophe: Practical progress with Deleuze and Guattari. *Qualitative Inquiry, 0*(0), 1–13. https://doi.org/10.1177/10778004241295745

Sternberg, R. J. (Ed.) (2018). *The nature of human intelligence*. Cambridge University Press.

Sternberg, R. J., & Kaufman, J. C. (Eds.) (2018). *The nature of human creativity*. Cambridge University Press.

Storr, R. (2016). *Intimate geometries: The art and life of Louise Bourgeois*. The Monacelli Press.

Sullivan, H., & Skelcher, C. (2017). *Working across boundaries: Collaboration in public services*. Bloomsbury Publishing.

Williams, R., Runco, M. A., & Berlow, E. (2016). Mapping the themes, impact and cohesion of creativity research over the last 25 years. *Creativity Research Journal, 28*(40), 385–394.

Chapter 5

The World Café Approach: Partnering Parents Towards a Deeper Understanding of Child Transitions

Charmaine Agius Ferrante and James Stack

Department of Social Work, Education & Community Wellbeing, Northumbria University, UK

Abstract

This chapter presents the development of a collaborative research methodology with staff and parents around supporting infants' transitions into nursery. The authors argue that attachment formation is a process that can take a protracted length of time, and therefore, propose an alternative approach that offers better support to infants and parents during the earlier stages of transition. The aim of our research was to identify the key characteristics of a model that supports infants' gradual transition into nursery from both parents' and practitioners' perspectives. However, within the chapter, we seek to provide a rich real-life example of a lived experience of collaborative research with parents and practitioners from one nursery. Collaborative research with parents opened new possibilities for understanding the perspectives around infants going into nursery by drawing on the expertise of parents and practitioners. As part of the study, we employed a collaborative methods approach and encouraged parents and practitioners to work together through their participation in baby social sessions. Data analyses were conducted through thematic analysis, identifying patterns and themes related to parent–practitioner collaboration around infants' transitions into nursery. The findings reveal significant emphasis on trust, care, mutual respect, and the development of warm relationships between

Public Involvement and Community Engagement in Applied Health and Social Care Research:
Critical Perspectives and Innovative Practice, 57–68

parents, practitioners, and infants with open communication. Having shared values and knowledge around infant care routines aligning home with the nursery supported the infant's gradual transition into nursery.

Keywords: Parent–practitioner collaboration; infant transition; relationships; interaction; attunement; nursery

Introduction

In this book chapter, we present our experience on a professional research journey, based upon shared knowledge and relationships, within a collaborative working approach with parents in supporting infants' transitions into nursery. As more is understood about the potential for learning from birth, further attention is given to what can be learnt from sensitively observing children's autonomous actions within transition into nursery alongside their caregivers. Trevarthen and Delafield-Butt (2016) acknowledged infants' autonomy by revealing that they have 'the spirit of an inquisitive and creative human being' (p. 17). Taking this crucial element into account, staff, parents, and researchers have collaborated on the research presented here to foster sensitive and inclusive transitions for infants aged up to 18 months. This has been achieved by providing socio-emotional and socio-cognitively framed interactions that support attuned infant–caregiver interactions and caregiving routines.

In our research we adopted a qualitative collaborative methodology (Degotardi et al., 2019), which required us to engage with, manage and work alongside the nursery management, staff, and parents of the infants throughout the research design phase and during data collection. Being able to engage with and include all the parents of the infants transitioning into the nursery at the time of the research, and the baby room practitioners in the data collection process was seen by us as an important way to ground our research within the stories and conversations around early transitions into nursery. Our engagement strategy and involvement work were rooted theoretically and methodologically in the World Café Approach. The World Café approach (Brown, 2010) is a particularly suitable data collection method, it is a method that relies on meaningful engagement and collaborative action. Our utilisation of this approach to collaboration and engagement facilitated accuracy, and recognition of the knowledge of the process and practice of the infant's gradual settling into nursery. Although based in the UK and adhering to UK early years policy (DfE, 2024) the nursery we conducted our research in offers an innovative continental approach, inspired by principles of the Reggio Emilia model of day care. The Reggio Emilia approach (Bove, 2001; Edwards & Gandini, 2018) places more emphasis on the roles of community and relationships with parents and children. Within this approach there is both a blurring of the boundaries between home and day care and, when contrasted with the UK, offering a more protracted and gradual timeframe for transitions into day care.

Our motivation was to work with parents and practitioners to assess whether current approaches to transitions, an approach framed around the importance of infant attachment formation with key persons within the setting, can be improved upon. In terms of our own theory and positionality, we reasoned that attachment formation is a process that can take a protracted length of time. Therefore, it is an alternative approach that offers better support to infants during the earlier stages of transition.

With these motivations in mind, we formulated an alternative theoretical model that outlines the benefits of providing socio-emotional and socio-cognitively framed interactions that support attuned infant–caregiver interactions and caregiving routines. In developing this research focus, both researchers relied heavily on their existing knowledge and research of attunement, infancy research and theory from developmental psychology (e.g., Bigelow, 1998; Moll et al., 2021; Terrace et al., 2022; Trevarthen, 1979). For example, would transitions into day care be smoother if the key person's level of social and emotional engagement with a new infant mirrored that experienced with their primary caregiver? In this chapter we worked with parents and practitioners by having a conversation to explore issues around how initial phase of a transition to nursery is experienced by the infant. In the first instance, we explored critical questions around the idea that if the key person's level of contingent interaction with the infant is not at a similar level to that experienced with the primary caregiver/s (Bigelow, 1998), then infants would experience a less-than-optimal start to day care.

Transitions Are Difficult for Parents

It is important to acknowledge that working with parents and practitioners as research partners can be difficult because both parents and practitioners can struggle emotionally during these transitional periods. Highlight that the competing demands between home, work and day-care setting can manifest in feelings of stress and tension as the parent seeks to find a new sense of balance and equilibrium (Monk & Hall, 2017). Parents can experience a sense of loss of control due to relinquishing caregiver responsibilities to the practitioner and feelings of fear, distress, and insecurity, especially if the transitional process is not managed with sensitivity and care (White et al., 2020).

Within the current research we adopted the key aspects of the Reggio Emelia approach in our attempts to help better understand how these types of stressors can be better managed for parents. For example, this approach advocates for a more community-based approach within which there is less of a delineation between home and day-care setting (Bove, 2001). Rather, emphasis is placed on what is termed 'inserimento'. This translates literally from Italian into English as 'insertion' and its key function is to allow parents and infants more time and space for a smoother adjustment during the settling period. Here parents are welcomed openly and encouraged to become part of the caregiving community. In doing so there is greater opportunity for the parent themselves to become acclimatised to the experience of transition and, in turn develop deeper supportive relationships with other parents and with practitioners in the setting.

Overview of the Research: Our Initial Theoretical Position

Our research falls very much within the early childhood education and care (ECEC) tradition. It was motivated by an attempt to develop an enhanced theoretical understanding of, and practical approach to, infant transitions from the parent, family home into formal day care. Of specific interest were the views and opinions of both parents and practitioners before, during, and after their infant had made the transition. Beyond these key sources of information, we were also motivated to observe how infants experienced all stages of the transitional process.

At the earliest stages of our research, at a time when we were still developing and refining the research focus, our theoretical lens was focussed exclusively on consideration of whether current DfE (2024) policy and practice was sufficient in adequately supporting all parties during the transition to day-care process. We reasoned that current policy, advocating the need for the formation of attachments with key persons within the nursery (Elfer, 2015; Elfer et al., 2012; Page & Elfer, 2013), offers more of a longer term 'outcome model' of day-care transition and does not adequately support all parties, especially infants during the earlier periods of transition. In contrast, we utilised a body of infancy theory and research evidenced from developmental psychology to argue that a different socio-emotional approach to transitions may be more suited. Specifically, we outlined an 'intersubjective' approach to transitions. This approach emphasises the importance of key persons adopting 'attuned', synchronous, and contingently organised emotional engagement with infants within both dyadic and triadic caregiving routines and play activities (e.g., Bigelow, 1998; Moll et al., 2021; Terrace et al., 2022; Trevarthen, 1979). Central to our views was that such practitioner attunement, with newly arriving infants, should be modelled on the rhythms and regularities in emotional displays and behaviours similar to what infants experience with their primary caregivers (Bigelow, 1998). We also reasoned that through such sensitivity and emotional and social attunement within routines, infants would be more readily placed to both navigate the trials and stresses of the transitional period and develop secure attachments (Field, 1985; Schore, 2001) with practitioners operating in key person roles.

It is important to note here both how and where each researcher developed the views that formed the basis of this research. Essentially, our views are a mixture of (1) significant reading of key academic sources within our field, which encompass developmental psychology, educational psychology and early childhood studies, and (2) our experiential learning having spent several decades working within and/or visiting day-care settings to carry out tasks such as data collection for research or to carry out assessments. Importantly, one staff researcher did not have any direct experience of working as a staff member or key person within the nursery subject to this research or recent practice. Therefore, we recognise that we could be criticised for being decontextualised from the real-life experiences of current staff members within settings.

Engaging with parents in involvement work and having conversations about the topic of transitions can be difficult because it also raises questions around attachment and parenting perspectives, values and beliefs about what is important. The synergy between parents and practitioners plays a pivotal role in influencing positive outcomes around transitions for the infant. As primary agents of socialisation, parents play an important part in shaping the transition process for their infant.

Our First Conversation with the Setting: Thinking About, Developing, and Revising Ethics

Our involvement in work and research conversations enabled us to understand more about practice, and it became apparent that the more practice-based approach being employed within the setting was different to, and yet compatible with, our own intersubjective model. The key difference was seen through the adoption of what is termed the Reggio Emilia approach Edwards and Gandini (2018), within which emphasis is placed on the importance of time and space with key practitioners focussing on a more gradual, community-based approach to transitions. Within the framework, the boundaries between home and day-care setting were blurred in a manner that emotionally and socially supported all parties as infants (and parents and practitioners) gradually acclimatised and emotionally adjusted to the parents' absence over sustained periods of time and other key aspects of the transition experience (Bove, 2001).

Both researchers came into this research process with a deep familiarity with early childhood developmental education, and although we were 'outsiders' to the setting, we had an 'insider' perspective on the debates around infant transitions into day care. Our first meeting with staff members was pivotal within our research journey, both at a theoretical and practical level. Importantly, in terms of the ethical issues we would immediately encounter and continue to engage with throughout the course of our data collection and analyses over the following months. Through our early negotiations with staff and involvement in work with them, it quickly became apparent that our own theoretical account (based solely on the importance of attuned socio-emotional caregiving and socio-cognitive forms of play and stimulation did not account for the full complexity of experience during the period of transition. Reflexivity during fieldwork is important, and our engagement in Parent-Practitioner Involvement (PPI) work with nursery staff led us to reconsider our own positionality and theoretical perspective. Rather, a more ecologically valid approach should situate such sensitive forms of practitioner provision within a wider socio-cultural framework that acknowledges the key aspects of the Reggio Emilia approach.

Once we felt that a firm theoretical grounding was established for the research, we began the process of completing a standard University ethics form. This took place alongside the relationship building. According to Lyndon (2023, p. 143), 'The ethics of research can all too often be reduced to a single form and a checklist of requirements.' This statement mirrored our own experience as we began to consider how we, as researchers, would look to minimise risk to participants, help maintain psychological well-being throughout, avoid deception and allow for transparency, help maintain confidentiality and anonymity and allow for debriefing and voluntary withdrawal at any stage during the research journey. For any academic who has conducted their own research and helped support numerous undergraduate and postgraduate dissertation projects, such ethical topics are routinely encountered as standard fare with such forms feeling a little like a one-size-fits all tick box exercise.

Innovation and the World Café Approach

Our idea of having professional conversations with parents was to understand their lived practice experience and then engage in a constructive dialogue around their experiences, perceptions, and practices around infant transitions into nursery. This approach builds on elements of the World Café (Brown, 2010). The World Café approach is an appropriate public involvement and community engagement tool and method. It is a conversational process that helps people to engage in constructive conversations around critical questions, whilst building personal relationships and fostering mutual learning. Some shared principles underpinning this approach, that we based our professional conversation around, were recognising the knowledge and expertise of the parents, baby room practitioners, and nursery management; a commitment to the collective wisdom of each group; allowing sufficient time and space for each conversation group to critically reflect, to form and share their views (Brown, 2010).

The nursery offers a friendly and welcoming atmosphere, like that of the World Café, where we encourage involvement and foster open discussions that encourage participants to freely share their perspectives, experiences, and expertise. The method enabled parents to reflect on their own values, beliefs, and experiences whilst digging deeper into the topic of transitions and generating new insights. Furthermore, the conversations helped us understand and compare the perspectives of parents alongside staff, as well as highlight the good practices occurring within the nursery. The World Café approach also serves as a catalyst for future practice (Ropes et al., 2020). This method played a pivotal role in stimulating conversations and encouraging parents to explore infant transitions in a deep and meaningful way.

Consideration of Ethical Complexities: Challenges to Current Beliefs About Praxis?

The nursery was selected due to its known good practices and reputation. The setting's ethos encourages children and parents to participate in decisions which affect them, mirroring the ethos of participatory research (Vaughn & Jacquez, 2020). Practitioners in this setting have been very active in reflecting on transitions and have been offering 'baby social' for over a year prior to this study, as part of their usual practice. Within these sessions, parents and newly arriving infants spend the morning interacting with other new arrivals, staff members, and infants who are now fully established within the setting. With the support of the different 'gatekeepers' such as the nursery management, baby practitioners, the parents, and the Board of Governors, we built trust and a collaborative research interest. Concerns with trust, mutual recognition, and authenticity are key characteristics of good and high-quality research.

It soon became apparent to us during our early discussions, with the nursery manager and senior staff, that this alternative framework, whilst theoretically grounded, was in fact lacking some aspects of ecological validity (Denner et al., 1999), and that there was a need for ongoing involvement and conversations around wider aspects of emotionally attuned support for infants. For example, staff members commented on the requirement that aspects of caregiving, such as feeding, comforting, and sleeping, also needed to be acknowledged within this attuned framework. Through such conversations, the initial questions that had been generated, and which were framed more around the more social and cognitive routines (such as play and stimulation), were modified and broadened to better capture the real-life experience of both infants and key persons during and beyond the initial periods of transition into day care. In effect, whilst getting professionals onboard, the experienced staff members had become integral partners in our attempts to develop a set of ecologically valid research questions that would be administered more widely within this setting and more widely across other settings.

Voluntary and Informed Consent

Our relationship with the nursery was of paramount importance, and to this end, we ensured that participation in this research project was not only based on voluntary, informed consent, but there was interest and motivation from the nursery. Informed consent was vital to our research, and so we talked through all the materials with the nursery manager and her deputy and sent all planning documentation to the nursery for all participants to read and approve. We provided all those involved with full and honest information about the content, purpose, and process of the research, and all parents were given the opportunity to agree or disagree to participate and have opportunities to guide and develop the research at all stages.

Baby Social Observations

Engaging in a meaningful way with parents as research partners and participants was key to our research, and naturalistic observation formed an essential part of both our planning and underpinned our research process. We adopted participant observation (Mayall, 2002), which is a form of observation that involves watching, listening, reflecting, and engaging the participants in conversation. This approach also helped us build our relationships with the baby practitioners, parents, and infants, and ensure equality in power and status within the research. Written observations were made using narrative descriptions of each session observed, with a focus on the structure of the session, relationships, attunement, joint involvement episodes (Schaffer, 1992), infant/adult interactions, infant/infant interactions, and conversation topics. Between us, we observed eight sessions of 'Baby Social' where we became familiar with the baby practitioners, parents, and their child, and other infants who joined in the session. It is important to note that throughout this initial stage of the project, there were several important issues that required full consideration.

The infants' key workers and parents were present throughout the observations. As researchers, we were sensitive to the needs of the infants, and there was no pressure for them to engage in anything other than usual play and settling-in activities. Had any child shown distress, we would have ceased the observation immediately. Parents were curious about the observations shared with them and keyworkers prior to our subsequent reflective conversations.

Developing Our Research Focus – Parents and Practitioners as Partners

Beyond these early conversations with the manager and deputy manager of this nursery, and over the coming weeks, we became more confident in our initial impressions of the setting. We became fully aware that there was a real synergy between this practice and our own views, which (1) also considered the need for a more protracted and sympathetic approach to transitions (inspired by the Reggio Emilia approach), but (2) went one step further to offer a framework that allows for infants to be supported by practitioners (key persons) who provide a form of emotional caregiving, social interaction, and cognitive stimulation that is similar to what each infant experiences within their primary caregiving relationships with parents (an intersubjective approach). Our conceptual model, emphasising relationships amongst contexts and persons, also informed the approach we took in conducting our research. If we were to understand transition for infants, parents, and practitioners, and if we were to facilitate interactions amongst participants in this process, then our success in this research endeavour was tied to forming relationships with the participants and building partnerships in inquiry, as stated in the introduction to this chapter.

It became apparent that some members of staff were reluctant to be interviewed by so-called 'experts' in this field. We had to address this issue to keep the professionals onboard, but we also did not want the staff to think that they were being assessed as they engaged in the sensitive transitions that they undertook on a daily basis. Doing so would tap into the power relations dynamic, which is evident within all human participant research (Hickey, 2018), resulting in a perceived sense of vulnerability and/or lack of competence of practitioners. It was important to note here that such concerns were not made directly to either researcher but emerged indirectly through dialogue with the nursery manager and deputy, and only after several sessions of attendance at the nursery. These conversations were invaluable for both researchers as they allowed us to reflect on our own position with both the research and the nursery. We also appreciated the honesty. Reflexivity is key to assessing trustworthiness in qualitative research (Dodgson, 2019). Reflexivity means that researchers should reflect and share with readers how their social positions vis-a-vis research participants may interfere with the researcher's ability to maintain objectivity. The effects of the researcher on the research participants and vice versa are both potential areas for bias and misunderstanding.

Through such reflection we became more aware of the impact of our presence during the daily working routines of caregiving practitioners. We concluded that such concern did not only reflect the silent number of practitioners within the setting but may also have been underlying, and very real concern of all current and potential participants within this research. With these issues in mind, we concluded that our approach to data collection within the setting would benefit by adopting a slower approach to that which was the actual focus of our research. This more considered approach allowed staff members to gradually become comfortable with our presence as we transitioned to becoming regular visitors within the setting.

Open-ended Research

With the issues considered above very much at the forefront of our thoughts, we, as researchers, felt that there was a need for an exploratory and open-ended approach at each stage of the research process. This issue was most evident during the formulation of the open-ended research questions. Initially, both researchers had utilised their own knowledge and academic understanding of the theory surrounding transitions into day care to help direct both the theoretical and empirical focus of the present study.

Thus, we adopted a qualitative approach, in which we conducted relevant research conversations with parents and practitioners. These data were then thematically analysed. We also felt that there was much that we as researchers could both learn and gain from having a collaborative approach within this project. We, therefore, developed a 'practitioners as partners' approach. As outlined below, this allowed for the development of the research questionnaires and has helped inform data collection and analyses. By conducting research in this manner, we aimed to help provide additional support to facilitate smoother transitions moving forward.

Conclusion

Within this chapter, we have described our engagement with the parents, professionals, and children in the nursery and engaged in a sympathetic, critical assessment of our own PPI approach and practice. In the future, we would advocate for more naturalistic public involvement approaches like 'World Café' and ongoing reflexivity to ensure that children and their parents are fully informed about and appreciated in the research process. In our work, the PPI approach we used enabled us to consider our approach, positionality, and practice in the setting in a way that resulted in deeper learning for us. This approach also enabled us to engage more productively with nursery staff and to move from 'outsiders' to 'insiders' in such a way that parents accepted out presence and that practitioners never felt (or were able to manage) that they were being assessed in relation to such a fundamental part of their practice: re-transitions. Trust is one of the basic and core components of good quality research and also trauma-informed research (see Adams, Ramsey, Cooper, and Lhussier in this collection) and is vital in collaborative processes and research with parents and public members. Trust was central to our public involvement work, and incorporated trust building within our research by consciously developing a reflexive and responsive way of working with parents and practitioners, which we describe as a trust-building approach.

Whilst we were motivated to offer a critique of the current attachment approach to day-care transitions, we were also aware that managing the transition from parent to professional and the attachment formation occupy a central role within parenting and infant emotional well-being. Therefore, in this instance, we had to ensure that both the nursery and we, as researchers, were aligned in our views regarding the importance of primary caregiver presence in supporting the infant during their initial experiences of new people in a new nursery.

It was important for us as infancy researchers to acknowledge that humans in general, and parents in particular, can not only be susceptible to their infants' perceived levels of anxiety and stress, but may elicit such behaviours themselves in a manner that is transmitted back to the infant. Importantly, transitional periods into day care, especially first-time parents, can be especially difficult. For example, there is the potential that such stressful emotions can be interpersonally transmitted from the primary caregiver and infants within such environments which may 'catch' their caregivers negatively heightened affective state (Waters et al., 2017).

As with the previous examples, this issue (an emotionally upset parent) can be the catalyst for the onset of an emotional stress response in the infant, which could possibly persist for several hours after the initial event. Beyond these issues, there is also the potential for infants to either remember (a cognitive interpretation) or become conditioned (a behavioural interpretation) to such experiences (a negative stimulus), and therefore, increase the possibility of similar stress responses in future situations. Nurseries are vibrant research contexts and places where professionals and parents nurture and foster warm and inclusive relationships within them. There are places where so much can be learned by engaging with parents, staff, and children, and those who are allowed to enter these settings should consider themselves privileged. Those challenged with entering and researching these types of areas need to be willing to manage a complex set of corresponding and competing beliefs, values, and perceptions of what is right and what is best for children in relation to their transitions. These issues and concerns can only be managed when research practice is informed by a willingness and ability to engage with different PPI approaches and participant groups and manage them as the research is designed, refined, and delivered in practice.

References

Bigelow, A. E. (1998). Infants' sensitivity to familiar imperfect contingencies in social interaction. *Infant Behavior and Development*, *21*(1), 149–162. https://doi.org/10.1016/S0163-6383(98)90060-1

Bove, C. (2001). Inserimento: A strategy for delicately beginning relationships and communications. In L. Gandini & C. P. Edwards (Eds.), *Bambini: The Italian approach to infant/toddler care* (Chap. 9, pp. 109–123). Teachers College Press.

Brown, J. (2010). *The World Café: Shaping our futures through conversations that matter*. ReadHowYouWant.com.

Degotardi, S., Johnston, K., Little, H., Colliver, Y., & Hadley F. (2019). "This is a learning opportunity": How parent–child interactions and exhibit design foster the museum learning of prior-to-school aged children. *Visitor Studies, 22*(2), 171–191. https://doi.org/10.1080/10645578.2019.1664849

Denner, J., Cooper, C. R., Lopez, E. M., & Dunbar, N. (1999). Beyond 'giving science away': How university-community partnerships inform youth programs, research, and policy. *Social Policy Report Society for Research in Child Development, 13*(1), 1–17.

DfE. (2024). *Statutory framework for the early years foundation stage: Setting the standards for learning, development and care for children from birth to five.* DfE.

Dodgson, J. E. (2019). Reflexivity in qualitative research. *Journal of Human Lactation, 35*(2), 220–222.

Edwards, C. P., & Gandini, L. (2018). The Reggio Emilia approach to early childhood education. In J. L. Roopnarine, J. E. Johnson, S. Flannery Quinn, & M. M. Patte (Eds.), *Handbook of international perspectives on early childhood education* (pp. 365–378). Routledge.

Elfer, P. (2015). Emotional aspects of nursery policy and practice – Progress and prospect. *European Early Childhood Education Research Journal, 23*(4), 497–511. https://doi.org/10.1080/1350293X.2013.798464

Elfer, P., Goldschmied, E., & Selleck, D. Y. (2012). *Key persons in the early years: Building relationships for quality provision in early years settings and primary schools* (2nd ed.). Routledge.

Field, T. (1985). Attachment as psychobiological attunement: Being on the same wavelength. In M. Reite & T. Field (Eds.), *Psychobiology of attachment and separation* (pp. 415–450). Academic Press.

Hickey, G. (2018). Co-production from proposal to paper: Share power in five ways. *Nature, 562*, 29–30. https://doi.org/10.1038/d41586-018-06861-9

Lyndon, H. (2023). Embracing the breadth of ethical complexities in early childhood research. *European Early Childhood Education Research Journal, 31*(2), 143–146. https://doi.org/10.1080/1350293X.2023.2208469

Mayall, B. (2002). Understanding childhoods: A London study. In L. Alanen & B. Mayall (Ed.), *Conceptualising child–adult relations* (pp. 128–142). Routledge.

Moll, H., Pueschel, E., Ni, Q., & Little, A. (2021). Sharing experiences in infancy: From primary intersubjectivity to shared intentionality. *Frontiers in Psychology, 12*, 667679. https://doi.org/10.3389/fpsyg.2021.667679

Monk, H., & Hall, H. (2017). New mothers transitioning to employment: Impact on infant feeding practices. In L. Li et al. (Eds.), *Studying babies and toddlers, international perspectives on early childhood education and development* (Vol. 20, pp. 63–80). Springer.

Page, J., & Elfer, P. (2013). The emotional complexity of attachment interactions in nursery. *European Early Childhood Education Research Journal, 21*(4), 553–567. https://doi.org/10.1080/1350293X.2013.766032

Ropes, D., Van Kleef, H., & Douven, G. (2020). Learning in the World Café: An empirical evaluation. *Journal of Workplace Learning, 32*(4), 303–316. https://doi.org/10.1108/JWL10-2019-0126

Schaffer, H. R. (1992). Joint involvement episodes as contexts for cognitive development. In H. McGurk (Ed.), *Contemporary issues in childhood social development.* Routledge

Schore, A. N. (2001). Effects of a secure attachment relationship on right brain development, affect regulation and infant mental health. *Infant Mental Health Journal, 22*(1–2), 7–66.

Terrace, H. S., Bigelow, A. E., & Beebe, B. (2022). Intersubjectivity and the emergence of words. *Frontiers in Psychology, 13*, 693139. https://doi.org/10.3389/fpsyg.2022.693139

Trevarthen, C. (1979). Communication and cooperation in early infancy. A description of primary intersubjectivity. In M. Bullowa (Ed.), *Before speech: The beginning of human communication* (pp. 321–347). Cambridge University Press.

Trevarthen, C., & Delafield-Butt, J. (2016). Intersubjectivity in the imagination and feelings of the infant: Implications for education in the early years. In E. J. White & C. Dalli (Eds.), *Under-three year olds in policy and practice* (pp. 17–39). Springer.

Vaughn, L. M., & Jacquez, F. (2020). Participatory research methods – Choice points in the research process. *Journal of Participatory Research Methods, 1*(1), 1–13. https://doi.org/10.35844/001c.13244

Waters, S. F., West, T. V., Karnilowicz, H. R., & Mendes, W. B. (2017). Affect contagion between mothers and infants: Examining valence and touch. *Journal of Experimental Psychology: General, 146*(7), 1043–1051. https://doi.org/10.1037/xge0000322

White, E. J., Rutanen, N., Marwick, H., Souza Amorim, K., Karagiannidou, E., & Herold, L. K. M. (2020). Expectations and emotions concerning infant transitions to ECEC: International dialogues with parents and teachers. *European Early Childhood Education Research Journal, 28*(3), 363–374. https://doi.org/10.1080/1350293X.2020.1755495

Chapter 6

Co-producing Better Mental Health Research with Young Researchers in Educational Establishments

Dave McPartlan

Institute of Health, University of Cumbria, UK

Abstract

This chapter explores the learning experience of a teacher who returned to his previous school to conduct research. The research aim was to investigate the efficacy of a recently introduced mental health school strategy from the students' viewpoint. Initial research concepts were to collect student data and draw conclusions. However, due to issues of power and trust, the study evolved into a collaborative exercise, which saw the researcher work with young people as partners. The research became a voyage of discovery as the working partnership between the researcher and young people matured into a transformational process for both parties. Young people's lived experience became a central tenant of the research methodology and process. What transpired was a better community research project that demonstrated benefits for both the individuals involved and the community. Whilst the focus of this work was school-based, there are lessons to learn for studies aiming for collaboration within communities.

Keywords: Schools; young researchers; youth participative action research; critical communicative methodology; community involvement

Public Involvement and Community Engagement in Applied Health and Social Care Research:
Critical Perspectives and Innovative Practice, 69–79
doi:10.1108/978-1-83608-678-920251006

Introduction

As a school teacher with over 30 years' experience, I have developed a focus on student welfare and the pastoral aspects of education. My career trajectory saw me transition from classroom teacher to Head of Year and then an Assistant Headteacher before leaving education to take up my PhD. My research journey for the purpose of this chapter is best described as a voyage of self-discovery where I learnt how 'me' the person contributed to 'me' the teacher and how both these identities helped me become a more inclusive and reflexive researcher. Transitioning from teacher to researcher was a steep learning curve, realising that, at times, my inclusive principles as a researcher were compromised as I had to navigate school systems, government initiatives and a neoliberal education system as a relative outsider. Neoliberalism here refers to how school performance and individual performance are prioritised over the needs and involvement of young people (Dunn, 2020). The four years I spent conducting research was a time for reflection, a time to ensure inclusive principles were front and centre of the research, which meant investing in young people as research partners as they have the ability and a right to contribute to the public involvement and community engagement (PICE) agenda in the context of schools.

Schools can be places of physical, practical, and emotional safety (McGovern et al., 2022); I recognise this, but in this chapter, I also recognise that schools can be places where children are marginalised. Children often live in and are expected to function in an adult world where their voice is rarely heard; even when professionals are well-intended and inclusive, it can often end with tokenistic and counterproductive practices (Kilkelly, 2004; Pleasance, 2016). Schools are also known as places of inclusion and social and psychological safety in some literature, but they are also traditional hierarchical structures of governance, where the power of adults remains largely unquestioned. As my research progressed and I became aware, I was forced to acknowledge my identity as a researcher coming from a career of 35 years of teaching who, through following the norms of an oppressive societal structure, had not always afforded young people their rights to:

- Express their views in all matters relating to them.
- Their views being given due weight, taking account of age and maturity.
- Be heard in administrative proceedings.
  (UNCRC, 2019).

Context

I started my doctoral studies in 2019, and in doing so, I returned as a researcher to my school of 30 plus years. Returning to the places where you once worked (or similar) will always be difficult for those who choose this route to doctoral study. I was concerned that my previous powerful position could negatively influence the research. Being the behaviour and attendance lead for the school for over 12 years had, on occasion, brought me into conflict with young people and families, and I was apprehensive that my previous position might obstruct the research. I wanted to draw on young people's experiences of the whole school mental health strategy (WSMHS), and to do this; I would need (as others have written in this collection, see Adams and Ramsey) them to trust me, something not straightforward for someone who used to be the pastoral lead in the school. Concerned about this, I arranged a series of consultation exercises with groups of young people from the school. As I had suspected, the younger students suggested I was unlikely to gain their trust. But they also started to inform the research design and strategy for my doctoral study, as it was they who came up with the idea of me partnering with sixth-formers who could then act as advocates and brokers in talking to the younger pupils who would become my participants.

The beginnings of a plan to take this research forward started to crystallise. The inclusive nature of youth participatory action research (YPAR) attracted me to it as my methodology. Now, I needed to develop a way of conducting this research with co-researchers from the sixth form as my partners. My recruitment strategy was purposeful and opportunistic (Dunning et al., 2021). I began the process by addressing a sixth-form assembly, explaining the project and recruiting 13 volunteers aged between 16 and 18. Initial discussions with my new young research team (YRT) made me realise they were all different and had varying needs. Some were more confident working with younger students, whilst others developed their analytical skills more quickly. Recognising the differentiated ability and attributes of the young people made it clearer to me that not every child needed to be involved or to support every aspect of the research design and implementation. To create a process that supported them as individuals and as a team, we jointly agreed that they could choose to work individually, in pairs or in small groups to collect data from their participants. The participants we identified for the study were then divided between the YRT, and a cycle of weekly meetings was devised to enable the research. This is explored more fully in the methodology section below.

Theory

Action research (AR) assumes correctly that those closest to a given issue are experts in understanding the root of the problem and are in the best position to help find solutions to such matters (Stringer & Ortiz Aragon, 2021). AR can be utilised as a methodology to explore real-life issues impacting people's lives through a systematic cyclical investigation incorporating observation, reflection, and action (Stringer & Ortiz Aragon, 2021). Participatory Action Research (PAR) is a collaborative approach to AR where the research team includes community members with lived experience of the research topic. At times, it is criticised as a 'non-scientific' and a subjective form of research which is unreliable when used to generalise results more broadly (Lindhult, 2019). Furthermore, critics suggest this research can exploit those people it aims to support by 'using' them for their own research needs (Jacobs, 2016). However, I aimed to use AR to glean greater depth and insight into the subject area, whilst involve the lived experience of young people and the reconstruction of knowledge through understanding and empowerment. The aim is to try and ensure social change is informed by the voice of such groups.

Whilst I was convinced AR was the most appropriate methodology, I was also searching for something more than this. This research enabled me to return to my principles of inclusivity by drawing on young people as the source of new knowledge. In my search for something more than AR, I turned to critical communicative methodology (CCM), which followed a dialogic approach (Latorre et al., 2005). CCM is based on the premise that everyone has the critical competency to analyse their own lived experience. It is influenced by the thinking of Habermas and three of his seven postulates (see here for further reading, Habermas, 1987). Everyone can interact and communicate; this is the 'universality of language and action'. The second postulate of relevance is the 'absence of interpretative hierarchy' that all interpretations coming from the research process are equally valid (see Jackson et al. in this collection), regardless of the position of the person putting them forward. The final postulate is where the researcher and researched work on an 'equal epistemological level', each an expert in their area, be that academic or lived experience (Puigverta et al., 2012). Whilst this methodology and approach had been developed and utilised more within economically disadvantaged rural communities, I was convinced these principles could be applied to the YRT. Understanding your positionality, values and beliefs about research and different research traditions and approaches is essential. In my research, I believed that if I was going to be true to my word and collaborate with young people in the search for new knowledge, I had to trust them and empower them to become decision-makers in the research process. I therefore blended CCM with YPAR to develop a novel methodology I named youth participative dialogic action research (YPDAR). The dialogic element became central to this work as we embarked on a series of weekly AR cycles over four months.

Methodology

The dialogic aspect of YPDAR was founded on developing two key sets of relationships, as shown in Fig. 6.1.

The AR cycle took a stepped approach:

Stage 1. I met with the YRT team, where they identified a research issue, discussed how it would be investigated, and then planned the YRT/participant meetings.

Stage 2. The YRT members ran separate meetings with their participants.

Stage 3. Meetings were held between individual YRT members and me immediately after their participant meetings. These meetings fulfilled several purposes: They allowed me to capture and transcribe the information from the Stage 2 meeting and enabled us to discuss the research meeting, exploring its challenges and successes. This was a time for reflexive and reflective thinking as we considered the processes and the data collected.

Stage 4. The YRT met as a group to explore further how the week's meetings and data collection had progressed. The process ensured that the team learnt from each other to improve practice. This was also the time that the team planned forward for the following week's meetings (McPartlan, 2023).

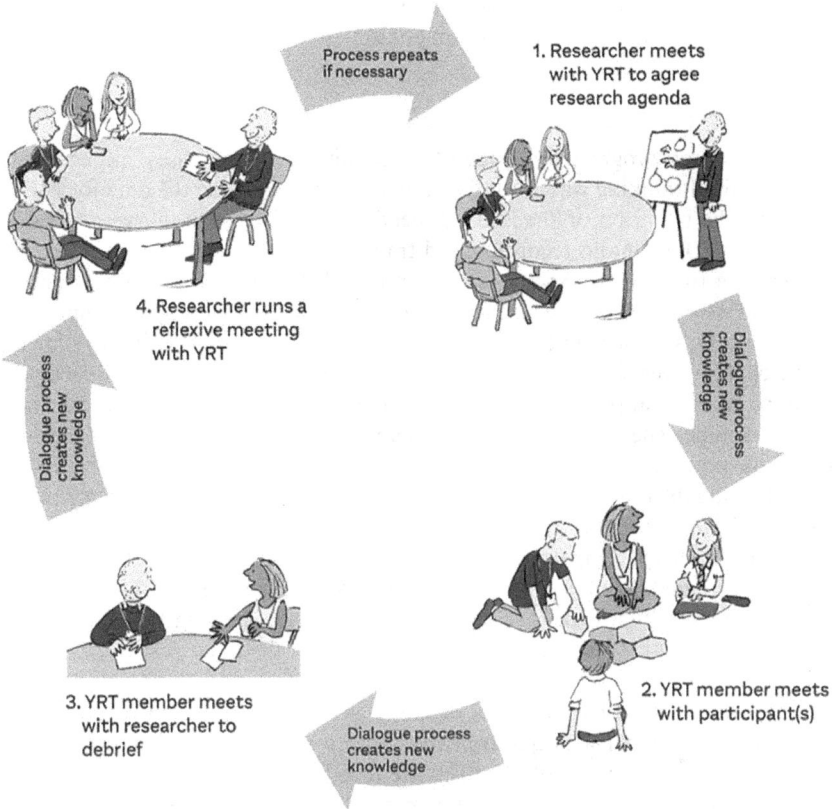

Fig. 6.1   Action Research Cycle (McPartlan, 2023).

Over time, Stages 1 and 4 merged into a single weekly meeting.

The central tenant of this research cycle was the two sets of relationships developing as part of the process: the researcher/YRT and the YRT/participant relationships. These relationships aligned closely with my values and ontological position as a social constructivist. Researching with people is about being reflective and reflexive: listening to and recognising/responding to. As a largely qualitative researcher, research is about building relationships, mutual understanding, and exploring issues whilst solving fieldwork and subject area-specific problems together. To do this, there needs to be a clear insight into oneself, one's core values and how these can impact research design and processes (Gilgun, 2006). My values were central to the research and fed into my decision to conduct YPAR and search to enhance this further with a stronger dialogic stance. By committing to collaborate with young people, I was morally invested in their well-being and welfare, further enhanced by the research process (Hipolito-Delgado et al., 2022). The way in which the two sets of relationships developed was influenced by my decision to empower the YRT. This started during the recruitment process, where

I was open and honest with the sixth-formers about needing their help to ensure authenticity during the data collection phase.

Whose Analysis Is It Anyway?

As the research progressed, I began to recognise these processes' impact on us all. My initial thinking was around 'using' the YRT to collect the data for ME to analyse. The intention of the Stage 3 meetings was for me to 'harvest' the data from the YRT by audio recording and transposing the conversations to extract the themes from them. As my relationship with the individual YRT members grew and we became an effective and cohesive team, I was torn by a conflict. This was my PhD, so I needed to complete the analysis to create the findings for my research. However, the more I worked with the YRT, the more I came to recognise them as an integral part of the research process; this was their research as much as it was mine. The whole process of collaborating with the YRT to analyse the data was, however, challenging in a number of ways. To begin, I had to consider the following dilemma: do I present my opinions to the group, impose my power to force these on the YRT (researcher analysis), or do I step back and allow the group to decide (participatory analysis)? There was also a compromise position whereby I offered my opinion and suggested it as just one voice within the group, and we analysed the work together. I found this a challenging time, and this is reflected in an extract from a reflexive diary I kept at the time.

> The tension I have is that I do not want to impose myself or my opinion, but I also question the validity of what the YRT may decide. The echoes of adultism are reverberating in my head as I ponder the correct decision for myself, the YRT and the research outcomes. If I am to be true to my values, then the YRT needs autonomy to make their own findings within a supportive structure, something I need to develop. Just because the YRT is made up of young people does not give me the right to disempower them and impose my will. I believe that by taking a 'middle road', I will offer opinions without imposing my will.

Keeping a reflective and reflexive diary and notes to self is a meaningful part of the research process. These types of diary entries become artefacts for progressing ideas over time, as the research progresses. The end approach was only possible because of the effort we had all made to develop our relationships during the research design and implementation. We had taken time, and reciprocal trust was developed through our relationship, which helped deepen truthfulness, morality and authenticity (van Lieshoult & Cardiff, 2011). This was multi-voiced research and required multi-voice analysis. At every meeting, I built on my experiences of managing discussions. I would openly encourage the YRT to ask questions, reflect, challenge me and put counterarguments to my points to provoke debate within the team. This was pivotal as in research contexts, children and young people will enquire and challenge to try to make sense of a situation if they feel safe enough to do so. I aimed for inter-subjective consensus (van Lieshoult & Cardiff, 2011) or mutual adequacy (Boog, 2007), a critical validity check in participatory AR. Ultimately, I was responsible for telling a story and reporting the findings as I saw them. Reflect-ing back now I would urge YOU the reader to recognise that investment in hard thinking about, the study population, the methodology and balancing your needs against those being researched needs to be done. At the outset of my research, my thoughts had been about completing a classic thematic analysis (Braun & Clarke, 2012). My initial view that this was my research, which I needed to ana-lyse. My thinking around the analysis developed as the research progressed and my relationship with the YRT matured. I realised that the young people had to be central to the analysis, which soon led to a collaborative effort involving the YRT and myself. At the outset of my research, I had also not considered that the YRT would be involved in the analysis, and it meant that I had to ask for more from my participants and ask them to engage in more technical aspects and usu-ally less enjoyable areas of research. I was open with the young researchers; we discussed the data and how it should be analysed. I explained how my thinking had developed during the research period, and we made a joint decision that the analysis would be a collaborative effort. What transpired was a thematic analysis approach informed by the dialogic processes between the three parties within the research, which led us to an interpretative rather than an objectivist standpoint (Ellingson, 2008).

The search for authenticity was less about triangulation and its objective over-tones and more about the intuitive flexibility of crystallisation (McPartlan, 2023). This brought another aspect into consideration in relation to the YRT. I had to lead them through the analysis. I introduced them to the intuitive data platform Quirkos. I input the data collected at Stage 3 meetings, and together, we worked through a cyclical process of identifying themes, discussing them, and testing them with the participants. In addition to this, I developed support sheets for the YRT to help their understanding of data analysis. I ran tutorials on data analy-sis, and we used a collaborative self-reflection tool to support the process. The YRT benefitted from their involvement; they were also encouraged to develop their self-reflective writing, contributing to a paper we published as part of the dissemination process (McPartlan et al., 2021). I was equally challenged about who should own the research findings regarding the WSMHS. However, having already worked through the arguments concerning the analysis, I quickly con-cluded that I could not compromise the research principles and that the YRT should write up these findings.

YRT Findings

The ethos of PICE is to guarantee that the community informs the research design, implementation, data, findings, and what is produced. PICE can poten-tially empower communities and develop lasting policy change (Kim et al., 2014). By working with the community and recognising their expertise, there is an opportunity to create long-term relationships and build trust (Schiavo, 2021).

It was incumbent on me to ensure that this work was authentic; it was essential the young people's lived-experience informed the findings. If I were to conduct an analysis and write up the findings by myself, there is a good chance I may misinterpret information, and my work would be informed from my 60-year-old 'self' rather than from the YRT lived experience. This was brought home to me whilst we were analysing a research section. I introduced a card-sorting activity to help us synthesise the data and themes. Whilst we discussed the data, the YRT arranged the cards according to their preferences; I wanted this writing up, but none of the team had time due to exam pressure. Therefore, I asked permission to write it up and get their feedback. What I got back both shocked and pleasantly surprised me. Two of the team took my write-up and rewrote it with a different focus. I was surprised, and I must admit, slightly affronted they did this (even though I had asked them to sense check my work) but also moving beyond 'ego' delighted they had! This justified my approach and reassured me we were getting genuine community feedback. Having decided that the YRT would write up the findings, we continued our cyclical meeting process, defining and refining our findings. Over weeks, we arrived at a series of findings that the YRT returned to the participants. They sense-checked these with their younger peers to ensure the validity of the findings. Alongside our weekly research team meetings, I also paid attention to individual YRT members to ensure that all were comfortable with the final validity check. I quickly realised that the YRT had all grown through the process and had become adept communicators and researchers who had built strong and mature relationships with their younger peers.

The process I described above was about how dialogue and relationships became central to the research and how the principles of CCM enabled a collaborative process that encouraged egalitarian relationships. It diffused and shared power whilst also challenging neoliberal processes. This, in turn, countered negative societal and school power relationships where adults dominate and make decisions impacting young people. The dialogic process between the three parties in my research ensured robust data collection and analysis. It then enabled us to produce findings and recommendations to present to the headteacher, with whom we had further dialogue before agreeing on an implementation strategy.

Writing Up and Dissemination

After the writing-up period, the most important work was relaying the findings and recommendations back to the school. The YRT and I met with the headteacher and senior school leaders. The school accepted most of the findings and recommendations, and adjustments were made to implement what could reasonably be. I had prepared and explored expectations with the YRT at the start of the research that whilst the school had promised to engage with the research, there may be aspects that could not be addressed due to circumstances beyond our control, such as budget.

As the research progressed, my ambition for the YRT and the research in general grew. As an ex-teacher and one who believed in young people's abilities, the research demonstrated to me there was a societal 'glass ceiling' in terms of what young people are capable of when trusted by adults. I had also become a victim of this, and the research instilled in me a determination to showcase the YRT's abilities. I was now clearly in the camp of this being 'our research', so we should disseminate this together. Moving beyond the research, we wrote and published papers and attended conferences where we presented our findings. I believe this was essential to the spirit of PICE. This was not just about harvesting information from the public and including them in the process; it was about creating capacity and opportunities for allowing children and their voices to be heard in a way which benefitted them and others.

Conclusion

This research applied approaches developed within a health context to an educational setting. During my journey, I learned that research is more than academics collecting information to further their agenda. It is about understanding positionality, values and then developing partnerships with communities and individuals within them to learn with and from them. Hierarchical structures such as schools and health organisations are dominated by power, and the need to utilise and adapt methodologies to redefine research relationships by empowering participants is more significant than ever.

In bringing my two identities together teacher/researcher I have always championed young people and their abilities, and this research emphasised their true capabilities. Children in research have ability, and their ability to adapt to situations, create resources, and synthesise information is apparent, as this chapter has described. During my 18-month project, I observed young people developing their self-awareness, self-concept, self-identity, and epistemic agency. I listened to them as they reported, and I observed increased confidence in decision-making. Children may often be overlooked or not heard within schools, but it is important to recognise that if they are supported and given opportunities, they will stand up and be involved.

I believe that approaches like mine offer innovation and then the potential to 'flatten' the hierarchical school power structures dominated by adults (McPartlan, 2023). In this context, staff can also recognise and appreciate the young people's work, and so do not feel threatened by them.

Community engagement should be about developing relationships and ensuring a dialogic approach. Reflecting on my overall research processes, I now realise I was informed but also naive. As a person interested in children, I did not realise the importance of time and relationship development at the conception of the research. Whilst I was focussed on transferring power to the YRT and the younger participants, I was not fully cognisant of precisely what this involved. Community involvement is about the investment of time with people talking and listening to each other and working together to solve problems. Trust between the researcher and YRT developed due to both sides' investment of time and effort. A symbiotic process developed.

The research process involved developing relationships within the school and between myself, the researcher, and the YRT. Their sense of self was enhanced as they grew into the research. They knew they were doing an important job and started feeling valued, knowing they were being taken seriously. The school would adopt their findings, and as a result, their confidence in the school and themselves started to grow. This, in turn, empowered them and their agency to act also flourished.

The skills the YRT built throughout the research also influenced their development and growth. They learnt about research, what it is, how types of research may differ, and how to conduct rigorous qualitative enquiry. Their communication skills were enhanced as they practised reflective and reflexive writing. They also had the opportunity to present findings at conferences and mix with professionals and academics from various fields; their social and cultural capital was enriched. The work they completed with the younger participants contributed to improved socio-emotional skills as they learnt how to build and manage meaningful relationships. The participants were almost unanimous in believing this was the best thing about the research.

There were also lessons related to the relationship between the YRT and the school. As the research developed, there was a two-way process whereby the YRT started to trust the institution and staff within the school began to recognise the abilities and insight of young people. The short-term nature of this project meant that the duration of the research was not extensive enough to draw material conclusions about the impact this type of research may have on an institution. Whilst further research is required to explore this, research of this nature can contribute to improved school climate and culture.

When this research started, I was an experienced educator but a naive and inexperienced researcher. I was unaware of how public health and community research would be central to my work; my research, therefore, took learning from the public health and community sectors. The PPI consultations with young people prior to the research commencing helped me shape a new methodology centred around a YRT.

YPDAR is an example of PICE in an educational setting but can be developed further into the broader community. The principle of fully involving community members in the research process can, I believe, be expanded. As highlighted above, the benefits to the individuals involved are clear to see, and there is potential for these to impact the community. During my journey, I learned that research is more than academics collecting information to further their agenda. However, it is about developing partnerships with communities and individuals within them to learn with and from them. Societal structures such as schools and health organisations are dominated by hierarchy. This work has the potential to break these traditional and sometimes archaic structures down for the betterment of our communities.

References

Bergold, J., & Thomas, S. (2012). Participatory research methods: A methodological approach in motion. *Historical Social Research, 37*(4), 191–222. https://doi.org/10.17169/fqs-13.1.1801

Boog, B. (2007). Quality of action research: Reciprocal understanding of (scientific) researchers and participating researchers. In P. Ponte & B. H. J. Smit (Eds.), *The quality of practitioner research: Reflections on the position of the researcher and the researched.* BRILL.

Braun, V., & Clarke, V. (2012). Thematic analysis. In H. Cooper, P. M. Camic, D. L. Long, A. T. Panter, D. Rindskopf, & K. J. Sher (Eds.), *APA handbook of research methods in psychology, vol 2: Research designs: Quantitative, qualitative, neuropsychological, and biological* (Vol. 2, pp. 57–71). American Psychological Association. https://doi.org/10.1037/13620-004

Dunn, A. H. (2020). "A vicious cycle of disempowerment": The relationship between teacher morale, pedagogy, and agency in an urban high school. *Teachers College Record: The Voice of Scholarship in Education, 122*(1), 1–40. https://doi.org/10.1177/016146812012200101

Ellingson, L. (2008). *Engaging crystallization in qualitative research: An introduction.* Sage Publications, Inc.

Gilgun, J. F. (2006). The four cornerstones of qualitative research. *Qualitative Health Research, 16*(3), 436–443. https://doi.org/10.1177/1049732305285338

Jacobs, S. (2016). The use of participatory action research within education-benefits to stakeholders. *World Journal of Education, 6*(3), 48–55. https://doi.org/10.5430/wje.v6n3p48

Kilkelly, U. (2004). *Northern Ireland commissioner for children and young people, & Queen's University of Belfast.* Children's rights in Northern Ireland: Northern Ireland Commisoner for Children and Young People (NICCY).

Kim, S., Hollowed, A. B., Barange, M., & MacKenzie, B. R. (2014). ICES and PICES strategies for coordinating research on the impacts of climate change on marine ecosystems. *Oceanography, 27*(4), 160–167. https://doi.org/10.5670/oceanog.2014.94

Latorre Beltran, A., & Gómez, J. (2005). *Critical communicative methodology. First international congress of qualitative inquire.* University of Illinois. http://www.iiqi.org/C4QI/httpdocs/qi2005/papers/beltran.pdf

Lindhult, E. (2019). Scientific excellence in participatory and action research: Part II. Rethinking objectivity and reliability. *Technology Innovation Management Review, 9*(5), 22–33. https://doi.org/10.22215/timreview/1238

McGovern, W., Gillespie, A., & Woodley, H. (Eds.) (2022). *Understanding safeguarding for children and their educational experiences.* Emerald Publishing Limited.

McPartlan, D. (2023). *Young researchers in schools: A participative action research study into the efficacy of a whole school mental health strategy.* University of Cumbria. https://insight.cumbria.ac.uk/id/eprint/7274

McPartlan, D., Burrus, A., Elder, K., Gregory, P., Hillary, M., McCrea, C., Bell, S., Greenup, C., James, C., Liddell, J., Liddell, K., Norwood, E., Rome, A., & Schollick, J. (2021). *The benefits of young researchers in a school YPAR project.* Social Publishing Foundation. https://www.socialpublishersfoundation.org/knowledge-base/

Pleasance, S. (2016). Student voice and its role in sustainability. In D. Summers & R. Cutting (Eds.), *Education for sustainable development in further education* (pp. 213–229). Palgrave Macmillan.

Schiavo, R. (2021). What is true community engagement and why it matters (now more than ever). *Journal of Communication in Healthcare, 14*(2), 91–92. https://doi.org/10.1080/17538068.2021.1935569

Stringer, E. & Ortiz Aragon, A. (2021). Action Research (5th ed.). Sage Publications.

Chapter 7

Community Asset Mapping: An Ethical, Strength-based Approach to Co-production and Inclusion

Kim Hall[a], Lydia Lochhead[a], Hayley Alderson[b],
Monique Lhussier[a], Ruth McGovern[b], Zeb Sattar[a],
Paul Watson[a] and William McGovern[a]

[a]*Faculty of Health and Life Sciences, Northumbria University,*
Newcastle upon Tyne, UK
[b]*Institute of Population Health and Life Sciences, Newcastle University,*
Newcastle upon Tyne, UK

Abstract

Community asset mapping (CAM) is a strength-based approach to re-engaging with and re-developing communities through research. The approach aims to identify and document a community's existing resources whilst recognising that people within a community hold valuable knowledge about the assets in their area. Generating knowledge and mapping resources from people who represent different parts of a community focusses on the area's strengths rather than its deficits. In this chapter, we report and reflect on our use of CAM whilst exploring the concept of 'recovery' within a local authority area in the North East of England. In doing so, we describe and critically appraise our own practices as we seek to co-produce and implement the research. However, we also report positively on our research and the ways in which we promote and achieve inclusion

Public Involvement and Community Engagement in Applied Health and Social Care Research:
Critical Perspectives and Innovative Practice, 81–91

doi:10.1108/978-1-83608-678-920251007

and implement an anti-stigma approach within our methods. We conclude this chapter by making suggestions for those who are considering this topic or type of research.

Keywords: Community asset mapping; marginalised communities; stigma; carers; strength-based approaches; ethics and inclusion

Introduction

The local authority we were commissioned by were incorporating Marmot city principles alongside an inclusive recovery city (IRC) framework and approach to improve health outcomes and reduce inequalities. As a basic concept, an IRC is defined as a city where recovery is promoted, is visible, challenges stigma, and champions multiple pathways of drug and alcohol recovery (Best & Colman, 2019). As part of their underpinning work, the Public Health Team in the city had also continued to support the city's Service User and Carer Forum and the development of a lived experience recovery organisation (LERO). LEROs have several distinguishing features: they generally endorse a rights-based approach to involvement in, and co-production of developing and facilitating community-based recovery services. Crucially, LERO's act independently but are also usually involved in working with traditional forms of drug and alcohol treatment providers. LEROs act in response to the needs and aspirations of their community, 'recognising and employing the assets and competences that already exist' (College of Lived Experience and Recovery Organizations [CLERO], 2024). When developing recovery-orientated care (Office for Health Improvement and Disparities [OHID], 2023), it is important for traditional treatment providers and commissioners to support the development of a LERO and recovery support services. Both a recovery-orientated care system (ROCS), and the support offered by treatment and recovery support services, are considered to be important to a person's recovery. The interaction of both services and the local community contributes to the effectiveness of a ROCS.

Our research was conducted in a large city in the United Kingdom. Within the city, there is a well-established drug and alcohol treatment system and recovery community; therefore, a lot was already known about different communities within the locality, such as their characteristics and their experiences whilst accessing formal treatment. Less was known about the recovery community and for the context of our research, recovery assets explored included: individuals known as leading recovery agendas and planning; organisations commissioned or who support people using drugs and alcohol and/or family members of people using substances; groups supporting people in recovery; and the recovery community's perspectives regarding prior and current efforts to create and sustain recovery assets. There was recognition in the city that some recovery groups were well established, but little was known about smaller community-led organisations and other services that offer peer-led and non-affiliated (not part of a national group or movement like alcoholics Anonymous or Narcotics Anonymous) groups. Our CAM project was undertaken in the context of the project addiction, diversion, disruption, enforcement, and recovery (ADDER), a specialist-funded project by the Office for Health Improvement and Disparities (2023), aimed at reducing drug-related crimes, drug prevalence, and drug-related deaths. As a research group, we focussed on inclusion and inequality, the perceptions, hopes, and aspirations of these groups, and how they contribute to the broader aim of building an IRC. Our key concerns aligned with project ADDER, insofar as we wanted to engage with and raise the profile of marginalised communities and make them and their needs more visible to commissioners and services. We also wanted to utilise a strength-based approach and methodology, which enabled us to challenge negative societal perceptions of people who used substances. But also to help others understand more about the contribution that people in recovery made to the communities, health, and social care services, and priorities.

CAM and Co-production

CAM enables researchers to move beyond traditional methods (interviewing and focus groups) to embody a strengths-based approach to engage and develop communities through research (Luo et al., 2023). The aim of CAM is to identify and document a community's existing resources whilst recognising that people hold valuable knowledge about the (sometimes intangible) assets in their area (Luo et al., 2023). Generating knowledge and mapping resources from people who represent different parts of a community focusses attention on the area's strengths rather than on the deficits (Luo et al., 2023). The ethos of co-production is embedded within CAM work. Co-production is a strength-based approach increasingly used by researchers invested in 'egalitarian, democratic or transparent' ways of working (Williams et al., 2020, p. 3). As a methodological tool it is an umbrella term that 'locates power and worth with citizens in order to address issues of social justice' (Williams et al., 2020, p. 3). Co-production is also a value-based approach encouraging people who share common values to come together and take ownership in facilitating change (Cahn, 2011). Co-produced research is valuable when researchers wish to work with a range of stakeholders to generate knowledge about an agreed focus and ultimately, bring about change (Tembo et al., 2019). Stakeholders, including People With Lived Experience (PLWE) public citizens or practitioners), policy makers, funders, and researchers bring their unique perspectives about their community, enhancing the richness of the project (Luo et al., 2023; Tembo et al., 2019). Honouring transparency means being clear about the roles and responsibilities of all involved in the research, which we outline in the section below. Defining co-production is challenging because of the myriads of similarities and differences across and within communities that will determine the agenda for this research. The ambiguity of co-production's multiple methodological designs, and the ubiquity of its use within communities means that there is no 'gold standard' (Williams et al., 2020) that we must adhere to. Rather, it is the principles and values based on philosophical concepts of equity, empowerment, respect, inclusivity, and democratic ways of working, that are foundational to its design (Pettican et al., 2023). The measure of quality within a project is the transformative possibilities for PWLE and its ability to affect social change (Cook, 2012). Co-production work is challenging and requires constant reflective and reflexive practice, it is something that will look and feel different on every occasion. Therefore, rejecting a gold standard notion of co-production enabled us to appreciate the opportunity to co-design a project, acknowledging the unique skill set brought by different partners, and the right of each to engage in different ways.

Issues of tokenism can arise in co-produced research when prior consideration is not given to the power dynamics and relationships between the stakeholders, particularly for people who are marginalised by their perceived status. Our definition of tokenism is drawn from Hahn et al. (2017, p. 291), who state it is the 'difference between … the empty ritual of participation and having the real power needed to affect the outcome'. This has been referred to as a 'genuine – token continuum' where attempts at engagement are those that seek bidirectional partner engagement throughout the project and tokenistic attempts are more unilateral, aligned with consulting and informing (Hahn et al., 2017, p. 291). Following the co-productions' philosophical values of empowerment, respect, inclusivity, and democratic processes, we strove to make attempts to engage from the early stages of the project (Pettican et al., 2023). This involved ethical considerations about our working practices, including reflecting on our positionality even before we entered the research field. We paid attention to the power dynamics that are inherent in any research project, including co-production, by utilising a reflexive approach to consider our positionality. Our endeavour for genuine co-production was incorporated into the research aims.

Implementing Co-production Principles

We implemented our research with the already existing community resource 'Service User and Carer Forum', which was both central to the research process and to the communities we were seeking to work with. In our attempts to be inclusive and avoid tokenism, we developed a semi-structured programme of work which involved consultation sessions. In developing the content and the focus of the sessions, we worked with colleagues, forum leaders, and researchers to consider what the sessions should include and how they should be delivered. What we were essentially doing was 'sense making' and considering our own positionality, in relation to what we needed to do, and then allowing others to help us by participating in a sympathetic critical appraisal of our ideas and practices. Here, we were primarily concerned with starting a dialogue with different stakeholders.

We were mindful that PWLE are less likely to be included in discussions about matters that impact their daily life (Luo et al., 2023; Williams et al., 2020). Additionally, platforms for the production and sharing of knowledge may previously have been limited or non-existent for PWLE who are marginalised and stigmatised (Cotterell & Buffel, 2023; Kulmala et al., 2024). Invisibility of marginalised groups is harmful because it perpetuates misrecognition, stigmatisation, and embedded social and political inequalities resulting from the limited understanding about different ways of living (Gordon, 2008). Embedding the ethos of co-production in CAM is a way to engage with PWLE who have typically been left out of discussions about their life (Cotterell & Buffel, 2023; Luo et al., 2023). In striving for an inclusive and transformative approach (Cook, 2012) we recognised this as ethical practice, enabling the generation of different perspectives and increasingly nuanced understanding of lived experiences. The reciprocal benefits of engaging with PWLE includes enhancing the quality of the knowledge generated (Tembo et al., 2019), enhancing feelings of empowerment, and instigating change at a local and/or national level (Heard, 2022). The potential for change in co-production is dynamic and can impact those on the inside of research partnerships, and equally it can extend to those in the public domain; particularly when PWLE are engaged publicly in sharing and disseminating their knowledge. Gordon (2008, p. 7) refers to the concept of 'haunting' to explain that when a marginalised and stigmatised hidden group becomes visible to others, this visibility enables pathways to 'seeing' the trauma, inequalities and social injustice. Gordon and Bengal (2018) explain that publicly seeing PWLE and hearing their accounts offers greater potential for their stories to 'haunt', leaving a lasting impression with the audience. The potential for change is greater because these voices carry the messages more powerfully than those without similar lived experience. When we engage with marginalised communities, we need to be mindful that we are not labelling, stigmatising or being tokenistic towards the groups we work with in co-production. Anti-stigma and trauma informed approaches (see Adams and Ramsay in this collection) also need to underpin all aspects of research conceptualisation, design and implementation. Therefore, we adopted an ethical stance to the idea of 'haunting'; on the one hand, we understood the importance of platforming unheard voices, whilst on the other, we were mindful that it can be tokenistic without facilitating change. The notion of change was embedded in the co-production work, therefore throughout the project, we embraced Gordon's (2008) notion of 'haunting' by engaging with PWLE of substance use to make visible and map the services and resources relating to recovery.

Workshops

We convened four formal workshops during the project. Workshop members were initially recruited via an advertisement shared with the city's service user and carer forum. We utilised this approach because we wanted to provide an opportunity to all forum members to participate. We were, however, mindful that we did not want to waste forum time and involve members when they did not feel inclined to work with us. Individuals who were interested in developing and supporting the research were asked to fill in a form outlining their motivations to be involved, what they thought they would bring to the research, and what they hoped to achieve by being involved. As we have seen in other chapters in this collection (Bidmead et al., 2025), community groups and organisations can become weary of research and do not always benefit from their involvement with research. Most of those we recruited, however, expressed a desire for more visibility of services to better help people looking for recovery and improve the way services are ran in the community to benefit others.

Three members participated in the first workshop session, and four attended the second workshop session. An additional 27 members of the wider forum attended the third workshop, and 13 attended the fourth and final workshop. Each member of the Public Involvement and Community Engagement (PICE) group was paid in relation to the time they spent in groups and activities: £40 per session (sessions one and two only in line with National Institute for Health and Care Research [NIHR] Guidance, 2024). Those in workshops three and four were paid £10 as a gesture of goodwill for listening to and engaging in discussions about the mapping process. Workshop members were informed via email of when the sessions were to take place. The workshops were organised to directly follow the already established service user and carer forum and were conducted in the same venue to facilitate ease of access. PICE members were given information about the study, and each signed a Public Involvement Group Consent Form. Data from the discussion was fed into the CAM process and later into the topic guide for the semi-structured interviews and focus groups.

The first workshop was an introductory and initial mapping session. In this session, we engaged in open discussions and reminded the group that they were not obligated to share experiences with us, but also that we were prepared to listen and support their involvement and experiences. In this session, PICE members were simply asked to consider and map out their own recovery journey and then to reflect on their needs and record the types of services they considered important to recovery. This session was also used to discuss and explore participants' perceptions of the types of organisations (e.g., peer support groups, non-affiliated services, etc.) that needed to be mapped as part of the research.

We wanted workshop members to have ownership over the mapping process and to be involved in the research. We knew that each of the forum members we engaged with was actively involved in their own communities and that they were tied into extensive recovery networks and communities. Armed with this knowledge and prior to session two, workshop members were asked to engage with their own extended recovery networks and communities and then to identify and record with them the different types of services that were utilised by the wider recovery community in the area. During workshop session two, members were asked to consider their experiences of accessing services and to identify what did and did not work for them and what they considered to be gaps within the current recovery community and provision in the city.

In the third workshop, an update was given to the wider service user and carer forum ($n = 13$ women; $n = 14$ men) on study progress, and an illustrative map of recovery services was shared, discussed, and reviewed to sense check the findings in relation to relevance and future uses. At this point, we wanted to bring the data we had generated back to the wider group and to start to involve the service user and carer forum again, and to keep the wider group involved in the research. Moving from the smaller group to the larger group was key for us to understand the varying perspectives of those involved directly or indirectly.

The fourth and final workshop involved sharing interim findings from the interviews with the service user and carer forum members ($n = 8$ women; $n = 5$ men). Findings were presented creatively in a poster format in which forum members were asked to discuss their thoughts around the findings; in particular, if they agreed or disagreed with anything that was presented. This helped the research group to sense check their findings from the wider reach work (interviews with individuals) and with those navigating recovery in the community.

Interviews and Focus Groups with Recovery Organisations and Services

In this project, it was key for us to bring the perspectives of PWLE and professionals together to explore their perceptions of the community assets that existed in the city. Interviews were conducted simultaneously with the workshops. The purpose was to invite those involved in delivering services to take the time to consider the positive attributes of the recovery community, their visibility, and role, in supporting their service and the wider community. In keeping with the strengths-based approach, any criticism was responded to by refocussing the interview to areas for improvement rather than what was wrong 'with recovery'. We engaged in semi-structured interviews and focus groups with those working in recovery organisations and services. A number of these were also PWLE working in the recovery community, but also accessing services. These individuals were practitioners who self-identified as 'being in recovery', and they were a valuable resource for us: not only had they navigated services themselves, they had also supported others who were going through the recovery process. About 13 semi-structured interviews and two focus groups ($n = 5$ participants in focus group 1; $n = 6$ in focus group 2) were conducted to further explore staff perspectives of the recovery community. Practitioners and service providers working in recovery were recruited using purposive sampling via the research teams' pre-existing networks. Professionals as representatives of the drug and alcohol treatment system were also invited to take part if they were working in the recovery community in any capacity. Our 'hands off' approach to recruitment meant that we were more likely to engage professionals who volunteered to come forward, either because they had something to say and/or because they wanted to join us in celebrating and championing the recovery work.

CAM As an Anti-stigma Approach

Stigma is a key determinant of exclusion and, whilst being an avoidable harm, it is associated with the maintenance of various forms of social and health-related harms and structural inequality (Addison et al., 2023). Stigma is conceptualised as a process of excluding and marginalising individuals or groups based on deficit perceptions of their characteristics, behaviours, motivations, acts, and attributes (Butler-Warke, 2020). Stigma is acknowledged to be a harmful act and can be a social factor of an individual's health, their sense of worth, belonging, and inclusion (Stockdale et al., 2022). Stigma occurs when people have an emotional response to a negative perception of others, and the subsequent prejudice they have leads to discrimination or the withholding of services and support from people. People who use substances (PWUS) are amongst the most stigmatised groups in society. Research and reviews have identified that PWUS are known to experience stigma in many forms, be these institutional, societal, public, and/ or private (Cazalis et al., 2023; McGovern et al., 2024). The stigmatisation of PWUS is highlighted as being weaponised to justify exclusion from involvement within society (Addison et al., 2023). This impedes opportunities for PWUS to engage and benefit from health and social care services, hindering opportunities for involvement in the support and development of health, and substance-specific treatment and recovery services (Cazalis et al., 2023).

PWUS are known to be aware of stigma and inequality and privileging their perspective and lived experience in co-production research, and in our case, CAM, provides a unique standpoint from them about what best serves them (Kulmala et al., 2024; Mendon et al., 2024). What we learned on a personal level is that co-produced research like ours encourages inclusivity in practice and benefits the individual by combatting stigma through empowerment and providing a sense of inclusion, worth, and agency (Kulmala et al., 2024; Mendon et al., 2024). In addition, our research helped us to understand CAM as a meaningful and authentic collaboration between PWLE and other stakeholders, enhancing the quality and relevance of strategies designed to reduce inequality and promote the uptake of public services. However, despite the benefits associated with co-production research, the lived experience of minoritised groups, such as PWUS, has often been under-represented in research design and development (Cotterell & Buffel, 2023; Kulmala et al., 2024). Our research has shown extensively that people are stigmatised as they use substances (McGovern et al., 2022) whilst they are in recovery (McGovern et al., 2024) and after they disengage with services (Lochhead et al., 2024). Co-producing research with PWUS and engaging with them in research and the development of public services enables possibilities for reducing stigma and inequality and is associated with a multitude of personal, social, and societal benefits (Gronholm et al., 2024). CAM asks individuals and community members to consider their strengths and the strengths of individuals and groups that are often stigmatised. It is a process in which professionals can be challenged to build their own knowledge about groups, but also to reconsider any negative and/or prejudicial perspectives they may have. Finally, PWLE who are involved in CAM can build their own self-worth and esteem from involvement (if reports from our group are accurate) and also increase an individual's sense of meaning and belonging if people feel they are making an active contribution to their community/society.

Conclusion

If you are engaging in research with marginalised communities we would encourage you to utilise a CAM approach. In research CAM can be utilised to surface knowledge embedded in communities of people whose voices are often unheard, with the focus of generating knowledge and documenting the existing resources of recovery services in a local area. Our CAM approach was rooted in constructivism and this enabled us to develop a more in depth and deeper understanding of how PWLE constructed knowledge and made meaning of their experiences of using substances, recovery and accessing recovery services. It allowed us to move beyond the lived experience of PWUS and to explore the contribution they made to their communities and others in recovery. In our research, we were not seeking to 'reinvent the wheel', rather we were interested philosophically with understanding how the wheel turned and how it functioned (Golder & Bengal, 2018). Our approach enabled us to engage with and understand PICE members' knowledge and their real-world experiences whilst enabling us as a research group to hypothesise together and ultimately draw themes and conclusion from their experiences (Golder & Bengal, 2018; Jonassen, 1994). In future whilst we advocate for the use of co-production, we advise being mindful of tokenism by taking measures to reflect in and on co-designing research with others. One such measure is by embedding the use of anti-stigma and trauma informed approaches (see Adams and Ramsey this collection) in all aspects of the research activity. We argue that co-production that uses CAM encourages inclusivity by disrupting and reducing stigma and inequalities through democratic and egalitarian practices, creating opportunities for feelings of empowerment, worth, and agency.

Our ethical approach in researching with PWLE, co-designing safe spaces, and building trusting relationships was rooted in our desire for activism rather than tokenism. We recognise that PWLEs are best placed to share their knowledge about the services in their community. The voices of PWLE enriched the quality of the CAM project, including the outcomes, and their voices carry greater potential to leave a lasting impression on others through a sense of 'haunting' those in the public domain, calling for a 'something to be done' and creating a demand for visibility and change.

References

Adams, A. A., & Ramsay, S. E. (2025). Embedding trauma-informed principles within involvement and co-production activities with people experiencing homelessness. In W. McGovern, H. Alderson, B. K. Bareham, & M. Lhussier (Eds.), *Public involvement and community engagement in applied health and social care research: Critical perspectives and innovative practice*. Emerald Publishing.

Addison, M. (2023). Framing stigma as an avoidable social harm that widens inequality. *The Sociological Review, 71*(2), 296–314. https://doi.org/10.1177/00380261221150080

Best, D., & Colman, C. (2019). Let's celebrate recovery. Inclusive cities working together to support social cohesion. *Addiction Research & Theory, 27*(1), 55–64. https://doi.org/10.1080/16066359.2018.1520223

Bidmead, E., Shenton, F., Brunskill, G., Whitmarsh, K., Barnes, S., & Capewell, S. (2025). Coproduction of a regional approach to community engagement in health and social care research in the North East and North Cumbria. In W. McGovern, H. Alderson, B. K. Bareham, & M. Lhussier (Eds.), *Public involvement and community engagement in applied health and social care research: Critical perspectives and innovative practice*. Emerald Publishing.

Butler-Warke, A. (2020). There's a time and a place: Temporal aspects of place-based stigma. *Community Development Journal, 56*(2), 203–219. https://doi.org/10.1093/cdj/bsaa040

Cahn, E. (2011). *It's the core economy stupid: An open letter to the non-profit community.* chrome-extension://efaidnbmnnnibpcajpcglclefindmkaj/http://ereserve.library.utah.edu/Annual/BSH/5000/Waitzman/cahn.pdf

Cazalis, A., Lambert, L., & Auriacombe, M. (2023). Stigmatization of people with addiction by health professionals: Current knowledge. A scoping review. *Drug and Alcohol Dependence Reports, 9,* 100196. https://doi.org/10.1016/j.dadr.2023.100196

College of Lived Experience Recovery Organisations. (2024). *About the college of Lived Experience Recovery Organisations.* Retrieved September 20, 2024, from https://www.clero.co.uk/

Cook, T. (2012). Where participatory approaches meet pragmatism in funded (health) research: The challenge of finding meaningful spaces. *Forum: Qualitative Social Research, 13*(1), Art. 18. https://doi.org/10.17169/fqs-13.1.1783

Cotterell, N., & Buffel, T. (2023). "Holders of knowledge are communities, not academic institutions": Lessons from involving minoritised older people as co-researchers in a study of loneliness in later life. *Qualitative Research in Psychology, 20*(3), 441–470. https://doi.org/10.1080/14780887.2023.2180463

Golder, J., & Bengal, W. (2018). Constructivism: A paradigm for teaching and learning. *International Journal of Research and Analytical Reviews, 5*(3), 678–686.

Gordon, A. (2008) *Ghostly matters: Haunting and the sociological imagination.* University of Minnesota Press.

Gronholm, P. C., Kline, S., Lamba, M., Lempp, H., Mahkmud, A., Morales Cano, G., Vashisht, K., Vera San Juan, N., & Sunkel, C. (2024). Exploring perspectives of stigma and discrimination among people with lived experience of mental health conditions: A co-produced qualitative study. *eClinicalMedicine, 70,* 102509. https://doi.org/10.1016/j.eclinm.2024.102509

Hahn, D. L., Hoffmann, A. E., Felzien, M., LeMaster, J. W., Xu, J., & Fagnan, L. J. (2017). Tokenism in patient engagement. *Family Practice, 34*(3), 290–295. https://doi.org/10.1093/fampra/cmw097

Heard, E. (2022). Ethical challenges in participatory action research: Experiences and insights from an arts-based study in the pacific. *Qualitative Research, 23*(4), 1–21. Retrieved August 4, 2022, from https://doi.org/10.1177/14687941211072797

Jonassen, D. H. (1994). Thinking technology: Toward a constructivist design model. *Educational Technology, 34*(4), 34–37.

Kulmala, M., Venäläinen, S., Hietala, O., Nikula, K., & Koskivirta, I. (2024). Lived experience as the basis of collaborative knowing: Inclusivity and resistance to stigma in co-research. *International Journal of Qualitative Methods, 23,* 1–13. https://doi.org/10.1177/16094069241236271

Lochhead, L., Addison, M., Cavener, J., Scott, S., & McGovern, W. (2024). Exploring the impact of stigma on health and wellbeing: Insights from mothers with lived experience accessing recovery services. *International Journal of Environmental Research and Public Health, 21*(9), 1189. https://www.mdpi.com/1660-4601/21/9/1189

Luo, Y., Ruggiano, N., Bolt, D., Witt, J.-P., Anderson, M., Gray, J., & Jiang, Z. (2023). Community asset mapping in public health: A review of applications and approaches. *Social Work in Public Health, 38*(3), 171–181. https://doi.org/10.1080/19371918.2022.2114568

McGovern, W., Addison, M., & McGovern, R. (2022). Final reflections on stigma and implications for research, policy, and practice. In M. Addison, W. McGovern, & R. McGovern (Eds.), *Drugs, identity and stigma* (pp. 271–278). Palgrave MacMillan.

McGovern, W., Addison, M., & McGovern, R. (2024). The adoption of a "diseased identity" in traditional 12-step groups: Exploring the implications of these processes for individuals and practitioners in health and social care services. *International Journal of Environmental Research and Public Health, 21*(10), 1297. https://www.mdpi.com/1660-4601/21/10/1297

Mendon, G. B., Gurung, D., Loganathan, S., Abayneh, S., Zhang, W., Kohrt, B. A., Hanlon, C., Lempp, H., Thornicroft, G., & Gronholm, P. C. (2024). Establishing partnerships with people with lived experience of mental illness for stigma reduction in low- and middle-income settings. *Cambridge Prisms: Global Mental Health, 11*, e70, Article e70. https://doi.org/10.1017/gmh.2024.69

National Institute for Health and Care Research. (2024). *Payment guidance for researchers and professionals*. Retrieved October 8, 2024, from https://www.nihr.ac.uk/payment-guidance-researchers-and-professionals

Office for Health Improvement and Disparities. (2023). *Part 1: Introducing recovery, peer support and lived experience initiatives*. https://www.gov.uk/government/publications/recovery-support-services-and-lived-experience-initiatives/part-1-introducing-recovery-peer-support-and-lived-experience-initiatives

Pettican, A., Goodman, B., Bryant, W., Beresford, P., Freeman, P., Gladwell, V., Kilbride, C., & Speed, E. (2023). Doing together: Reflections on facilitating the co-production of participatory action research with marginalised populations. *Qualitative Research in Sport, Exercise and Health, 15*(2), 202–219. https://doi.org/10.1080/2159676X.2022.2146164

Stockdale, K. J., Addison, M., & Ramm, G. (2022). Navigating custodial environments: Novel psychoactive substance users experiences of stigma. In M. Addison, W. McGovern, & R. McGovern (Eds.), *Drugs, identity and stigma.* (pp. 147–172). Palgrave Macmillan. https://doi.org/10.1007/978-3-030-98286-7

Tembo, D., Morrow, E., Worswick, L., & Lennard, D. (2019). Is co-production just a pipe dream for applied health research commissioning? An exploratory literature review [review]. *Frontiers in Sociology, 4*, 1–10. https://doi.org/10.3389/fsoc.2019.00050

Williams, O., Sarre, S., Papoulias, S. C., Knowles, S., Robert, G., Beresford, P., Rose, D., Carr, S., Kaur, M., & Palmer, V. J. (2020). Lost in the shadows: Reflections on the dark side of co-production. *Health Research Policy and Systems, 18*(1), 43. https://doi.org/10.1186/s12961-020-00558-0

Chapter 8

Applying a Public Health Lens to Co-production with the Military Connected Community

Paul Watson, Emma Senior, Robin Hyde and Mark Telford

Faculty of Health and Life Sciences, Northumbria University, Newcastle upon Tyne, UK ·

Abstract

Addressing emerging public health emergencies within the military-connected community requires a culturally informed, value-driven, and collaborative approach to service development and implementation. Drawing on insights from several studies, this chapter explores the synergy between public health theory and co-production methodology. We introduce a method of systematically layering Beattie's model of health promotion with a stepped iteration of the co-production process, creating a nuanced understanding of the experiences within this community. Key considerations for bridging the gap between rhetoric and reality are examined through a value-based approach, emphasising trust and rapport building, a commitment to impact, and a drive for meaningful change.

Keywords: Co-production; public health; service improvement; military; value-based practice

Public Involvement and Community Engagement in Applied Health and Social Care Research: Critical Perspectives and Innovative Practice, 93–104
doi:10.1108/978-1-83608-678-920251008

Introduction

In this chapter, we demonstrate and reflect on how co-production as a research method can be applied to health and social care research within the military-connected community and offer an interpretation of how co-production could be practised within service development and service implementation. Presented is a method of systematically layering Beattie's model of health promotion with a stepped iteration of the co-production process used to create a bricolage of understanding into the experiences of conducting research with the military-connected community. As a research method, co-production is complex; however, applying a public health lens using Beattie's model provides clarity and conceptualises a bottom-up trajectory to address the areas of public health need within this community. The conceptual application of theory and process is a favoured methodology. It is used across multiple national projects within the northern hub for veterans. Family research, such as the one, is too much (Kiernan et al., 2024) (reducing military suicide), developing a common approach to assessment (Watson et al., 2024), and reducing social isolation and loneliness in the veteran population (Watson & Farrell, 2023). Using a scaffolded approach, this chapter demonstrates the iterative process of how findings emerge and inform the subsequent phases of research.

Military Connected Community

The military constitutes a distinct cultural entity, characterised by its own history, legal frameworks, values, traditions, language, and customs (Meyer, 2015). Individuals are socialised into military culture from an early stage, with this cultural immersion influencing nearly all aspects of their lives and resulting in a high degree of acculturation. Notably, veterans who served for only a few years frequently report a strong identification with the military even decades after leaving service (Johansen et al., 2013). As Heward et al. (2024) describes, military culture is a dynamic construct shaped by shared beliefs, values, behaviours, norms, symbols, and practices, which in turn influence individuals' identities, worldviews, and social interactions. The military's pervasive role in the lives of its personnel is designed to ensure operational effectiveness; however, this also entails a reduction in personal freedoms and privacy; constraints that civilians may find difficult to comprehend (Dandeker, 2021). Military culture does not only reside within serving and veteran personnel, but it also permeates the family and significant others surrounding that individual. For military families, military life presents a range of situations that others seldom face and embodies a culture that is unique to them (Mancini et al., 2020). Their private family life is synonymous and not separate suggesting all family members collectively play a role in military life (Watson & Osbourne, 2025) and very often display the same militarised values (Cree, 2020). Due to the complexities of military culture, health and social care providers often navigate dual responsibilities, balancing the needs of the patient, and their families alongside the broader operational requirements of the military.

Beattie's Model of Health Promotion

Beattie's (1991) model of health promotion offers a theoretical public health lens, and provides the conceptual framework for this work, due to its ability to identify the 'level' of health promotion, health protection and identify areas within health and social care to prevent poor health outcomes using contemporary and future intervention. The rationale for Beattie's model over other health promotion models, such as the health belief model (Rosenstock, 1974) or Tannahill (2008), was the model's ability to make clear links between the underpinning values and principles of public health practices, in line with co-production methodological practices. Moreover, unlike other models of health promotion, Beattie's model allows theory to drive the development of health promotion interventions and is not purely a description of existing activity (Rowe et al., 2009). Crucially, Beattie's model provides an understanding of collaborative intervention, which is important as it recognises the influence and involvement of the individual, their family, their communities, and those who deliver services (Hubley et al., 2021).

Beattie's (1991) model describes four paradigms for health promotion, including health persuasion, legislative action, personal counselling, and community development. Moreover, the four paradigms are generated by two axes, 'mode' and 'intervention', that range from authoritative (top-down) to negotiated (bottom-up) on the vertical axis. The horizontal axis focusses on intervention, which ranges from individual to the left, moving right to groups of people. Moreover, Beattie's model allows for the layered practicalities of the co-production process to be placed within each corresponding part of the health promotion model. Importantly, Beattie's (1991) model allows the health promoter (micro, meso, and macro levels) to locate existing activity and then consider action at the individual level, recognising the impact of the broader social and cultural practices on health, specifically in this case, military culture.

Co-production

Service users' and their families' expectations of quality health and social services being provided to them continue to grow amidst increasing demands on service provisions, caused by an ageing population and a significant rise in long-term chronic health conditions (McMullin & Needham, 2018). This increase in service demand and quality has compelled policymakers to highlight the importance of and develop more patient and public involvement in service design, delivery, and research (Involve, 2012). One method of service user involvement is co-production.

Co-production is not a new concept however, co-production has renewed importance in contemporary policy reform and is widely considered as best practice for dealing with current health and social care sector issues; especially when practical and financial resources are significantly reduced (Marsilio et al., 2021). Originally coined in the 1970s by economist Elinor Ostrom, 'co-production' became a designation of process, in which contributions from 'individuals who are not "in" the same organisation are transformed into goods and services'

(Ostrom, 1996). This process according to Ostrom, also included the assessment, management, and delivery of public services by 'users' and 'providers'. Academics and social activists such as Cahn (2000) developed the idea of co-production from Ostrom's work and identified that participation and the involvement of all within any sector was indispensable to getting real results and was the only way to truly maximise effectiveness in completing any mission (Cahn, 2000). Cahn later proposed in a letter to the non-profit sector, that the only way the world is going to address its problems is by enlisting the very people who are now classed as clients and re-enlist them as co-workers, partners, and rebuilders (Cahn, 2005). Cahn's (2005) work provides a radical shift in the thinking among those who 'help', to move away from a top-down approach to an environment where change is value-based. This then blurs the barriers between the state, services, and its people; and involves relationships of reciprocity and mutuality; therefore, becoming an asset-based model for change (Boyle et al., 2010). As an asset-based model, Marsilio et al. (2021) explain policy makers have created new relational models, in which service users, their families, and local communities share responsibility with care providers and local governments bodies. That is, service users and their families are asked to actively participate in service design, its development, and the implementation processes. Therefore, service users work next to and in interaction with service providers and other stakeholders to enhance service provisions (Durose et al., 2017) thus being a collective for positive change.

Over the last 20-plus years, there has been an exponential growth of academic publications on all aspects relating to co-production (Loeffler & Bovaird, 2021) and an increase in the discourse of what co-production means (Fusco et al., 2020). Health and social care within the United Kingdom (UK) has become a continually changing landscape, which is awash with policies, strategies, practices, and mission statements stating that change within this sector must be developed through co-production (Repper & Eve, 2023). There is much talk about co-production and its need; however, as Repper and Eve (2023) explain, there are multiple descriptions of what co-production is and what co-production does, along with added complications that are sector-dependent. The discourse of what co-production is and what it does has been a continual historical discussion and continues today. Filip et al. (2017) explain that despite the apparent consensus regarding the potential for co-production, it is not always clear as to what counts as or what it means to co-produce services, for development, and/or practice change.

According to Boyle and Harris (2009), co-production means delivering public services in an equal and reciprocal relationship between professionals, people using services, their families, and their communities. Penny et al. (2012) extend Boyle and Harris's work by emphasising that all those involved become effective change agents. Slay and Stephens (2013) further describe the concept of co-production as one of equal and reciprocal relationships, to a relationship where professionals and citizens share power and plan and deliver support together, recognising the synergy in equal contributions to improve life for people and communities. Co-production continues to be a hot topic in policy making, governance, and research. In health, alongside user and community participation, co-production is described as improving health and creating user-led, people-centred services (Kickbusch & Gleicher, 2012). As Wilton (2021) explains, there is a desire for people to have more control over decisions which affect them and that system leadership and public service management need to diverge from traditional 'top-down' approaches to service development and delivery, to more inclusive and collaborative practices, which are more suited to achieving change in complex systems.

In their systematic scoping review Masterson et al. (2022) map the different definitions of co-production and its partner co-creation, stating these are terms which have been used individually, interchangeably, and collectively. As Masterson et al., note from the works of Williams et al. (2020), the increasing interest in co-production has also seen the emergence of a plethora of 'co' words, which has promoted a conflation of meanings and practices. For example, the term co-design has also been considered interchangeable with co-production and co-creation. The concept of the development of 'co' words is not something new, and several authors including Van Eijk and Steen (2014) and Bradwell and Marr (2017) break down co-production into its component parts with terms such as *co-creation, co-management, co-planning-*, and *co-assessment* to highlight the different stages of which service user involvement can occur. It can therefore be argued there are a range of perspectives and typologies on each working element of the co-production process based on its component parts.

Method

When the aforementioned parts are identified as a methodological concept, there is a layering of understanding to the practicalities of co-production delivery. For example, the breakdown of co-production allows us to see; who is co-producing; how many people are involved; at what stage co-production takes place; what is contributed; and how co-production relates to other forms of citizen participation (Needham & Carr, 2009; Pestoff, 2014) which provides further credence for the use of Beattie's model with this community. Even with the continual development of co-production theory, the origins of co-production as a 'whole' methodological process revisits the understanding of public service provision, suggesting that services are joint products of providers and users, that is, it emphasises of users in the design, implementation, and/or delivery of services (Ostrom & Ostrom, 2019).

Within this section, we look to use a scaffolded approach to provide a stepped guide to illustrate each aspect of our approach to the iteration processes of co-production, resolving some of the typologies of the co-production process while using Beattie's (1991) model to support its development and implementation through a public health lens. As highlighted earlier, this methodological approach has been used in several projects. Ethical approval must be *in situ* prior to any co-production process.

Phase 1: Co-design

The studies conducted within the Hub start with an initial phase, which is primarily where the research team explores the experiences of those affected or impacted by the identified phenomenon, for example, lack of holistic assessment of need, military families bereaved by suicide, and reducing social isolation and loneliness within the veteran population. Within this phase of the study, members of the research team meet with those at the heart of the issue, the veteran, their family, and those who are close to the family to listen to their ideas to understand how best to prevent or change current practice by those delivering service provisions. This consultation informs the beginning of the co-production process, which identifies the starting point for and the development of an appropriate research method. Moreover, this phase of the project allows those affected by the phenomenon to identify who they believe are the most appropriate stakeholders to engage with.

The methodological approach underpinning this phase is Narrative Inquiry, due its abilities to enquire into the meanings people make of their lived experiences, in the context of their social environment, and where the study relates to a new and relatively unexplored area within the existing academic literature (Patton, 2002). To support the capture of narrative data, a modified 'life-grid' (Richardson et al., 2009) approach can also be used for the interviews in this initial phase. A 'life grid' provides a structure from which to elicit a narrative and diagrammatic chronography of the significant events in a person's life. In addition to the 'life grid' a series of structured prompts serves to scaffold the storytelling and map the temporal journey of the phenomenon. Within the wider co-production process this element has been labelled the co-design element. Co-design sits between the collective and negotiated axes and within the community development quadrant of Beattie's model. It is this positioning which has underpinned a bottom-up approach to identify, explore, and understand the presenting phenomenon.

Phase 2: Co-managing

The goal of Phase 2 is to build upon the findings from Phase 1 and integrate overarching factors to co-produce an evidence-based intervention model. In line with the co-production methodology, it is essential to involve stakeholders who have relevant experience and expertise (Involve, 2012). This requires a purposive sample of individuals with direct experience of the phenomenon to ensure the study's aims are met (Campbell et al., 2020). For example, one study involved surviving families of military veterans who had died by suicide, health and social care sector representatives, statutory agencies, third sector organisations, politicians, retired military personnel, funding bodies, and other key stakeholders. With such diverse representation, event management is critical from the outset.

For the research team facilitating these events, the first step is to set the agenda and establish clear expectations, ensuring that all delegates understand the co-production methodology and the importance of exploring viewpoints and experiences. Facilitators must reassure participants that their contributions are equally valued, heard without discrimination, and documented. Given the diversity of delegates, there is a risk that some may dominate discussions, and conflicting views may arise, potentially making others uncomfortable. Facilitators must ensure that all participants have an opportunity to contribute in an open, non-judgemental setting.

Co-production events can be held in-person or online, each with its own set of advantages and challenges. In-person events offer opportunities for networking, greater engagement, and deeper exploration, but come with higher costs and time commitments for delegates. Online events, while more accessible and cost-effective, require considerations around digital literacy and technology access. In our co-productions, we have used a combination of both, starting with online events to reach a broader audience and followed by in-person events for more in-depth discussions. To ensure national coverage, each in-person event was held in a different devolved nation.

Each co-production event in Phase 2 is designed to answer specific questions arising from Phase 1's findings. The process is iterative, with each event informing the next. For instance, the superordinate themes from Phase 1 shaped the questions for the co-production event 1, which then influenced the focus of event 2, and so on. This iterative, collaborative process helps build a holistic understanding of the findings and contributes to the co-development of a solution-focussed framework for addressing the identified challenges.

Events 1 and 2: Co-creation

Within the co-production cycle, this phase is labelled the co-creation phase, as it involves not only those who have experienced the phenomenon but also stakeholders such as public health commissioners, military-connected service providers at various levels, frontline staff, and specialists. This phase spans both collective and individual axes of Beattie's (1991) model, covering the community development and personal counselling quadrants, while remaining firmly on the bottom-up axes.

Phase 1 focussed on collecting narratives from those who directly experienced the phenomenon. Key themes were extrapolated from these narratives, such as in the One is Too Many study, where themes on the breakdown in care formed the superordinate themes of service provision and care coordination. These themes then guided the questioning in the co-production event 1.

Event 2 built on the themes identified in Phase 1 and Event 1, exploring the barriers and responses from multiple stakeholders. These discussions led to more informed, solution-focussed conversations later in the event.

To better engage delegates at both co-production events, evidence is presented at the start of each session, recapping progress and providing reminders of the initial narratives. In some cases, these narratives are brought to life through vocal performance, where anonymised quotes are performed by an actor. This approach effectively enhances the emotional and visceral impact of the participants' stories.

Event 3: Co-assessment

Within the co-production cycle, this phase moves into the co-assessment phase as it requires the attending delegates to assess the presenting issues of the solutions discussed previously, conduct root cause analysis, and develop solutions to the presenting issues. This phase of the co-production process continues across both collective and individual axes of Beattie's (1991) model, while also moving and residing in the health persuasion quadrant. Within this event, the participants' specific recommendations surrounding the phenomenon arising in Phase 1 are addressed, for example, what would have worked for them during their experience? What are the complexities that need to be considered?

Event 4: Co-planning for Co-implementation

In the co-production cycle, we label this phase the co-assessment and co-planning phase, which leads into the co-implementation phase. This phase brings together findings from previous stages, contributing to the development of an evidence base and identifying key components of the emerging concept. During this final event, the data from earlier co-production stages are assessed and analysed by senior public health advisors, service providers, and government officials. Delegates use this data to solve problems and discuss the development and implementation of the intervention or framework.

The focus is identifying implementation barriers and defining 'good' practice – what factors are essential to creating positive or preventative environments at all levels of service delivery, from government policy to frontline care. This phase spans both collective and individual axes and includes negotiated axes, allowing a move towards the authoritative axes of Beattie's (1991) model. The completion of the co-production cycle ensures that Beattie's model is maximised, addressing all four quadrants: community development, personal counselling, health persuasion, and legislative action.

Reflections on Lessons Learnt

Working with the military-connected community highlights the importance of cultural insight for those engaging with this population. For external stakeholders, understanding military values, language, and experiences is essential to building trust. Without this, service design risks being superficial, and research may feel like an external imposition rather than a meaningful collaboration. The military community values authenticity, and trust is earned when service providers and researchers demonstrate a genuine commitment to their needs.

Trust-building requires consistency, integrity, and transparency. The military-connected community has faced repeated consultations with what some note has had little meaningful change, leading to scepticism and resistance. Our research shows that honesty, active listening, and a commitment to real impact will gain their trust. Researcher positionality – whether having an 'insider' connection to the community – also aids in trust-building.

A key lesson is the importance of value-based practice. Research should drive improvements in policy and service delivery for the population. Co-production should be more than a tick-box exercise; it must be a process for real change. This requires an iterative, long-term approach where findings inform future innovations. We recognise that no single organisation can fully meet the needs of the military community, so cross-sector collaboration is vital. However, accountability must be shared to ensure tangible action.

Setting clear expectations is crucial. Co-production takes time, and sustainable change does not happen quickly. Honest, transparent communication helps manage expectations and prevents disillusionment. While co-production identifies gaps and proposes solutions, implementation requires commitment beyond the design and assessment phases. Collaborative relationships that address limitations and challenges help maintain trust.

Co-production bridges the gap between policy rhetoric and reality, bringing the lived experiences of military personnel, veterans, and families to the forefront. By including diverse stakeholders, co-production can identify gaps, challenge assumptions, and foster solutions (National Institute for Health and Care Research, 2024). Ultimately, research must drive meaningful change, ensuring policy aligns with the lived experience of the military-connected community.

Conclusion

This chapter presents a compelling case for the use of co-production with the military-connected community, focussing on health and social care service design, development, research, and implementation science. The significance of co-production is particularly apparent in addressing public health challenges, where engaging communities directly in the creation of solutions ensures the relevance and impact of interventions. As demonstrated, each phase of the co-production process facilitates the development of trust and collaboration between the military-connected community, service providers, and researchers, which is crucial for successful outcomes.

We recognise that, as cultural insiders, we have some 'buy-in' to the military-connected community, a group that can be sceptical and resistant to external services. However, our experience shows that involving the military-connected community from the outset in the co-design process empowers them as active participants, rather than passive subjects. This shift in agency allows the community to have a central role in defining and addressing issues that are significant to them, resulting in more sustainable and effective solutions. This approach aligns with the argument that the success of co-production is contingent upon the meaningful inclusion of all relevant stakeholders, particularly those directly impacted by the issues under consideration. Therefore, our work demonstrates the power of collaborative, value-based approaches in transforming health and social care services for the military-connected population.

References

Beattie, A. (1991). The evaluation of community development initiatives in health promotion: A review of current strategies. In *Community Development and Health Education: Occasional papers of the health education unit 1991* (Vol. 1, pp. 61–86). Open University.

Boyle, D., Coote, A., Sherwood, C., & Slay, J. (2010). *Right here right now.* NEF/NESTA.

Boyle, D., & Harris, M. (2009). *The challenge of co-production.* NEF/NESTA.

Bradwell, P., & Marr, S. (2017). Making the most of collaboration an international survey of public service co-design. *Annual Review of Policy Design, 5*(1), 1–27.

Cahn, E. (2000). *No more throw-away people: The co-production imperative.* Essential Books Ltd.

Cahn, E. (2005). *It's the core economy stupid: An open letter to the non-profit community.* Time Banks. Retrieved February 12, 2025, from https://efaidnbmnnnibpcajpcgl-clefindmkaj/http://ereserve.library.utah.edu/Annual/BSH/5000/Waitzman/cahn.pdf

Campbell, S., Greenwood, M., Prior, S., Shearer, T., Walkem, K., Young, S., Bywaters, D., & Walker, K. (2020). Purposive sampling: Complex or simple? Research case examples. *Journal of Research in Nursing, 25*(8), 652–661.

Cree, A. (2020). People want to see tears': Military heroes and the 'Constant Penelope' of the UK's Military Wives Choir. *Gender, Place and Culture, 27*(2), 218–238.

Dandeker, C. (2021). On 'the need to be different': Recent trends in military culture. In H. Strachan (Ed.), *The British army, manpower and society into the twenty-first century* (pp. 173–187). Routledge.

Durose, C., Needham, C., Mangan, C., & Rees, J. (2017). Generating 'good enough' evidence for co-production. *Evidence & Policy, 13*(1), 135–151.

Filipe, A., Renedo, A., & Marston, C. (2017). The co-production of what? Knowledge, values, and social relations in health care. *PLoS Biology, 15*(5), e2001403.

Fusco, F., Marsilio, M., & Guglielmetti, C. (2020). Co-production in health policy and management: A comprehensive bibliometric review. *BMC Health Services Research, 20*, 1–16.

Heward, C., Li, W., Chun Tie, Y., & Waterworth, P. (2024). A scoping review of military culture, military identity, and mental health outcomes in military personnel. *Military Medicine, 189*(11–12), e2382–e2393.

Hubley, J., Copeman, J., & Woodall, J. (2021). *Practical health promotion.* John Wiley & Sons.

Involve, N. I. H. R. (2012). *Briefing notes for researchers: Involving the public in NHS, public health and social care research.* INVOLVE Eastleigh.

Johansen, R. B., Laberg, J. C., & Martinussen, M. (2013). Measuring military identity: Scale development and psychometric evaluations. *Social Behavior and Personality: An International Journal, 41*(5), 861–880.

Kickbusch, I., & Gleicher, D. E. (2012). *Governance for health in the 21st century.* World Health Organization: Regional Office for Europe.

Kiernan, M. D., McGill, G., Watson, P., Farrell, D., Oxburgh, G., Arnfield, J., Rebair, A., Knibbs, L., Allen, S., Gettings, R., Nicholson, L., Tailyour, H., & Senior, E. *A conceptual framework for safety planning within service delivery for veterans and their families.* Armed Force Covenant Fund Trust.

Loeffler, E., & Bovaird, T. (2021). *User and community co-production of public value.* In E. Loeffler, & T. Bovaird (Eds.), *The Palgrave handbook of co-production of public services and outcomes* (pp. 31–57). Palgrave Macmillan.

Mancini, J. A., O'Neal, C. W., & Lucier-Greer, M. (2020). Toward a framework for military family life education: Culture, context, content, and practice. *Journal of Applied Family Science, 69*, 644–661.

Marsilio, M., Fusco, F., Gheduzzi, E., & Guglielmetti, C. (2021). Co-production performance evaluation in healthcare. A systematic review of methods, tools and Metrics. *International Journal of Environmental Research and Public Health, 18*(7), 3336.

Masterson, D., Areskoug Josefsson, K., Robert, G., Nylander, E., & Kjellström, S. (2022). Mapping definitions of co-production and co-design in health and social care: A systematic scoping review providing lessons for the future. *Health Expectations, 25*(3), 902–913.

McMullin, C., & Needham, C. (2018). Co-production in healthcare. In T. Brandsen, T. Steen, & B. Verschuere (Eds.), *Co-production and co-creation* (pp. 151–160). Routledge.

Meyer, E. G. (2015). The importance of understanding military culture. *Academic Psychiatry, 39*, 416–418.

National Institute for Health and Care Research.(2014). *Briefing notes for researchers – Public involvement in NHS, health and social care research*. Retrieved February 20, 2025, from https://www.nihr.ac.uk/briefing-notes-researchers-public-involvement-nhs-health-and-social-care-research

Needham, C., & Carr, S. (2009). *Co-production: An emerging evidence base for adult social care transformation* (pp. 1–24). Social Care Institute for Excellence.

Ostrom, E. (1996). Crossing the great divide: Coproduction, synergy, and development. *World Development, 24*(6), 1073–1087.

Ostrom, V., & Ostrom, E. (2019). Public goods and public choices. In E. S. Savas (Ed.), *Alternatives for delivering public services: Toward improved performance* (pp. 7–49). Routledge.

Patton, M. Q. (2002). *Qualitative research and evaluation methods*. Sage.

Penny, J., Slay, J., & Stephens, L. (2012). *People powered health co-production catalogue*. NESTA.

Pestoff, V. (2014). Collective action and the sustainability of co-production. *Public Management Review, 16*(3), 383–401.

Repper, J., & Eve, J. (2023). Embedding coproduction in organisational culture and practice: A case study. *Leadership in Health Services, 36*(1), 39–58.

Richardson, J., Ong, B. N., Sim, J., & Corbett, M. (2009). Begin at the beginning … using a life grid for exploring illness experience. *Social Research Update, 57*, 1–4.

Rosenstock, I. M. (1974). Historical origins of the health belief model. *Health Education Monographs, 2*, 328–335.

Rowe, C., Bannerman, M., & Church, N. (2009). Health promotion. In K. French (Ed.), *Essential skills for nurses* (pp. 9–24). Wiley-Blackwell.

Slay, J., & Stephens, L. (2013). *Co-production in mental health: A literature review*. New Economics Foundation.

Tannahill, A. (2008). Health promotion: The Tannahill model revisited. *Public Health, 122*(12), 1387–1391. https://doi.org/10.1016/j.puhe.2008.05.009 [Corrected and republished in: (2009, May). *Public Health, 123*(5), 396–399].

Van Eijk, C. J., & Steen, T. P. (2014). Why people co-produce: Analysing citizens' perceptions on co-planning engagement in health care services. *Public Management Review, 16*(3), 358–382.

Watson, P., & Farrell, D. (2023). *Developing a holistic intervention to reduce social isolation and loneliness in Veterans treated for PTSD*. The Armed Forces Covenant Fund Trust. https://covenantfund.org.uk/resources/developing-a-holistic-intervention-to-reduce-social-isolation-and-loneliness-in-veterans-treated-for-ptsd/

Watson, P., & Osborne, A. K. (2025). Being a military child in Denmark: Young people's experiences of living with a parent with PTSD. *PLoS Mental Health, 2*(1), e0000144.

Watson, P., Senior, E., Hyde, R., Telford, M., & Cottam, E. (2024). *Transformation-collaboration and consensus: Co-production report*. Royal Marines Association.

Williams, O., Sarre, S., Papoulias, S. C., Knowles, S., Robert, G., Beresford, P., Rose, D., Carr, S., Kaur, M., & Palmer, V. J. (2020). Lost in the shadows: Reflections on the dark side of co-production. *Health Research Policy and Systems*, *18*, 1–10.

Wilton, C. (2021). Coproduction and partnership with people and communities. *BMJ Leader*, *5*(2), 79–82.

Section 3

PICE Work in Marginalised Communities

Chapter 9

Embedding Trauma-informed Principles Within Involvement and Co-production Activities with People Experiencing Homelessness

Emma A. Adams and Sheena E. Ramsay

Population Health Sciences Institute, Newcastle University, Newcastle upon Tyne, UK

Abstract

Drawing on several studies, this chapter explores the potential application of trauma-informed principles in meaningful involvement and engagement with people who experience(d) homelessness and trauma. The chapter starts with exploring trauma and contemporary trauma theory and co-production in research to set the context. In this chapter, we draw on key issues related to trauma and homelessness to explore the application and practical strategies for undertaking research. Particular aspects include acknowledging past and current experiences of trauma while preventing re-stigmatisation and ensuring meaningful involvement. We suggest that concerns with safety, trustworthiness and transparency, collaboration and mutuality, peer support, empowerment, voice and choice, and cultural, historical and gender issues need to be considered in the context of involvement and engagement. This chapter concludes with considering the need for ongoing reflective practice, which will ensure that researchers can maintain an awareness and understanding

Public Involvement and Community Engagement in Applied Health and Social Care Research: Critical Perspectives and Innovative Practice, 107–117

doi:10.1108/978-1-83608-678-920251009

of trauma and its consequences, while ensuring meaningful and positive involvement in research takes place.

Keywords: Trauma-informed principles; homelessness; co-production; lived experience; trauma; marginalised communities

Introduction

Increasingly, meaningful involvement of the people directly impacted by health and social care in research has become an expectation (Russell et al., 2020). Historically, for populations facing marginalisation, this has been accomplished through participatory approaches, particularly for people experiencing homelessness (Anonson et al., 2022; Feen-Calligan et al., 2009; Rogers, 2021). More recently, this has been accomplished through co-production or involvement across the research process or in specific components (Adams et al., 2024a, 2024b, 2022; Crooks et al., 2024). When collaboratively undertaking research with people experiencing homelessness, issues of marginalisation are even more pressing. Additionally, an awareness and understanding of trauma, which is very common in people with experience of homelessness, is equally as important. In this chapter, we will draw from several empirical research studies with varying levels of involvement in research of people with lived experience, to reflect on the implications of trauma and then ways to embed trauma-informed principles in the approaches used when working with people who have experience of trauma and homelessness.

Trauma and Contemporary Trauma Theory

Trauma is the psychological response to an event or an experience that is out of the ordinary and has lasting impacts on all aspects of well-being, particularly mental health (Substance Abuse and Mental Health Services Administration, 2014). The Substance Abuse and Mental Health Services Administration (2014) explains that trauma is comprised of three main components: the event, experience, and the effect. Traumatic events can be singular or repetitive (Sweeney et al., 2016). When someone is unable to recover from one experience of trauma before another takes place, they experience cascading trauma (Center for Substance Abuse Treatment, 2014). The way someone experiences an event or events determines whether something is traumatic (Substance Abuse and Mental Health Services Administration, 2014). Trauma is personal, and one person could experience an event as a trauma, whereas another person experiencing the same event does not. In addition to recognition at an individual level, understanding trauma and its impacts requires a societal and political context that supports this (Herman, 2015). Historically, the lack of supportive societal and political contexts has led to challenges in investigating psychological trauma. However, the current supportive contexts have led to an increase in current research and evidence related to trauma and thus changes in practice (Herman, 2015).

One of the major shifts in our understanding of trauma and its impact is tied to the trauma-informed practice movement pioneered by Harris and Fallot (2001a). This shift led to a greater recognition that many people accessing health and care services are survivors of trauma, and therefore, services need to be mindful of the role they have in preventing re-traumatisation and encouraging access to support. We would argue that the same applies to people involved in research. Harris and Fallot (2001a) acknowledged the importance of appropriate referrals to trauma-specific support, while highlighting that health and care services and the wider system must have awareness and understanding of the trauma and its consequences. They proposed a shift for all services working with survivors of trauma to become trauma-informed. Building on the original principles highlighted by Harris and Fallot (2001a), Substance Abuse and Mental Health Services Administration (2014) in the United States of America (USA) further refined this understanding through developing a model for conceptualising trauma, four key assumptions for applying trauma-informed approaches, and six key principles for trauma-informed approaches. The four Rs highlight the basic assumptions that need to be met when implementing trauma-informed approaches (Substance Abuse and Mental Health Services Administration, 2014). These assumptions suggest that services need to have a basic *realisation* of trauma and its effects, *recognition* of the signs of trauma, *respond* in a way that applies to the six principles of trauma-informed approaches, and finally *resist re-traumatisation*. Based on prior research (Elliott et al., 2005; Harris & Fallot, 2001b), six principles fundamental to trauma-informed approaches were created: (1) safety, (2) trustworthiness and transparency, (3) peer support, (4) collaboration and mutuality, (5) empowerment, voice and choice, and (6) cultural, historical, and gender issues (Substance Abuse and Mental Health Services Administration, 2014). These principles are applicable to a range of types of services and were not designed to be prescriptive, but rather generalisable. Although designed for service provision, the concepts, assumptions, and principles are applicable to research, particularly in research involving people who have faced trauma and/or homelessness, where the researcher has the responsibility to reduce the risk of re-traumatisation from taking part in the research.

Defining Co-production and Involvement in Research

Recently there has been an increasing body of health research that has moved beyond doing research *about* people to research *with* those who are impacted. The range of terminology used to capture research undertaken with those impacted reflects the ambiguity of consensus on what is meant by involvement (Tritter & McCallum, 2006). Much of the current understanding stems from Arnstein's ladder of participation (Arnstein, 1969), which although has merit in the context of research involvement, it was not designed with this nuanced use in mind, but rather citizen participation. Our research focusses on public health and inequality issues related to homelessness and other forms of disadvantage and is often qualitative in nature and incorporates the voice of lived experience into different elements of the research process from co-creating information sheets and study materials to analysing transcripts and presenting findings. In the context of our research, active participation or involvement involves a partnership between researchers and those who are impacted by the condition or experience being investigated across the research process, including in the design, conduct and implementation (Rahman et al., 2022). Although this approach is concerned with justice and fairness and aims to create equity, there are still concerns that barriers (including trauma) could prevent involvement and this approach could perpetuate marginalisation when the approach is applied inappropriately (Foster et al., 2021; Williams et al., 2020). Recently, there has been the development of the UK standards for public involvement, which highlights six standards for involvement: inclusive opportunities, working together, supporting and learning, communications, impact and governance (Hickey et al., 2018). These standards provide a starting point for understanding what is *good* or *meaningful* involvement. While acknowledging the need for adaptation these standards are commonly used within UK health research.

Involvement and the Role of Trauma-informed Principles

There is substantial overlap in the principles behind co-production and trauma-informed practice (McGeown et al., 2023). This is particularly the case when considering addressing power dynamics through collaboration and empowerment. However, there is no trauma-informed framework to guide co-production approaches between researchers and people with lived experience. This is particularly concerning given the need for approaches to acknowledge and understand trauma and its potential impact on the people that researchers are working with (Fulfilling Lives South East Partnership, 2021). When undertaking research in sensitive subject and topic areas, the onus is often on the researcher to understand how trauma and marginalisation are connected in the context of their research.

Trauma and traumatic events are often discussed or expressed by study participants. This means that when we involve people in research who have experienced trauma, they are very likely to be exposed to further discussions related to and about trauma. This can impact someone by being reminiscent of a past trauma, a concept known as retraumatisation (Sweeney et al., 2018). Alternatively, where events are discussed that are not reminders of one's own experience, there is still a risk that hearing or reading these experiences can lead to emotional or psychological responses. This puts someone at risk of secondary traumatic stress, the emotional and psychological responses from hearing about trauma, originally thought of as compassion fatigue and focussed on those treating or supporting people who experience trauma (Figley, 1995). Having this awareness of the types of trauma(s) that arise while undertaking work collaboratively is imperative to reducing negative psychological consequences for those involved in research.

The value of trauma-informed principles in co-production has been explored in the context of service design (McGeown et al., 2023). Despite an overall recognition that co-production principles are highly suitable when developing trauma-informed services, there is a need for greater consideration to be given as to the implementation of specific principles around sharing lived experience, creating safe spaces, and balancing empowerment with safety among other areas (McGeown et al., 2023). With co-production being increasingly applied within research, the potential application of trauma-informed principles in co-produced research warrants further consideration. Throughout the remainder of this chapter, we will explore the potential application of the six key principles of trauma-informed care into co-production and involvement activities in research. This is based on empirical research studies we have conducted on homelessness applying co-production (Adams, 2023; Adams et al., 2022, 2024a, 2024b; Harland et al., 2021; Perry et al., 2021). Although our experience has been mainly around qualitative studies and people who have experienced homelessness and trauma, the reflections and learning are applicable to other study designs and can be considered in the context of other populations who have experienced trauma.

Safety

Safety focusses on ensuring you are safe as a researcher and that the people you involve are protected and feel physically and psychologically safe to engage (Substance Abuse and Mental Health Services Administration, 2014). In research, this can be supported through an open conversation about what safety means to the people we are working with and how they would like us all to work together.

Ensuring physically safe spaces requires open and collaborative discussions to firstly determine where meetings take place and what they will look like (Adams, 2023; Adams et al., 2022, 2024a, 2024b; Harland et al., 2021; Perry et al., 2021). Irrespective of the location, it is important to think about the physical space from the outset of your research. Physical space is not only a factor for meetings when working together directly, but also when people are working independently on tasks outside of meetings. In the context of our work, we will ask people to complete tasks in the place where they are currently living. Although we have less control over what those settings and spaces look like, in our experience, it was equally important to have open conversations around what support people need to be able to do this, in relation to the support we could provide.

Psychological safety during research is important, and this can also be supported through implementing trauma-informed check-ins and check-outs for those involved in or co-producing research (Hackney et al., 2023). These will be structured times to build relationships, and end on a positive statement of accomplishment. To facilitate completing this independently, there is the potential to use journals to facilitate this (Adams, 2023). Researchers need to be mindful of their own practice, and part of the reason why check-ins and check-outs are important is to identify if someone is already dealing with a lot and may need additional support during the research process (McGeown et al., 2023). With independent working, active effort needs to be made to collaboratively understand how to tell if someone is not in a position psychologically to continue with their work. There also needs to be an agreed-upon process that is clear and transparent for communicating safety concerns. As part of this, discussions around what the role of the lead researcher is and where situations arise outside of what that researcher can support, what the appropriate escalation channels are. Interlinked with this will be creating a clear post-support process. For independent working, we have previously used messaging channels and apps, based on the recommendations and preferences of the people involved, for an ongoing channel whereby someone can reach out if they ever feel their safety is at risk (Adams, 2023; Adams et al., 2022, 2024a, 2024b).

Trustworthiness and Transparency

Transparency in the way research is undertaken and how decisions are made, enables trust to be built and maintained between the researcher and those involved in the research process (Substance Abuse and Mental Health Services Administration, 2014). Trust and transparency are common principles in research involvement and engagement (Devonport et al., 2018; Foster et al., 2021; Hayes et al., 2012; Hickey et al., 2018). Building trust takes time (Devonport et al., 2018; McGeown et al., 2023). An initial step in developing transparency is co-creating a group agreement (Adams, 2023). This can range from having clearer processes, such as confidentiality and safeguarding, to less standardised processes, such as group behaviour, ways of working, and what involvement will look like, to having clear transparency across the people you are working with on how things will be done. As a researcher, there also needs to be flexibility to ensure that the people you are working with can contribute and identify any items that missing. One element that is particularly pertinent, is having clear expectations about the role of the lead researcher. The potential for blurring in the role of the researcher in the minds of those we are working with should also be considered, as this boundary or relationship blurring is challenge in many dynamics between people experiencing homelessness and those who support them (Kidd et al., 2007; McGrath & Pistrang, 2007). The reason we feel this is important in the context of research is the time restrictions around research and the natural endings that take place. Ensuring clarity in the role of the researcher from the outset ensures issues relating to safety are reduced and that trust is built in such a way that someone does not feel let down when a study ends.

Transparency in how feedback and involvement are shaping research has supported this. Researchers need to avoid tokenistic practices in research (also see Jackson et al in this collection) because tokenistic involvement leads people involved to feel as though they are not seeing the impact of their involvement. Our research practice experiences have enabled us to understand that people we work with share frustration around constantly repeating themselves or feeling unheard. One way we address this is by ensuring that when we receive feedback or specific input, we return to the person or group and clearly communicate how this has changed or shaped the research (Adams et al., 2022, 2024a, 2024b; Harland et al., 2021; Perry et al., 2021). Not all input will always be incorporated, but being honest about the thought behind the decisions increases transparency and ensures a trusting relationship is built. It often comes down to ensuring that when researchers say they are interested in hearing from the lived experience members, that is then acted upon or given serious consideration.

Collaboration and Mutuality

Good collaboration in research involvement requires a researcher to understand what partnership or meaningful involvement looks like and a recognition that there needs to be an active effort made to address power. Power in this context is concerned with how decisions are made and priorities are set. One of the first things to consider with this is how to create inclusive opportunities for involvement and co-production in research (Hickey et al., 2018). A collaborative partnership between a researcher and the people they are working with means that there are appropriate measures in place to support people to be involved. In our experience, this has involved early conversations on everything from providing transportation to attend activities in person, offering printed or digital copies of documents based on preferences, and providing ways to support joining activities remotely (Adams et al., 2022, 2024a, 2024b).

Effective collaboration requires a shared understanding of aims and goals in discussions or meetings. Unstructured approaches can lead to people feeling as though nothing was accomplished and things were difficult to follow. On the other hand, when it was overly structured, discussions could feel rigid and stagnated. Researchers can come in with an initial idea of what the session will focus on. However, it is important to have a conversation with the people who you are involving so that the goal is reflective of everyone's priorities. When in-person, it is important to have a visible means of recording and illustrating the overall aim of the day and to capture key points/areas of the discussion (Adams, 2023; Adams et al., 2022, 2024a, 2024b). To respect that sometimes discussions would move away from this central area of discussion, we had a 'parking lot' for other ideas where we would write things down that could be returned at a different time, so that we could return to the original discussion area.

As a researcher, ensuring there is a shared mutual respect for everyone involved, but also a constructive way to voice distrust, disagreements, and discomfort, is essential. Working with colleagues and agreeing on strategies and responses to in-group conflict is key, as is maintaining an open line of communication to speak about concerns, so that we can put measures in place to address them.

Peer Support

In the context of co-producing research, peer support and shared lived experience encompass several elements in involvement activities. Instinctively, through having people involved in research studies based on their own lived experience, experiences will be shared. The way in which researchers handle the sharing of experiences within a group context without causing harm to the person sharing or others is challenging. We have often worked with networks of groups and employed buddy systems in our studies, where people involved are put in self-identified pairings to ensure people have access to someone to speak to outside of the context of regular meetings (Adams, 2023; Adams et al., 2024a). The value of peer support outside and within the research activities is important. Similarly, a lot of the techniques used in creating psychologically safe environments ensure that any sharing is done in a way that does not risk oneself or others. Many of the people we work with have experience with peer support groups, so having an understanding of how those experiences might be different or the same as peer support in the context of a study is extremely important.

Empowerment, Voice, and Choice

Empowerment, voice, and choice can be operationalised differently for everyone. In early stages of our studies where there can be a greater degree of involvement, we have often had one-to-one conversations with the people who would be involved to understand if they have been involved with research in the past, what skills they bring to the study, and what they hope to achieve from being involved (Adams, 2023; Adams et al., 2022, 2024a, 2024b). Having discussions like this is empowering, and they enable people to identify their role, their needs, and how they want to be involved. From this, we start to understand the learning needs and training requirements for each person. Training can be formal and informal in orientation and process, and ensuring people have the choice of appropriate training, resources, and understanding to actively participate in involvement activities ensures people are empowered to be involved. An example of this is where we have provided bespoke training sessions on the six steps of reflexive thematic analysis (Adams et al., 2022, 2024b). Although framed as 'sense-making', these sessions provided the base skills for people to be actively involved in the data analysis process.

People may also want to opt out, and ensuring people have a voice in the research they are involved in is essential. How this looks will be different for each person, but having open and ongoing reflections on the different activities and how things are done will support this. This is also relevant when we are looking to consider how we share the findings of the work. Having the relationship built over the course of a research project ensures we can have open conversations about the best ways to share what we have learned.

Cultural, Historical, and Gender Issues

Researchers need to move beyond an awareness of past experiences of stereotypes or biases and to creating spaces that address and reduce stereotypes and bias and ultimately reduce the trauma linked to these experiences. This will be different for every study, but might involve gender inclusive or gender specific spaces, recognition of variations in cultural or religious norms for group discussions. The best way to identify biases and stereotypes is through open communication with the people you are working with, but to also explore your own positionality, possible biases and then constantly engage in a sympathetic critical appraisal of your own motivations, and practices. For the communities we work with in our studies, one of the biggest challenges we face is around previous experiences and perceptions of stigma (real and anticipated), labels and the terms used to describe people. In our research, the terminology used to represent those involved in the research process has changed over the past few years, starting out with terms like 'peer researcher' and 'Expert by Experience' to more recently using 'a person with lived experience' (Adams et al., 2022, 2024a, 2024b; Harland et al., 2021; Perry et al., 2021). Our shift towards focussing on using a person or people with lived experience(s) is that the people we worked with did not always feel happy saying they were an Expert in something. Some have identified they would not want to be an Expert in something like homelessness or trauma. The most important learning from this is having flexibility and ongoing conversations to ensure the terminology we are using is reflective of what people feel most comfortable with.

Negative past experiences of research may impact the confidence someone might have in engaging with a researcher or in the ability to develop a trusting relationship. On the other hand, a positive experience can set a precedent for what can be expected and lead to disappointment. One thing that can help is to complete an assumption mapping exercise for both the researcher and the people involved in co-producing research (Bland & Osterwalder, 2019). Having a clear idea of what people can expect from being involved and ensuring the ways we are involving people do not further perpetuate stereotypes and biases is essential.

Conclusion

Being aware of trauma and using trauma-informed approaches to research is important to people who engage in research and to us as a research community. It is also a central concern if we consider that the groups we may be involved with want to build capacity and get involved in more research. This chapter presents some of the ways we have introduced these principles in the research we have undertaken with people who experience homelessness. However, it is meant to be a starting point for researchers to consider how this may shape and inform their own involvement or co-production activities. Underlying all the principles described are concerns around power, assumptions, and expectations, but we argue that collaboration and open communication can begin to address these. No approach will ever be perfect, but ongoing reflective practice on the concerns we raise here will ensure researchers can maintain an awareness and understanding of trauma and its consequences, while ensuring meaningful involvement takes place.

References

Adams, E. A. (2023). *The impact of trauma on mental health in people experiencing homelessness: A qualitative study exploring the role of system factors and social networks*. National Institute for Health and Care Research [online]. Available https://www.fundingawards.nihr.ac.uk/award/NIHR302470

Adams, E. A., Brennan-Tovey, K., McGrath, J., Thirkle, S., Jain, N., Aquino, M. R. J., Bartle, V., Kennedy, J., Ogden, M., Parker, J., Koehne, S., Kaner, E., & Ramsay, S. E. (2024a). A co-produced international qualitative systematic review on lived experiences of trauma during homelessness in adulthood and impacts on mental health. *Trauma, Violence, & Abuse, 26*(3), 510–527. https://doi.org/10.1177/15248380241286839

Adams, E. A., Hunter, D., Kennedy, J., Jablonski, T., Parker, J., Tasker, F., Widnall, E., O'Donnell, A. J., Kaner, E., & Ramsay, S. E. (2024b). Exploring perspectives on living through the COVID-19 pandemic for people experiencing homelessness and dealing with mental ill-health and/or substance use: Qualitative study. *Advances in Dual Diagnosis, 17*(1), 1–13.

Adams, E. A., Parker, J., Jablonski, T., Kennedy, J., Tasker, F., Hunter, D., Denham, K., Smiles, C., Muir, C., O'Donnell, A., Widnall, E., Dotsikas, K., Kaner, E., & Ramsay, S. E. (2022). A Qualitative study exploring access to mental health and substance use support among individuals experiencing homelessness during COVID-19. *International Journal of Environmental Research and Public Health, 19*(6), 3459.

Anonson, J., Bae, H., Anderson, J., Kaczur, M., Mishak, B., & Galbraith, S. (2022). A collaborative approach to studying homelessness in rural Saskatchewan through participatory action research. *Journal of Interprofessional Education & Practice, 26,* 100482.

Arnstein, S. R. (1969). A ladder of citizen participation. *Journal of the American Institute of Planners, 35,* 216–224.

Bland, D. J., & Osterwalder, A. (2019). *Testing business ideas: A field guide for rapid experimentation* (Vol. 3). John Wiley & Sons.

Center for Substance Abuse Treatment. (2014). Chapter 2 trauma awareness. In *Trauma-informed care in behavioral health services*. Substance Abuse and Mental Health Services Administration.

Crooks, J., Flemming, K., Shulman, C., Casey, E., & Hudson, B. (2024). Involving people with lived experience of homelessness in palliative and end of life care research: Key considerations from experts in the field. *Research Involvement and Engagement, 10,* 16.

Devonport, T. J., Nicholls, W., Johnston, L. H., Gutteridge, R., & Watt, A. (2018). It's not just 'What' you do, it's also the 'Way' that you do it: Patient and public Involvement in the development of health research. *International Journal for Quality in Health Care, 30*(2), 152–156.

Elliott, D. E., Bjelajac, P., Fallot, R. D., Markoff, L. S., & Reed, B. G. (2005). Trauma-informed or trauma-denied: Principles and implementation of trauma-informed services for women. *Journal of Community Psychology, 33,* 461–477.

Feen-Calligan, H., Washington, O. G., & Moxley, D. P. (2009). Homelessness among older African-American women: Interpreting a serious social issue through the arts in community-based participatory action research. *New Solutions: A Journal of Environmental and Occupational Health Policy, 19,* 423–448.

Figley, C. R. (1995). *Compassion fatigue: Coping with secondary traumatic stress disorder in those who treat the traumatized*. Routledge.

Foster, R., Carver, H., Wallace, J., Dunedin, A., Burridge, S., Foley, P., Pauly, B., & Parkes, T. (2021). "PPI? that sounds like payment protection insurance": Reflections and learning from a substance use and homelessness study experts by experience group. *Research Involvement and Engagement, 7,* 82.

Fulfilling Lives South East Partnership. (2021). *Trauma-informed practice in co-production*. Fulfilling Lives South East Partnership. https://www.bht.org.uk/wp-content/uploads/2021/10/4-FLSE-TIP-in-Co-production.pdf

Hackney, A. J., Jolivette, K., & Sanders, S. (2023). Integrating trauma-informed practices into check-in/check-out for use in alternative education settings. *Intervention in School and Clinic, 59,* 227–235.

Harland, J. M., Adams, E. A., Boobis, S., Cheetham, M., Wiseman, A., & Ramsay, S. E. (2021). Understanding the life experiences of people with multiple complex needs: Peer research in a health needs assessment. *European Journal of Public Health, 32*(2), 176–190.

Harris, M., & Fallot, R. D. (2001a). Envisioning a trauma-informed service system: A vital paradigm shift. *New Directions for Mental Health Services, 89,* 3–22.

Harris, M., & Fallot, R. D. (2001b). *Using trauma theory to design service systems.* Jossey-Bass.

Hayes, H., Buckland, S., & Tarpey, M. (2012). *Briefing notes for researchers: Public involvement in NHS, public health and social care research [online].* INVOLVE. https://www.invo.org.uk/wp-content/uploads/2014/11/9938_INVOLVE_Briefing_Notes_WEB.pdf

Herman, J. L. (2015). *Trauma and recovery: The aftermath of violence – From domestic abuse to political terror.* Basic Books.

Hickey, G., Brearley, S., Coldham, T., Denegri, S., Green, G., Staniszewska, S., Tembo, D., Torok, K., & Turner, K. (2018). *Guidance on co-producing a research project.* INVOLVE.

Kidd, S. A., Miner, S., Walker, D., & Davidson, L. (2007). Stories of working with homeless youth: On being "mind-boggling". *Children and Youth Services Review, 29,* 16–34.

McGeown, H., Potter, L., Stone, T., Swede, J., Cramer, H., Horwood, J., Carvalho, M., Connell, F., Feder, G., & Farr, M. (2023). Trauma-informed co-production: Collaborating and combining expertise to improve access to primary care with women with complex needs. *Health Expectations, 26,* 1895–1914.

McGrath, L., & Pistrang, N. (2007). Policeman or friend? Dilemmas in working with homeless young people in the United Kingdom. *Journal of Social Issues, 63,* 589–606.

Perry, R., Adams, E. A., Harland, J., Broadbridge, A., Giles, E. L., McGeechan, G. J., Donnell, A., & Ramsay, S. E. (2021). Exploring high mortality rates among people with multiple and complex needs: A qualitative study using peer research methods. *BMJ Open, 11,* e044634.

Rahman, A., Nawaz, S., Khan, E., & Islam, S. (2022). Nothing about us, without us: Is for us. *Research Involvement and Engagement, 8,* 39.

Rogers, J. D. (2021). *Homelessness and mental health: A participatory action research approach.* James Madison University.

Russell, J., Fudge, N., & Greenhalgh, T. (2020). The impact of public involvement in health research: What are we measuring? Why are we measuring it? Should we stop measuring it? *Research Involvement and Engagement, 6,* 63.

Substance Abuse and Mental Health Services Administration. (2014). *SAMHSA's Concept of Trauma and Guidance for a Trauma-Informed Approach.* HHS Publication No. (SMA) 14-4884. Substance Abuse and Mental Health Services Administration.

Sweeney, A., Clement, S., Filson, B., & Kennedy, A. (2016). Trauma-informed mental healthcare in the UK: What is it and how can we further its development? *Mental Health Review Journal, 21,* 174–192.

Sweeney, A., Filson, B., Kennedy, A., Collinson, L., & Gillard, S. (2018). A paradigm shift: Relationships in trauma-informed mental health services. *BJPsych Advances, 24,* 319–333.

Tritter, J. Q., & McCallum, A. (2006). The snakes and ladders of user involvement: Moving beyond Arnstein. *Health Policy, 76,* 156–168.

Williams, O., Sarre, S., Papoulias, S. C., Knowles, S., Robert, G., Beresford, P., Rose, D., Carr, S., Kaur, M., & Palmer, V. J. (2020). Lost in the shadows: Reflections on the dark side of co-production. *Health Research Policy and Systems, 18,* 43.

Chapter 10

Co-production from the Perspectives of People Who Have Experienced Homelessness

Monique Lhussier and Christina Cooper

The School of Communities and Education, Northumbria University, UK

Abstract

Homelessness is a growing and highly mediatised issue. Based on a project developing a community of practice to tackle homelessness in Northern England, this chapter presents reflections on the research processes, forefronting experts by experience's (EbE) views.

We highlight the sense of value, identity, and belonging that can be generated, the importance of stories, how and when to tell them, and the practicalities of being involved in research. We provide five key lessons for researchers working with people with experience of homelessness (PEH) and/or those from marginalised communities or with multiple and complex needs. This includes being cognisant of EbE histories, ensuring EbE always feel in control, taking a flexible and inclusive approach to engagement, being aware of the potential impact of the project on EbE, and careful consideration of practicalities, such as payments.

Public involvement has to be understood as having value in and of itself rather than solely as informing the research. Further critical public involvement

Public Involvement and Community Engagement in Applied Health and Social Care Research: Critical Perspectives and Innovative Practice, 119–131

research should explore the complexity and richness of the relationships created through Public Involvement and Community Engagement (PICE).

Keywords: Homelessness; expert by experience; meaningful engagement; authenticity; valuing involvement; storytelling

Introduction

Homelessness typically attracts a lot of attention from the media and policymakers, for example, being equated to a 'health catastrophe' in the most recent review of the National Health Service (NHS) (Darzi, 2024), highlighting the pressing need for change. We define homelessness as sleeping rough, living in shelters, hostels, and temporary or unsuitable accommodation, with the implicit recognition that before becoming homeless, people have often faced sustained periods of severe difficulties, which are both a cause and a result of poor health and well-being. The longer or more often people are homeless, the worse their health becomes and the harder, and more costly, it is to get their life back on track. Despite a range of good initiatives in the UK,[1] PEH have an expected lifespan of just 45 years for males and 43 years for females (Office for National Statistics [ONS], 2019), and homelessness continues to rise, increasing by 26% in 2023 alone.

This chapter presents a reflection on a recent UK Research and Innovation (UKRI)-funded project, which aimed to build a practice network to tackle homelessness in the North East and North Cumbria. We partnered with a group of eight people with lived experience of homelessness (EbE), who between them had experienced many of the complex needs typically faced by PEH, including experiences of addictions, trauma, mental and physical health issues, challenges with learning, and past criminal convictions.

Meaningful public involvement in research can present a range of positive benefits for EbE, the researchers, and research outcomes. Studies have found that involvement can generate feelings of empowerment (McLaughlin, 2009), improved self-esteem, self-efficacy, and self-control (Pawson et al., 2022). Involvement can increase knowledge and support the development of other life skills (Brett et al., 2014). However, few researchers have produced critical reflections of public involvement, including negative aspects (Russell et al., 2020). Few yet have forefronted the voices of particularly marginalised groups in their reflections on the research process. This is precisely what we aim to do in this chapter. After giving the reader an overview of the research that led to the data we are presenting here, we let the voices of the EbE we worked with do the talking, purposefully taking the back seat of the critical reflection endeavour.

The Project

The data presented here was collected at the end of a research project funded by the Arts and Humanities research council (AHRC)–UKRI, which aimed to develop a consortia to address homelessness across the North East and North Cumbria. It consisted of four activities, in which PICE was key:

1. Workshops with practitioners and decision makers from across the North East and North Cumbria to promote knowledge exchange. EbE decided on the focus of each workshop and contributed to its organisation.
2. Developing a network of organisations supporting people experiencing homelessness, and identifying a host website (Signpost) for further development in a subsequent project.
3. As part of the funding, £10,000, referred to as the innovation pilot fund, was ringfenced to enable EbE to improve the integrated care offer for the residents in their housing association. They developed five projects, which provided sustainable and varied opportunities for self-care, learning, and exercise.
4. EbE also had the opportunity to take part in an accredited module focussed on peer and participatory research to support their involvement in research.

On completing the project, we interviewed the six EbE who shaped this project, as well as the key support lead in their housing association ($n = 7$ interviews), to reflect on the process of working together. Interviews were conducted face-to-face and lasted 32 minutes on average; they were transcribed and thematically analysed. These interviews created a reflective space where we openly discussed our feelings about the project. While it must be acknowledged that social desirability bias may have guided some of the answers, all six EbE have subsequently chosen to continue working with us on a different project, which is testimony to their positive experiences.

In the following paragraphs, we present key themes arising from those conversations, giving most prominence to EbE voices, rather than superimposing our own. They spoke about getting involved in research, identity and belonging, how important it was to be in control of their stories, to have an opportunity to inform practice and have an impact, and the pragmatic aspects of taking part in research.

Involvement in Research

It was important that we recognised that PEH lead complex lives and often have multiple and intersecting needs, meaning that taking part in research may not be a priority. Reaching the right balance between being inclusive and respectful of more urgent needs was important. There was a sense that this had been achieved:

> The cohort of people that we helped you select were real people with real lived experience, with real issues, with real multiple needs, with real challenges ... we picked the right kind of people. That they weren't just people who were sorted, they had ongoing issues. (Interview 7)

While all EbE were housed, they had all experienced chronic or repeated homelessness, all had had experiences of trauma, and some had ongoing issues with their mental health or addictions. As a team, we had an explicit, very flexible approach to participation and attendance. This was particularly helpful for Interviewee 6, who knew that he was welcome any time, but that no questions would be asked when he could not attend a meeting.

> I do have mental health issues. I have bipolar, so sometimes I'm really good, and sometimes really bad. Even when I'm in the middle, I feel guilty for the things I've said or done when I was up or down. So I like volunteering, because then I'm not putting anyone out of joint and I can add something when I want to, but I'm not letting anyone down if I'm not. (Interview 6)

The opportunity to take part in research meant having a purpose, contributing to changing practice to support people, and giving a voice to others.

> [Support worker] said there was some research coming up and I thought I would, not just something to do but something that would make a difference ya knaa [you know]? Opportunity arises at 36 years of age and I thought why not give it a go. (Interview 2)

The opportunity to help others was a key driver in decisions to take part in the research for others too.

> People fall between the cracks – sometimes because they don't know what they're entitled to. The project empowered me to have a positive feeling of helping people I don't really know. It was great to be involved directly in such a massive project. (Interview 4)

The project inspired Interviewee 3 to want to learn and do more about homelessness.

> I want to understand how we can make things better for people who are living on the streets and being homeless. I just find the whole thing heartbreaking and very sad in the 21st century. (Interview 3)

Value, Identity, and Belonging

Data highlighted that the participants came from a perspective of having been disenfranchised, undermined, devalued, or distrusted throughout their lives. As researchers, we aimed to be as inclusive, valuing, and respectful as possible; this did not go unnoticed by EbE:

I am proud of being involved in this, [...] because it's like people saying [Interviewee 3] we like you, we trust you, you have good ideas that are worth hearing you know. And that gives me self-worth and a reason to get up in the morning, [...] I need a will to live, I know that sounds dramatic but doing this work gives me that and that is important. I am wanted and that is important. And I can make a difference, hopefully. (Interview 3)

Interviewee 3 further explained that in one of the workshops (activity 1), he decided to stand up and explain what being part of the project had meant for him. One of the attendees later approached him, saying they had been really touched, and he felt proud to have been able to make someone understand his perspective. While this may seem insignificant to many readers, this made him feel heard and valued.

Similarly, having the opportunity to be a student (activity 4) was a particular source of pride:

It's been nice to be called a student. When you lose your home when you lose everything in life you don't get to be given very nice labels. If you told people you were living in a hostel they automatically summarise, wrongfully that you're a drug addict, or you're a waste of space, or your problems are self-inflicted. It's only you to blame for the situation you're in. So it's nice to be labelled a student instead of something else when you're in that position. (Interview 6)

Reflecting on the same idea that, having been homeless, they had faced discrimination and stigma, Interviewees 4 and 5 noted how they felt respected during the research process.

I have lost a lot of confidence, but everybody made me feel welcome. I would like to be involved again if you do more work. Everybody was very respectful to our team. You couldn't have been any more respectful. You didn't look at us as if I had two heads. We didn't feel as if we stood out. Yous were lovely. Your main aim and priority was to help, that's why we felt at ease. (Interview 4)

You've always been respectful from day 1. I felt really respected. It was just hard to talk in a group. You always seem to be courteous. That was important. (Interview 5)

In order to operationalise the innovation pilot (activity 3), EbE pitched their ideas to each other and took collective decisions as to what to fund.

This was a level of autonomy that they had not been used to, and they reflected on this:

> It was just a huge honour to be involved in that process and it was lovely to be involved every step of the way, like our, it felt like we really mattered, that we decided where the money would go. Fabulous. It gives you lots of self-esteem and purpose and makes you feel like you're wanted, [...] But getting involved with stuff like this gives you something to be proud of and I am proud of myself. (Interview 3)

Interviewee 6 concurred:

> It was nice to be asked to take that amount of responsibility and have a say in how the money should be spent. It means a lot to a lot of people in our position, it really does. And to see people having a good time from the money, that's great, it really is. (Interview 6)

The EbE's reflections on the respect and trust they were met with were partly a function of the journey they had come from. In that respect, the research journey was itself valuable in ways we had not anticipated.

Telling Stories

From the outset, cognisant that the EbE were likely to have been through traumatising experiences, and that services often require them to repeat these, we made a point of being very clear that full participation in the project was not dependent on any personal disclosure, and this was important, as Interviewee 2 explains.

> I haven't telt [told] my story as much, you know what I mean, I didn't want to, it wasn't...I wasn't pushed to share it or not share it, it was off my own back. It's like with my psychologist every time I see her it's like gan [going] back gan [going] back, and I divent [don't] want to dee [do] that, I cannot you know, it's like I divent [don't] want to gan [go] back and keep repeating mesel [myself] about what happened, I wanna [want to] move on and go forwards and I won't, I just wanna put it to the back of my mind, and people are saying no you need to speak about this and speak about that but yous weren't like that. You made it perfectly clear that if I wanted to share my story that was fine but I just didn't want to. (Interview 2)

For others, it was important to be able to recount their experiences in order to help practitioners help others.

I don't mind talking about my life story, you know why? It's reality. And I have no problem, I am not embarrassed about it. I have had to live with it all my life and if I can say something, and any of them people out there whether they be social workers, mental health, psychiatrists, if they can take something away from what I have said and it helps them to help somebody else, wow, job done. (Interview 3)

Interviewee 6 agreed with this, though also highlighted how for them it was important to share their emotions and be open about them:

When you recover from any addiction, you need to get out of that denial basically, you've got share things that are painful, be honest with yourself and share about things that are painful. I used to not share my emotions, thinking that people would use that against me, but that's not the case. (Interview 6)

This shows differing preferences EbE had in disclosing their story while being involved in the project, and how important to them it was that they felt in control of what they shared, and how they shared it.

Impacts of the Research

The EbE reflected on the impacts of the research, both at an individual and collective level. For example, EbE highlighted how the project had enabled them to have a more positive outlook, and be and feel healthier:

I have been off cannabis now for 4 and a half month and I feel, I go and play football every second Tuesday of the month now and I am able to run around the pitch a lot better, I don't use my inhaler as much, and I am not as paranoid. I am quite happy. (Interview 1)

Being involved in the whole project has really helped me health, it helped a hell of a lot, gave me a purpose to get up in the morning and go and do something meaningful rather than just sitting about doing nowt [nothing] and feeling sorry for myself. (Interview 2)

The support lead noted how involvement in the project had enabled EbE to become more confident:

[XX] had no background of ever having been engaged by anyone; he had never been interviewed by researchers, he had, I don't think he had ever participated in anything like this and then got up as you know at that first event. (Interview 7)

This was true of others:

> [YY] is volunteering at the farm now, that wouldn't have happened before this project [...] He is doing well, when he first came he was angry, he is not like that now. [...] and now he is working with [...] the employability coach and he has jumped through all the hoops, going to interviews for volunteering. (Interview 7)

The project offered EbE opportunities to engage in positive activities that were not directly linked to their traumatic pasts. It has enabled them to begin to grow from beneath the umbrella of homelessness and its correlates.

> It's helped me, because I have issues that I haven't been able to resolve, so to learn about research helps me improve mesel [myself]. I need to improve me [my] mind, because no one else is helping us. (Interview 5)

Interviewee 5 felt the project had been transformational:

> 18 months ago I thought I was going back to jail. But now I've turned myself around. The university helped with that. (Interview 5)

The project increased some of the EbE's confidence in a way they had not anticipated.

> I would definitely do this again. It is a bit sad it's coming to an end, it has, like I said before it's given me purpose. It's not like I dee nowt [do nothing] you know I have me kids and I play football but this was something different you know, I could get up in the morning and look forward to going. If it wasn't for [Housing association] I wouldn't have thought never in a million years I'd be going to uni and doing research and that, I didn't even go to school man. (Interview 2)

> But as a therapeutic, positive distraction, it's been a 1000%. Everybody needs a sense of responsibility and achievement, even if they don't realise it. I had lost a lot of confidence. Social isolation was bad and has had a long-term effect on me. It's been a personal journey and it's an ongoing one. It's making me – not obsessed with it, but – it's actually opened my mind to a positive 'why not, why can't I do more courses. Why can't I?' (Interview 4)

Interviewee 2 commented on the usefulness of the workshops (activity 1), which brought together researchers, practitioners, decision makers from across the region, and EbE. This gave them a platform to be listened to in a way they had not experienced before.

> [The workshops] were a good idea. 100%. Cos normally you go for an appointment or whatever like with your doctor and they look at you like you are dead funny and that, but in there, where everybody was there to hear what we had to say you knaa [know], they were actually listening and then they can go back and tell their colleagues or whatever and it can have a ripple effect, hopefully it gets back to the doctors and the ones in services on the front line and hopefully they will start and look at us a bit differently. (Interview 2)

In activity 2, we explored the possibility of setting up a live interactive online directory, using an existing website called Signpost as an example. The EbE saw this as a positive ambition:

> When [XX] and [XX] talked to us about Signpost, that was good, I was like this should have been out years ago cos when you move from one area to the other they don't tell you about what mental health services there are in that area you have got to try and search up for yourself and you can't always find the right service for the mental health condition you have got or advice about it and now there is that signpost website its quite good. (Interview 1)

This reflection shaped a subsequent bid, which incorporated the development of the website, demonstrating a very tangible impact of EbE's input and reflections.

The innovation pilot projects (activity 3) had unplanned ripple effects, in that they inspired other residents to take charge and organise groups, such as a men's health and a women's group, supported by their housing association. The project thus demonstrated to residents that they could self-organise, and the housing association would support any development that would support its residents' health and well-being. With many people having chronic low self-esteem and being distrustful of organisations, this level of agency and proactivity was particularly welcomed by the housing association.

Other innovation pilot projects (activity 3) have outlived the funded research. For example, some of the funding enabled the housing association to finish equipping a kitchen and to teach people how to cook for themselves. Interviewee 4 took charge of this project, enrolled external course deliverers, and started to teach lessons himself.

> I'm helping other people. I'm on my second block booking of the Jamie Oliver thing. People want to come back and back and back. I'm now involved with the learning trust – I did that this morning.

It wasn't even in my idea. What you did is, you involved me in deciding how to help people's future, which is important to me … In 2 weeks' time, I'm doing a 6 week course for people coming out of prison, so they can learn to cook. It's gone off in all different directions. (Interview 4)

This level of growth in autonomy and confidence was not something the research aimed for, but an important finding, demonstrating that the research process itself can be transformational, at both an individual and collective level.

PICE Practicalities

It was important for us as researchers to think about the practicalities of organising meetings and workshops, ensuring that everyone was comfortable throughout.

It was sound, aye, sound, not too much or nowt [nothing]. We had plenty of opportunities for breaks and stuff like that, you didn't have us stuck in a room for 4, 5, 6 hours you know, we could have a break every hour or something you know and that was good. (Interview 2)

A key practical aspect of working together was payment. We followed the National Institute for Health and Care Research (NIHR) involve guidance of paying £25/hour, but came to an agreement with our partner housing association that the money would be negotiated individually, and spent towards people's employability to avoid giving cash, which might have impacted their receipt of benefits. All EbE reflected positively on this.

I am not very good with maths or money so I didn't get it at first and [XX] was saying you will get paid but you won't get money and I was thinking well how does that work? So it took me a little while to get it but in the end I understood, the penny dropped. So I didn't get cash but I did benefit and it was wonderful. (Interview 3)

I got a mobile phone […] I tried to work, but I was getting into a bigger hole, so the project helped that. (Interview 5)

It wasn't money we could spend on drugs and alcohol and that was a good thing. We spent it on practical things and that was good. (Interview 6)

Beyond this, the EbE reflected on the fact that we dedicated some time to scaffold them as they were engaging in a new environment:

You didn't treat us like children but you were there for us in an environment that really we never expected to find ourselves in [the university] so we were really very well looked after by all of the staff, the professors, yourself, we were looked after very very well. Any problems and you were there and that meant we felt comfortable in an environment that was pretty alien. (Interview 3)

Interviewee 3 highlighted a crucial need to reach a balance between support that could be felt as patronising or condescending, and courteous and supportive at all times. For example, we always made a point of meeting them where they were getting dropped off by taxi, and walking with them to the meeting room. This meant they had a friendly face to welcome them on campus and never had to worry about finding their way around.

Over the course of the project, the EbE learned to work together, as a team, in a way they had not had the opportunity to do before.

We didn't click at first. We were mostly doing it for ourselves at first. We knew each other, but we didn't really. The research has enabled us to work together as a group. (Interview 5)

This process alone was a learning experience that had not been anticipated.

Everybody got the chance to share, everyone got a fair crack of the whip and you were free to say things and you were listened to, it wasn't that you were cut off or anything so yes, absolutely. You were never pressured, if you didn't want to say anything then you didn't have to say anything and if you did say anything your view was respected, in fact that was the main thing when we started the group you know, to listen to other people's opinions and what they have to say, it might not be what you agree with but respecting that everyone has an opinion and a view. (Interview 3)

While these practicalities may seem trivial, they were key to making the relationships work and developing the trust we needed to make the project a success.

Conclusion

From these reflections, we have identified several key lessons to inform PICE with particularly marginalised groups, such as people who have experienced homelessness. Researchers need to be cognisant of EbE's histories and how their own actions might be perceived. We did not anticipate our common-sense inclusive and respectful approach to have quite the impact it had on them, and yet it did. This is likely to apply to other marginalised groups. Linked to this, researchers need to ensure that EbE always feel in control of the terms of their participation. This includes the telling of their stories, but also the frequency and shape of their participation. It is also important to reach the right balance between engaging people who are settled enough for participation (however that judgement is made), but close enough to the issues to inform the conduct of the project.

The EbE involved in this project were not always in a place that enabled them to be reliable, but we made it clear that participation was flexible at all times. The remaining part of the research team was neither contingent on them telling their stories, turning up to meetings reliably, nor always participating. No one was ever put on the spot or made to feel awkward if they had missed some activities. All were invited to all activities consistently. Other practicalities were important too. For example, while national guidance on payment is welcomed, individuals live in an environment that has to be factored in, as much as possible, in order to ensure that research does not do more harm than good, or is not solely transactional. Payments need to be carefully considered on an individual basis, applying flexibility and working with an organisation they trust wherever possible.

Conducted in this way, research can in itself be part of a process of healing and learning, which has benefits for individuals. For example, the opportunity to practically help others, when one has been seen as 'in need' for a long time, was particularly valued and valuing. Research drawn from occupational therapy has shown the positive effect of this, for groups with limited opportunities to engage in 'meaningful occupations' (Smith, 2018). Public involvement with marginalised groups, such as those who have experienced homelessness, cannot be conducted meaningfully as a purely transactional endeavour. It has to have authenticity, trust, respect, and meaning embedded at its very core. Our experience suggests that it works best when understood as not a means to an end (the research), but an end in itself (engaging with people because they matter), which can, as we have demonstrated here, have impacts beyond the original remit of the research.

Our project demonstrated that achieving meaningful engagement with PEH requires a thoughtful approach, but it is entirely possible.

Note

1. See, https://www.homelessnessimpact.org/publications.

Acknowledgement

This project was funded by the Arts and Humanities Research Council (UKRI); grant ref: AH/X005836/1. *With special thanks to Carl, Lee, Barnie, Stephen, Porl, Karl, Terry and Bryan, and in memory of Ben.*

References

Brett, J. O., Staniszewska, S., Mockford, C., Herron-Marx, S., Hughes, J., Tysall, C., & Suleman, R. (2014). A systematic review of the impact of patient and public involvement on service users researchers and communities. *Patient, 7*, 387–395. https://doi.org/10.1007/s40271-014-0065-0

Darzi.(2024). *Independent investigation of the National Health Service in England (2024) Lord Darzi of Denham*. Retrieved September 20, 2024, from https://www.gov.uk/government/publications/independent-investigation-of-the-nhs-in-england

McLaughlin, H. (2009). What's in a name: "Client", "patient", "customer", "consumer", "expert by experience", "service user"—What's next? *Journal of British Social Work, 39*, 1101–1117.

Office for National Statistics (ONS). (2019). *Deaths of homeless people in England and Wales 2019.* Retrieved July 9, 2023, from https://www.ons.gov.uk/peoplepopulationandcommunity/birthsdeathsandmarriages/deaths/bulletins/deathsofhomelesspeopleinenglandan dwales/2019registrations

Pawson, C., Bolden, R., Isaac, B., Fisher, J., Mahoney, H., & Saprai, S. (2022). Learning from collective lived experience: A case study of an experts by experience group. *Housing, Care and Support, 25*(3), 223–235. https://doi.org/10.1108/HCS-12-2021-0048

Russell, J., Fudge, N., & Greenhalgh, T. (2020). The impact of public involvement in health research: What are we measuring? Why are we measuring it? Should we stop measuring it? *Research Involvement and Engagement, 6*, 63. https://doi.org/10.1186/s40900-020-00239-w

Smith, H. C. (2018). Finding purpose through altruism: The potential of 'doing for others' during asylum. *Journal of Occupational Science, 25*(1), 87–99. https://doi.org/10.1080/14427591.2017.1371633

Chapter 11

Collaborating to Explore the Reproductive Health and Social Care Needs of Women Who Use Drugs: A Doctoral Research Study

Claire Smiles[a] and Donna Kay[b]

[a] *Population Health Sciences Institute, Newcastle University, UK*
[b] *Recovering Justice Women's Project, UK*

Abstract

Collaborative approaches to research, public involvement, and community engagement (PICE) have become an expectation when undertaking research in public health. An often-forgotten fact is that doctoral studies are essentially research training and career development programmes of work. In addition, little guidance is available to them when conducting research with underserved populations, particularly for those doctoral students, who like me, were at the beginning of their research career. This chapter provides a reflective and reflexive account of the approach to PICE I adopted when researching the sensitive topic of reproductive health and well-being amongst women who use drugs. This chapter explores the challenges of PICE work and also makes suggestions for how best to engage with this sensitive subject and topic area. Throughout the chapter, reflective narratives from Donna Kay bring the work to life and also allow you, the reader, to consider the impact and implications PICE may have for those collaborating with lived experience communities. The chapter

Public Involvement and Community Engagement in Applied Health and Social Care Research: Critical Perspectives and Innovative Practice, 133–144

doi:10.1108/978-1-83608-678-920251011

concludes with a discussion about the practical considerations and planning needed to undertake PICE in doctoral research studies.

Keywords: Lived experience; community engagement; women; drug use; reproductive health; motherhood

Introduction

This chapter aims to give a detailed account of the approach to PICE and the way in which it shaped my exploration of the reproductive health and social care needs of women who use drugs. Within this chapter, we give a detailed account of the impact PICE had on the lead author's doctoral research, supported by the reflections of a co-author, who at the time was involved in the research as a community activist. This chapter is a sympathetic critical self-appraisal of practice with a focus on the importance of positionality, relationship building, and incorporating the voices of underserved and marginalised populations in research. We provide a context for this chapter by discussing the ways in which women with lived experience of substance use became involved in the research. We use the chapter to illustrate how we utilised the experiences and expertise of these women in a collaborative way to refine and shape the study and co-produce our research. The chapter concludes with reflections on the importance of planning and communication when undertaking community involvement in doctoral research, and if done well, this can be helpful in forging meaningful and lasting relationships between communities and researchers.

PICE in PhD Research

PICE is an important part of contemporary research and is often stipulated as essential in funding bids (McGrane et al., 2023; NIHR, 2024). Evidence of the benefits of PICE in qualitative research has been well documented (Brett et al., 2014; Gilchrist et al., 2022; Gray et al., 2021); however, there are few publications that relate to PICE in doctoral research (Troya et al., 2019). The National Institute for Health and Care Research (NIHR) amongst other national funding bodies (and charities and regulatory bodies, such as Health and Care Professional Council) have led the way in promoting and ensuring PICE work in research and research practice, recommending that it is undertaken 'with' or 'by' members of the public rather than 'to' or 'about' them (NIHR, 2021). This approach advocates for the involvement of underserved groups and the incorporation of their views and perspectives in the design of research projects (NIHR, 2021).

Women who use drugs and other marginalised population groups are sometimes considered 'harder to reach', meaning their voices and experiences are often excluded from research (McGrane et al., 2023). Some researchers report they have difficulty in reaching participants to engage in PICE, and it is largely accepted that this creates difficulties in capturing the insider perspectives

(Islam et al., 2021). Whilst underserved populations may be difficult to engage with because they may be at risk of harm, be disenfranchised, excluded because of their location, or due to digital poverty, they are experts in their own experiences. For this reason, every effort should be made to include and incorporate them in research studies (Ellard-Gray et al., 2015). As discussed in depth by other authors in this collection, some marginalised populations have experienced stigma within the communities they live in, and this may further prevent them from coming forward and participating. They may also be concerned about whether researchers have their best interests and will listen to their perspectives and views (Islam et al., 2021). Previous research has identified that marginalised populations are unlikely to participate in research without referral (Liamputtong, 2019; Padgett, 2017). One potential way to overcome this barrier to engagement is to liaise with gatekeepers (e.g., third sector voluntary organisations who may support them).

> The community I represent in research and support have experienced stigma and shame and they are often not only forgotten, but also silenced. Giving women space to voice their experiences and what is important to them is important for making future changes in practice. We think research is important and to be given a voice, to be listened to and to be heard is important if these experiences are to be incorporated into research and practice. For me as an activist, I want to see changes made in the future in relation to changes for mothers, fathers, working class families and children. As an activist and a mother, I want to reduce the harms and trauma of families as they engage with services and for services to learn (through research) that others do not have to go through the same experiences. (Donna Kay, Community Activist)

One of the key lessons I have learned as a doctoral researcher relates to the importance of nurturing, developing, and maintaining a range of fieldwork relationships with organisations, communities, and individuals that serve and support the community you are researching. This requires serious introspection, skill and ability, however, if done with authenticity, it can lead to a range of fieldwork and research related outcomes. Good quality PICE work offers up the potential to positively affect the quality of research and strengthen the methodological rigour of the results (Brett et al., 2014; Gray et al., 2021; Gilchrist et al., 2022; McGrane et al., 2023; Troya et al., 2019). Incorporating PICE into research has been identified as having a positive impact which enhances the quality and appropriateness of research, an important aspect for early career researchers (Brett et al., 2014). PICE also gives cultural relevance and a broader understanding for the researcher undertaking the study, which is in turn translated into the findings, making them potentially more relevant and more likely to impact and inform policy and practice (Brett et al., 2014; Gray et al., 2021; McGrane et al., 2023). Credibility of findings with stakeholders is important when attempting to influence policy and practice, and PICE allows researchers and its public contributors to identify gaps and plan future collaborative research projects (Brett et al., 2014). This was further demonstrated by Troya et al., whereby her PICE group had informed her PhD research on self-harm in older adults (Troya et al., 2019). The incorporation and prioritisation of PICE are clear, however, this requires researchers to engage in quality PICE, moving beyond what some have referred to as 'tokenistic' PICE (Gray et al., 2021; Gilchrist et al., 2022; Islam et al., 2021). In research 'tokenism' is best understood as a process were research PICE work becomes perfunctory or symbolic to the subject area of community. Researchers can overcome tokenistic PICE by establishing a pre-defined model and involving PICE from inception to dissemination (Gilchrist et al., 2022).

Co-producing Sensitive Research with Women

Reproductive health and the social care-related needs of women who use substances are a sensitive subject area (McGovern et al., 2024). In recent years, there has been a focus on researching the lived experience of people who use drugs in the North East of England (Adams et al., 2022; Alderson et al., 2021; McGovern et al., 2021, 2023; Spencer et al., 2023), however, few studies have focussed only on women's experiences. A 2023 report focussed on 'Dismantling Disadvantage' for women with multiple unmet needs in the North East, including deprivation and poverty, the 'toxic trio of vulnerabilities' (mental health, drug use, and domestic abuse) and child removal, however, the report did not consider women's reproductive health and sexual well-being (Agenda Alliance & Changing Lives, 2023, p. 42). My PhD research, which was conceptualised in 2020, sought to begin to address the gap in knowledge about the reproductive health and social care of women who use drugs in the North East and practitioners who support them.

PICE was central to the design and development of this qualitative study, and I endeavoured to incorporate the expertise of women with lived experience early in the project. At the beginning of my PhD, I actively attended and participated in community and research events relating to women's health. The purpose of this was to increase my visibility within the community and highlight the importance of the research I was undertaking. Being known by others and attending to the more (commonly referred to) mundane aspects of networking, attending events, having and re-having conversations, and turning up are important to early career researchers. After attending many organisational and community events and discussing and presenting my research to a range of audiences, I was introduced to one person who has experience of activism and advocacy for women who have lived experience of substance use. Upon meeting to discuss the research aims and objectives, she helped me to begin to identify community members from her own personal and professional networks who shared our passion and enthusiasm for understanding and improving women's experiences of services. Through discussion, negotiation, and a shared understanding, she then decided to vouch for me within her networks and recommended I approach three other women to consult on the research study.

An Expert Advisory Group (EAG) was formally established in January 2022, with four women from the North East of England who had lived or lived experience of substance use. Aside from all women having experience of substance use, the four women involved in the EAG had many other lived experiences which they drew upon to support and inform the development of this research. These lived experiences included: mental ill health; domestic violence and abuse; sexual abuse; adverse childhood experiences; child removal and involvement with the criminal justice system. All four women involved in the EAG were known to each other through peer support networks and community organisations they accessed in the North East.

The women involved in the EAG had no previous experience of PICE work or research involvement, however, they felt the topic of reproductive health and well-being was important for the communities they represented. Previous research has reported that public involvement in research is more likely if it contains an 'action agenda for reform' which address issues such as empowerment, inequality, oppression, domination, suppression, and alienation which may encourage them to design questions, collect data, analyse information, or reap the rewards of the research (Creswell, 2013). Given their understanding and own lived experiences, the EAG felt this research offered an opportunity to empower other women.

Whilst the process of involvement was interesting and new to the women, it was also important to us that our EAG did not become fatigued by their involvement in our research, and we were flexible in opportunities to contribute to aspects they felt comfortable with and had the time to do so. A group messaging app (WhatsApp) was used to organise meetings on online video conferencing (Zoom). Both platforms were identified by the EAG as the best methods to support our communication throughout our work on the study. We also met in person for coffee mornings to discuss the research in community organisations the women identified as safe spaces. The gendered nature of safety has been explored theoretically and empirically in research (Lewis et al., 2015), and for us, it was about coming together to explore sensitive concerns without fear of judgement. We had discussions regarding the sensitivity of the topics covered in this research, and that it may be triggering for women involved in the EAG. Research with participants in sensitive subject areas and the involvement of people with lived experience can lead to trauma and also compassion fatigue, particularly when they engage with fieldwork elements of research (Steenekamp & Barker, 2024). Therefore, at the open and close of all meetings, I made members aware they could contact me directly if they had any concerns; additionally, I could facilitate onward signposting to access further specialised support. As recommended in published PICE guidance (NIHR, 2021), all of the women involved in PICE in this research were offered remuneration for their time and contribution to the study (NIHR, 2021).

Reciprocal Learning Opportunities in PICE

When incorporating members of the public with lived experience in research, it is important to listen to their views and perspectives and consider suggestions they make to the study. In the early stages of this research, the EAG was key to ensuring the research (including the language used) was accessible and free from stigma (a prerequisite for this collaborative work). Positive group identity was also of importance to them, and our consultation with the EAG led to a very simple, but also very important change (in terms of ownership) to the study being renamed as the 'Women's Sexual Wellbeing' study. We had in-depth discussions about the term reproductive health, and they felt using the initial research title was 'too academic' and specifically, they felt the term reproductive health was 'too clinical' and would not appeal to potential participants. The individual and group identities of individuals in marginalised communities are important (McGovern et al., 2024), and the EAG also felt that having the study titled 'Women's Sexual Wellbeing' was a way to empower women and increase the likelihood of participation. This also allowed us to illustrate partnership involvement and demonstrated to our PICE group that their perspectives and contributions were 'heard' and valued.

> What is important to me as an activist is the way the women have been treated during the whole project. They have been respected and listened to. It's really helped to build some confidence and there is that cliché saying that "talking in safe spaces, takes the shame away from them". (Donna Kay, Community Activist)

The EAG supported and challenged the research design and development processes including aspects of the topic guide and the relevance and importance of the questions in relation to the research. The EAG were also key to making fundamental suggestions for improvement throughout, including adding a retrospective question to explore how women's views may have changed on relationships and family planning due to drug use. They were also interested in incorporating a question relating to children's social services (based off their own lived experiences). We came together to discuss this between the team and after critical reflection, we decided to see if this topic would come up naturally during interview as opposed to probing the subject with participants. As our research developed, we found that working collaboratively on the development of the topic guide, built rapport between the team and demonstrated that their suggestions were important to the research and also improved the quality of the data collected (Hoddinott et al., 2018). It also highlights the reciprocal learning opportunities PICE afforded to both the researcher and the women with lived experience. As we reflected on at various stages of this chapter, doctoral study is a research training programme that is concerned with both the generation of knowledge and development and training of early career researchers.

During the participant recruitment process, the women in the EAG shared the study across their networks, encouraging participation in the study. They also demonstrated the importance of this research and validated that other women's views and perspectives were important to capture, to give the research the best opportunity to influence change. The importance of being creative and allowing the women to share the study on their social networks was fundamentally important to the success of the study: this was a clear endorsement of the study and one which was most effective for recruitment. The support of the EAG expedited recruitment, meaning most of the data collection for women was complete within the first four weeks of the fieldwork element of the study.

The EAG was not involved in the coding of data or anonymised transcripts. Other research studies have collaboratively undertaken the task of coding anonymised transcripts; however, given the sensitivity of the topic and that women had supported recruitment across their networks, we felt this may make women identifiable, but also, this may be triggering to members of the EAG. In other chapters in this collection (Adams and Ramsey), you can read about concerns with trauma-informed practice and research, whilst also considering the implications of involving participants in the process or learning and coding in relation to sensitive subjects and data areas. The women involved in our study did collaborate on sense-making of the codes and findings in an online workshop. During the initial workshop, we reviewed and discussed codes and emerging themes. We used these emerging themes to co-design an upcoming presentation, recognising this conference dissemination as another opportunity to review our interpretation of the findings. The final themes workshop took place in July 2023, and during this meeting, we discussed the relevance of the findings to ensure they included a cultural and broader understanding of the reproductive health and social care of women who use drugs (Brett et al., 2014).

Collaborative Dissemination

Throughout this study, it was important for us to involve women in every aspect of the research, and this included the dissemination of the findings. We discussed and planned how the results could be translated to improve policy and practice and how they could best be disseminated to maximise impact. This included considering the ways in which the findings were communicated with lived experience communities and members of the public to 'bridge the translational barrier' between academic writing and wider public literature (Melvin et al., 2020, p. 232). The EAG has undertaken a variety of collaborative dissemination opportunities, which have allowed us to share our PICE work and study findings with a wider audience. Collaborative and co-produced dissemination included: blog posts; podcasts, people with lived experience conference, and International Women's Day (IWD) conference. Events and opportunities like those mentioned above can be fashioned and utilised to raise the profile of marginalised communities and raise the awareness of the needs of these communities to practice partners and policymakers.

On IWD 2023 we organised and co-facilitated a research event which focussed on embracing equity by celebrating resilience and showcasing the lived experiences of women in the North East of England. This event featured research and community involvement from academic institutions, voluntary third sector and community organisations. The overall aim of the IWD 2023 research event was to give an overview of current research exploring women's health inequalities, how this was experienced, and the current unmet need within the region. Handing over power to research participants and allowing them to shape research design, implementation and then dissemination event can be both tricky and rewarding for them. With trust, good communication and support the EAG took ownership over the conference and focussed on making the conference as accessible as possible, to attract a diverse range of people with an interest in women's health and well-being. This included researchers, stakeholders, policy and practice and people with lived experience. In order to make the conference inclusive for as many to attend as they could, the EAG recommended the timings be considerate of those with caring responsibilities (during school time), that the location was accessible via public transport, that all information about the event be in plain English and free of stigmatising language. We co-facilitated our presentation, which included two members of the EAG reading poetry they had written about our research.

> It's a privilege to be able to work in an area I am interested in and passionate. The whole process has been an empowering, enriching experience. I have learned and enjoyed it all. The opportunities that have come from it. The opportunity from the first initial piece of works, brought other opportunities to work with other researchers. It has built a special relationship with 'Recovering Justice' and has been a big part of the 'Women's Project'. The people I have met (Professor Ruth McGovern and Dr Hayley Alderson), having the Spotify Podcast, going to York University to present our work, International Women's Day 2023. Being involved in other research projects and feeding back on research from a lived experience perspective. I am really looking forward to being involved in future research projects that are on the horizon. (Donna Kay, Community Activist)

Those who attended the IWD event reported it to be a positive experience, which had in excess of 80 attendees who listened, contributed, and supported a range of research projects. From a PICE perspective, the event was an invaluable knowledge exchange event and opportunity to evidence how co-production can be achieved through careful planning and engagement with people with lived experience. For all of the EAG involved in this research, they found the event to be an affirmative way to represent their community in research and reported it to be a valuable experience, which they were proud to be a part of.

Critical Reflections From PICE in PhD Research

As a researcher, whether doctoral, early career, or established, it is important to reflect on the privilege that is afforded to researchers by PICE insights and contributions. Previous guidance on PICE in research has evidenced that the incorporation of the voices of lived experiences can add value to the methods and findings of this research (Hoddinott et al., 2018). In the context of the 'Women's Sexual Wellbeing' study, the EAG's involvement added depth, richness, and rigour to the findings, but this did not come without significant time investment and communication between the EAG and I.

Taking stock of your own practice as a PICE researcher is important and reflecting on your own positionality and values is key for your practice and future learning. We believe the incorporation of the EAG enhanced and improved the study; however, it is important to acknowledge there has been challenges associated with PICE. Although PICE in research has become expected, there is little guidance for how to undertake PICE in PhD research. Incorporating the voices of lived experience individuals in research design and development brings about the responsibility of managing expectations both of the research parameters and of the PICE involvement, which many PhD students may have little experience of. Having a pre-defined plan for PICE involvement may help mitigate some of these challenges, but good quality research requires flexibility from the researcher, to ensure PICE members are not overwhelmed or burdened by participation (Steenkamp & Barker, 2024).

Conclusion

PhD students are often new to the field as researchers, and some may have little or no experience in engaging with the populations they are researching. They may also have no gauge to understand what is expected of them in relation to doctoral study and for this reason, they 'may require expert advice and support on how best to work with vulnerable populations sensitively' (Troya et al., 2019, p. 627). The first author's professional experience of working with vulnerable communities in the context of substance use was useful, but even here, there were barriers that had to be overcome to engage with women on the subject of social care and reproductive health. PICE requires time, planning, and resources in order to build meaningful engagement and rapport. This investment can help build collaborative partnerships with members of the public and those with lived experience. Incorporating the voices of lived experience in PhD research adds value and richness, and overcoming the challenges associated with PICE is achievable and worthwhile. Understanding your subject areas and the experiences of your research population is key to research design and implementation, but also understanding what is important to the communities you serve as a researcher. Taking time and building rapport to connect and understand the priorities, beliefs, and qualities of these communities is also important.

As demonstrated from this PhD research, incorporating PICE requires practical considerations, and it is fundamental that researchers consider these in advance of commencing research (McGrane et al., 2023). PICE work should be celebrated, but it is important to recognise that it can be both rewarding and burdensome for both researchers and, more importantly, for members of the public (Gray et al., 2021). Further reflection should also be given to the needs and capacity of PICE members; the extent of involvement and resources required, which should be undertaken prior to approaching or working collaboratively with lived experience communities (Troya et al., 2019). Discussions about the roles and responsibilities of participation are essential to avoid overburdening PICE members, alongside consideration of their well-being and safety (Gray et al., 2021; Islam et al., 2021). Reimbursement for PICE members should be ring-fenced in funding (if available), and communication about all aspects of involvement, research design, analysis, development of findings, and outcomes should be prioritised in order to ensure PICE members feel included and valued at all times (NIHR, 2024).

Women who have been involved in the EAG have been invited to co-author a publication related to this research and also to co-produce further research supporting their interests in this sector. This is intended to encourage them to exercise their lived experiences and reinforce the importance and value of their voices in future research. One of the most important concerns for newer and more established researchers in relation to PICE is to make sure that their involvement is meaningful and that they maintain good working relationships with the groups they do PICE work with. Essentially speaking, leaving the door open for the person who follows you in social care research is fundamental to the process of building capacity and the creation of new research communities.

> Communication and trust is key to community involvement in research. Speaking to people who are open minded, and nonjudgemental has been the pinnacle of it. On one occasion there was a research project were one of the researchers upset a mother and issue was immediately resolved over the telephone. Mothers who I represent have often battled with self-esteem issues because of past experiences, with drugs, self-worth, services and unable to use their voice at specific times. Being able to come to the research team and say I was upset about it. The researchers were able to reflect and consider the concerns and take on board with humbleness and humility – that was an amazing piece of work for us. It helped with confidence because as an advocate I was able to approach them and challenge the perceived power dynamics. (Donna Kay, Community Activist)

References

Adams, E. A., Parker, J., Jablonski, T., Kennedy, J., Tasker, F., Hunter, D., Denham, K., Smiles, C., Muir, C., O'Donnell, A., Widnall, E., Dotsikas, K., Kaner, E., & Ramsay, S. E. (2022). A qualitative study exploring access to mental health and substance use support among individuals experiencing homelessness during COVID-19. *International Journal of Environmental Research and Public Health, 19*(6), 3459.

Agenda Alliance & Changing Lives. (2023). *Dismantling disadvantage*. Retrieved December 20, 2023, from https://www.agendaalliance.org/documents/148/Transforming_Services_Final_Report.pdf

Alderson, H., Spencer, L., Scott, S., Kaner, E., Reeves, A., Robson, S., & Ling, J. (2021). Using behavioural insights to improve the uptake of services for drug and alcohol misuse. *International Journal of Environmental Research and Public Health, 18*(13), 6923.

Brett, J., Staniszewska, S., Mockford, C., Herron-Marx, S., Hughes, J., Tysall, C., & Suleman, R. (2014, October). Mapping the impact of patient and public involvement on health and social care research: A systematic review. *Health Expect, 17*(5), 637–650.

Creswell, J. W. (2013). *Research design: Qualitative, quantitative, and mixed methods approaches* (4th ed.). SAGE Publications, Inc.

Ellard-Gray, A., Jeffrey, N. K., Choubak, M., & Crann, S. E. (2015). Finding the hidden participant: Solutions for recruiting hidden, hard-to-reach, and vulnerable populations. *International Journal of Qualitative Methods, 14*(5). https://doi.org/10.1177/1609406915621420

Gilchrist, K., Iqbal, S., & Vindrola-Padros, C. (2022). The role of patient and public involvement in rapid qualitative studies: Can we carry out meaningful PPIE with time pressures? *Research Involvement and Engagement, 8*, 67.

Gray, R., Brasier, C., Zirnsak, T. M., & Ng, A. H. (2021). Reporting of patient and public involvement and engagement (PPIE) in clinical trials published in Nursing Science Journals: A descriptive study. *Research Involvement and Engagement, 7*(1), 88. https://doi.org/10.1186/s40900-021-00331-9

Hoddinott, P., Pollock, A., O'Cathain, A., Boyer, I., Taylor, J., MacDonald, C., Oliver, S., & Donovan, J. L. (2018). How to incorporate patient and public perspectives into the design and conduct of research. *F1000Research, 7*, 752. https://doi.org/10.12688/f1000research.15162.1

Islam, S., Joseph, O., Chaudry, A., Forde, A., Keane, A., Wilson, C., Begum, N., Parsons, S., Grey, T., Holmes, L., & Starling, B. (2021). "We are not hard to reach, but we may find it hard to trust" ... involving and engaging "seldom listened to" community voices in clinical translational health research: A social innovation approach. *Research Involvement and Engagement, 7*(1), 46.

Lewis, R., Sharp, E., Remnant, J., & Redpath, R. (2015). "Safe Spaces": Experiences of feminist women-only space. *Sociological Research Online, 20*(4), 105–118.

Liamputtong, P. (Ed.). (2019). *Handbook of research methods in health social sciences.* Springer Singapore.

McGovern, W., Addison, M., & McGovern, R. (2024). The adoption of a "diseased identity" in traditional 12-step groups: Exploring the implications of these processes for individuals and practitioners in health and social care services. *International Journal of Environmental Research and Public Health, 21*(10), 1297.

McGovern, R., Newham, J. J, Addison, M. T., Hickman, M., & Kaner, E. (2021). Effectiveness of psychosocial interventions for reducing parental substance misuse. *Cochrane Database of Systematic Reviews, 3*(3), CD012823.

McGrane, N., Dunbar, P., & Keyes, L. M. (2023). To summarise the approach to and findings of the PPIE undertaken as part of a programme of secondary research with a vulnerable, hard to reach population during the COVID-19 pandemic. *Research Involvement and Engagement, 9*(1), 31.

Melvin, C. L., Harvey, J., Pittman, T., Gentilin, S., Burshell, D., & Kelechi T. (2020). Communicating and disseminating research findings to study participants: Formative assessment of participant and researcher expectations and preferences. *Journal of Clinical and Translational Science, 4*(3), 233–242.

NIHR. (2021). *Briefing notes for researchers.* NIHR. Retrieved October 10, 2023, from https://www.nihr.ac.uk/documents/briefing-notes-for-researchers-public-involvement-in-nhs-health-and-social-care-research/27371

NIHR. (2024). *Ethical practice guidelines for public involvement and community engagement.* NIHR. Retrieved November 11, 2024, from https://arc-nenc.nihr.ac.uk/wp-content/uploads/2024/08/Ethical-Practice-Guidelines-FINAL-July-24.pdf

Padgett, D. K. (2017). *Qualitative methods in social work research* (2nd ed.). Sage.

Spencer, L., Alderson, H., Scott, S., Kaner, E., & Ling, J. (2023). 'The addiction was making things harder for my mental health': A qualitative exploration of the views of adults and adolescents accessing a substance misuse treatment service. *International Journal of Environmental Research and Public Health, 20*(11), 5967.

Steenekamp, B. L., & Barker, S. L. (2024). Exploring the experiences of compassion fatigue amongst peer support workers in homelessness services. *Community Mental Health Journal, 60*(4), 772–783. https://doi.org/10.1007/s10597-024-01234-1

Troya, M. I., Chew-Graham, C. A., Babatunde, O., Bartlam, B., Higginbottom, A., & Dikomitis, L. (2019). Patient and public involvement and engagement in a doctoral research project exploring self-harm in older adults. *Health Expectations, 22*(4), 617–631.

Chapter 12

A Queer Engagement: Navigating the Twists and Turns of Public Involvement and Multiple Marginalisation

Mark Adley

Population Health Sciences Institute, Faculty of Medical Science, Newcastle University, Newcastle upon Tyne, UK

Abstract

Ongoing critical reflection holds value within research, helping to embody learning and ethical literacy. This chapter presents the experiences of public involvement and community engagement (PICE) from the perspective of an early career researcher and holds them up for critical reflection and shared insight. Professionals working with people who have faced social inequality, marginalisation, disadvantage, or trauma may experience moments of ethical dissonance or uncertainty. Whereas clear policies are in place within many workplaces, these have been less apparent within some academic settings, although recently released guidance for researchers helps to address this. Public and community contributors brought benefits far greater than anticipated to this three-year doctoral study in the North East of England with LGBTQ+ people facing disadvantage, in which a total of 72 people aged above 18 years took part. By highlighting personal 'blind spots' and areas of epistemic bias within the study design, public involvement afforded invaluable insights and personal development. This chapter aims to illustrate how collaborations with people on the margins, who occupy queer or oblique positions in social space, can offer meaningful

Public Involvement and Community Engagement in Applied Health and Social Care Research: Critical Perspectives and Innovative Practice, 145–155

doi:10.1108/978-1-83608-678-920251012

contributions to research and bring fresh perspectives to established methodologies and methods. In turn, this hopes to encourage further evaluation of some established, yet perhaps rarely questioned research practices.

Keywords: Marginalisation; disadvantage; LGBT; reflexive; ethics; trauma; public involvement literacy

Introduction

Within this chapter the acronym LGBTQ+ (lesbian, gay, bisexual, transgender, queer or questioning, intersex, asexual, and more) is used to refer to people who are minoritised along axes of sexual orientation and/or gender identity. This acronym was selected over others due to its common usage within the UK. In doing so, it acknowledges that it may exclude the explicit naming of certain groups internationally, and that outside of global north and global western settings the term LGBTQ+ may represent concepts of personal identity that are not universal.

It takes time – a time that has to be acknowledged – to foster authentic relationships with people with lived experience of stigma, discrimination, exclusion, and marginalisation (Adley et al., 2024). At least that was my experience while conducting a PhD which aimed to explore the health and social care pathways of multiply marginalised LGBTQ+ people in North East England. By multiply marginalised, I refer to those LGBTQ+ people who have experience of, for example homelessness, substance use requiring treatment, or domestic violence. The study's underpinnings were an intersectional, queer, feminism which aimed to enhance consideration of marginalisation across multiple axes, and offer a framework of social justice from which to address inclusivity, privilege, and discrimination (Evans & Lépinard, 2020). One of the driving factors behind my choice of this topic was that, despite having over 30 years' experience working or volunteering in prisons, substance use, and homelessness services, I could count on two hands those who had disclosed that they were LGBTQ+. This, despite the increased awareness both within the UK and internationally of the significant health inequalities experienced by LGBTQ+ people (Dinos et al., 2021; Henderson et al., 2022) and the risk, impact, and structural invisibility of their homelessness and substance use (England & Turnbull, 2024; McCarthy & Parr, 2022). The study therefore sought to explore the health and social care pathways of this multiply marginalised group, to identify blocks and facilitators within these pathways, and use its findings to inform future service provision. Reaching those on the margins of these groups involved many queer twists and turns, and I wish that I could now re-run the study with the benefit of hindsight. Perhaps that is my aim here: to summarise my experiences of PICE, and in doing so lay down some breadcrumbs for others who may be walking behind.

Some of this is not flattering. However, ongoing critical reflection holds value within research, helping to embody learning and emotional and ethical literacy (Adley et al., 2024). It also holds value within the field of public involvement, where reflexivity can not only help develop researcher skills but also foster genuine, meaningful involvement with the communities under study (Gillard et al., 2012; Howe et al., 2017). This chapter, therefore, seeks to share some examples of public involvement within this PhD and to hold these up for critical reflection and shared learning.

Innovations and Concerns

Queer(y)ing 'Professional Advisors'

Although some universities may have developed networks of public advisors readily available to researchers, it is important to question whether they are representative of the population you are planning to work with. For this study, the professional public advisors that I met did not seem to have the lived experience I was looking for. I needed a queer bunch – not just in terms of minoritised sexual and gender identities, but people who occupied oblique angles from the normative. Having decided to look elsewhere, I initially found it relatively easy to access LGBTQ+ people outside of the professional networks of Public Advisors. However, I was aware of the tendency within LGBTQ+ research to draw from specific cohorts such as those whom researchers can reach through social networks or community events (Cochran, 2001). Although finding the right people has been highlighted as good practice in successful public involvement (Pollard et al., 2015), in this instance, reaching LGBTQ+ people with experience of stigma and marginalisation across multiple axes of discrimination took significant time and persistence.

The study's four public advisors, who were eventually assembled, brought a rich mix of lived experiences. Two had lived experience of homelessness, one of substance use requiring treatment, and one of the criminal justice system. Two were from non-White British backgrounds, two were cisgender, one was transgender, and one was non-binary. One had a long-term physical health condition, two had diagnoses of neurodivergence, and there were multiple permutations of sexual orientations. However, by the time we all met, the study design had been practically set in stone, and the Advisors could only offer minor suggestions, such as changes to the topic guide wording. This meant that the level of their involvement was not adequately negotiated, and therefore their roles and purpose were, as Dean (2017) described, '*imposed upon the participants, who thus have little scope to determine the conditions of their participation*'. A participatory approach and an earlier approach would have improved the integration and depth of public involvement (Felner, 2020).

Working alongside a group of Advisors who had themselves experienced significant marginalisation, and in some cases trauma, meant that their psychological safety was paramount. This involved facilitating a setting in which they felt safe psychologically, both individually and within the group; one in which people could disagree and take risks (Clandinin, 2007). In our initial meeting we explored power and hierarchy, and I invited challenge from the group, sharing my hope that we could create a knowledge space '*where different forms of knowledge can interact on an equal basis*' (Kok, 2018). Of specific note was that two out of the four Advisors were from populations that are ethnically minoritised in the UK (but are majority populations globally, and henceforth referred to as people of colour). Both commented how, when outside of their own communities, they often found themselves the lone black or brown face. They, however, found strength in numbers within the group, facilitating discussions around racism, bias, and power imbalance that each said they would not have shared had they been the only non-White person present.

Community Involvement and Reciprocity

My professional background brought benefits to recruitment as I was able to draw from pre-existing relationships with public and professional stakeholders, established and maintained over several years. Indeed, building and sustaining connections with people from marginalised populations can take considerable time, effort, and skill. I admit to feeling annoyed when, several months into the study, I began to be contacted by researchers and services who had been tasked with accessing LGBTQ+ populations and wanted to tap into the network I had been developing. I later reflected on the irony of my annoyance, as this was exactly what I had myself done. My initial consultations with community organisations had revealed that they were overwhelmed with incessant requests from researchers wanting to access their networks. While they could see the benefits for the researchers, there was little apparent benefit for them or their organisations. Research projects were time-consuming, there was rarely talk of adequate reimbursement, and many organisations were therefore reluctant to become involved.

There are a number of issues to consider here. Firstly, this highlights the importance of initial 'listening exercises' across marginalised communities, and, where possible, finding ways to address concerns. Secondly, there is the uncomfortable reflection of the potentially uneven rewards from this study. While I may have hoped for improved service provision for LGBTQ+ people in the North East, the most likely beneficiary was me, in terms of the study's potential boost to my academic career prospects. Avoiding tokenism in PICE work is key.

Attempting to redress this imbalance, I decided to adopt a reciprocal approach to community engagement. I took part in activities which offered no direct benefit for the study, such as joining and contributing to LGBTQ+ staff networks, running stalls at the weekends at community events, and helping out at Health Zones at local Pride and Mela events. I contributed to and delivered substance use training at evening LGBTQ+ groups and delivered a series of LGBTQ+ awareness sessions to a local housing provider. This approach brought its own rewards. Demonstrating a commitment to the communities I was working with raised the profile of the study with key individuals and organisations. Professionals promoted the study and supported people, many of whom were new to research, to take part in interviews. As identified within a previous project (Adley et al., 2024), connecting with marginalised populations may well require, or indeed demand, a concerted and heartfelt effort. This reciprocal approach supported Logie's (2021) position that it is the responsibility of researchers to take additional steps to move towards marginalised groups, rather than the other way around.

Grey Areas

At times the field of public involvement felt uncertain: as if there might be the potential for harm to researchers, members of the public, or academic institutions. Thankfully I had access to excellent support from supervisors, PICE leads, and fellow researchers over the course of my study and this guidance from skilled and experienced people who shared my ethical concerns and mindset proved invaluable. I also developed contacts with other researchers across the country working with marginalised populations, and discussed ethical grey areas within PICE across multiple sites. For example, there appeared to be a lack of cohesive approach to disclosure and barring service (DBS) checks, with one researcher mentioning that a member of their university's ethics panel had asked what the acronym meant. One early career researcher, more concerningly, had never been asked for a DBS and had therefore worked extensively with a marginalised population without any criminal records check having been completed. The recent publication of a set of Ethical Practice Guidelines that addresses some of these issues is therefore greatly welcomed (NIHR ARC NENC, 2024).

This touches upon the issue of ethics of public involvement with marginalised populations, and the grey areas within the boundaries of researcher-Public Advisor relationships led me to further reflections. This was a new type of working relationship for me. My experience within criminal justice and substance misuse services in particular had trained me to maintain specific boundaries with clients that would have been out of place here, and might have established a power imbalance with Public Advisors that I aimed to avoid or minimise during our collaboration. The study's Public Advisors were neither clients nor colleagues – I felt a duty of care towards them, and checked on their well-being and access to support much more frequently than I would have done in other roles. This felt justified, however, and the right thing to do in this circumstance, aligned with recommendations that public contributors should feel supported in their roles (WEAHSN, 2016). The Public Advisors were also keen to meet in each other's homes: settings that supported their psychological safety, which, as Sciolla (2017) highlights, should not be something set by the researcher but rather '*defined by those served*'. While perhaps less comfortable for me, these discussions and decisions around places of safety were important in supporting the levelling of power imbalances.

Working with this group required an intersectional approach that recognised the interactions between the Advisors' different social categories and identities, as well as the impact of additional processes of oppression such as sexism, racism, or ableism. It also called for an awareness of potential experiences of trauma, for example, the extent to which participant interviews could raise powerful emotions. Being trauma-informed, therefore, meant close consideration of psychological safety, providing ongoing 1:1 support, monitoring for power imbalances, allowing Advisors to go at their own pace, and taking a strengths-based, affirmative approach.

Shimmin et al. (2017) detailed the advantages of disrupting the identity of 'researcher' when working within a trauma-informed, intersectional framework.

I shared this experience: the study's four Public Advisors indeed troubled the power dynamics between 'researcher' and 'public'. By holding information that was hidden from me, particularly around the intersection of sexual orientation and/or gender identity and race, they became the teachers and I the student. There was a tricky balance within this, however. For example, my initial plan had been for group members to take it in turns to facilitate our meetings, with the idea that this strengths-based approach would support their self-efficacy. In spite of this intent, I stepped in and enforced my position of power after our first meeting due to my concerns about emerging power dynamics within the group. Whether I should have let them sort this out for themselves is a matter of debate, and over time, I may become more comfortable with the nuanced nature of this relationship. As an early career researcher, however, I continue to reflect and advocate for others to reflect on these blurred lines.

While the term ethical literacy describes a live, pragmatic, and flexible approach to the assessment and application of risks and ethical issues as they emerge during research projects (Wiles, 2012), this concept may not fully encompass some of the issues that may emerge during PICE work with marginalised groups. It is important therefore, particularly when working with marginalised communities, to consider a researcher's level of *public involvement literacy:* their ability to navigate nuanced boundaries and practical grey areas, and to assess the potential for power imbalances not only within the group but also between the group and researcher. We return again to the importance of supervision, of embodied learning within the academy, and the potential value of reflective and reflexive space in which to explore such issues.

The Rear View Mirror

> White bodies do not have to face their whiteness; they are not orientated "toward" it… By not having to encounter being white as an obstacle, given that whiteness is "in line" with what is already given, bodies that pass as white move easily. (Ahmed, 2006)

In her book *Queer Phenomenology*, Ahmed challenges us to draw our attention away from established, common practice towards that which may not immediately be in view. Conversations with the study's two Public Advisors who were also queer people of colour particularly troubled some of my assumptions and blind spots, drawing my gaze from what was immediately ahead of me towards the study's 'rear view mirror' and those not immediately in view. Having 'enough' representation of non-White participants was no longer 'enough'. Hoping to increase the representation of black and brown people, I decided to consult further with some of the other LGBTQ+ people of colour I had met during the study, and in this way, the Public Advisors shaped the study's recruitment strategy.

These consultations revealed several areas of epistemic bias embedded within my research methods. For example, I had designed the study's initial recruitment flyers with a white background and the acronym LGBTQIA+ in large type, alongside the 'progressive' rainbow flag that is widely used as LGBTQ+ branding in many global North or global Western nations. Where I had assumed that the rainbow branding was representative of all LGBTQ+ people, I learned that this was not true for all groups, even signalling to some that they were not welcome. Subsequent recruitment flyers therefore used wording that prioritised racialised identities above LGBTQ+ identities, with a brown rather than white background, the rainbow flag replaced by line drawings of black and brown people that specifically represented them.

Over time, I also developed a greater appreciation of why some marginalised groups may actively avoid or refuse to contribute to health and social care research. Having been excluded from systems and services designed without consideration of their needs, they are then approached by researchers who add insult to injury by trying to find out about their experiences of exclusion. Keeping a close eye on the demographic make-up of study participants highlighted other gaps in recruitment, for example, low numbers of lesbians and gay or bisexual women. This too calls for further consultation with community members and a considerate approach to recruitment – navigating complex cultural schisms around the meaning of the words 'women' or 'cisgender women' to different LGBTQ+ groups.

These consultations led to some revelatory interviews with sexual and gender minority women, LGBTQ+ people of colour, and people seeking asylum. A longer period of consultation at the start of the study with people on the furthest margins of this population group would have brought longer-term rewards. Doing so would not only have reduced epistemic bias within the study but would also have saved the need for further applications to ethics and the additional time required to redesign study materials. Researchers should therefore carry out as much preparatory groundwork as possible, dedicate ample time to co-creating study designs with marginalised communities, and when in doubt, ask rather than assume.

Things to Consider

The Advisors' main role was to analyse study interviews and to create their own set of recommendations for their report, and our initial meeting balanced time for the group to get to know each other with a set agenda. Much of this was dedicated to the informal training session in qualitative research methods that I had designed for this purpose. Aware of the emotionally charged nature of the subject matter and its potential to trigger trauma, the topic of emotional safety featured heavily: I advised them to stop reading if they were becoming upset, that they could choose not to read particular interviews, and indeed that they were free to take a 'time out' or withdraw from the study completely. Advisors could contact me on a one-to-one basis, and they also provided each other with ongoing peer support in their WhatsApp group to which I sent regular check-in messages and offers of one-to-one help over the course of our year-long collaboration. During this time, we held four in-person group meetings and two over videoconferencing: each meeting began and ended with a 'check-in' to see how people were feeling, with space for the group to discuss emotions brought up by the research.

We also discussed the process of analysing interviews. I explained that I would be providing transcribed versions of interviews that would be edited down to reduce the word count and therefore their workload, both in terms of time and emotional load. Then, at the end of the meeting, the four Advisors were given a short exercise in thematic analysis to complete on their own that they later discussed with me on a one-to-one basis. This aimed both to give them the opportunity to develop their approach to analysis and also to allow for any gaps in understanding to be reflected back individually so that any additional support needs could be identified and met. I had given thought to their learning styles, literacy issues, and neurodivergence at the start of our work together, and the group were offered the choice of transcripts in printed or digital form. We also discussed ways of easing the process of analysis, such as using their computer to read out text. In our final meeting, the Advisors identified their three main themes and recommendations, with their contributions placed into their report for distribution along with the wider study report.

After their analysis had been completed, I was curious about the Advisors' experiences, and with no apparent procedures in place to collect their feedback, I invited the group to share their reflections on their involvement in the study. Although I had assumed that they would be more comfortable speaking critically to a third party, the results of the anonymous poll I set up revealed that all four favoured meeting with me directly. Two of the Advisors attended this feedback meeting, and the main issue they raised was around the formatting of the interviews. Although they complimented the introductory 'scene-setting' paragraphs and trigger warnings I had added to the start of each transcript, they mentioned how a lot of important context had been lost and that they would have preferred to hear the interviews in their entirety and in the original audio. Sharing the original audio files would, however, have breached participants' confidentiality. I also had concerns about drawing on them too much, both in terms of their emotions and workload, and of them not being recompensed fairly for their time, given the study's 66.5 hours of interview data. There was a balance to be reached here, and also a reality to be acknowledged in terms of ownership of the research process.

The Advisors mentioned that they had enjoyed the informal settings of our meetings and our discussions about researcher power and privilege, and how these had supported open and honest conversations. Emotional safety was also an important topic: they noted how the interview transcripts had at times stirred powerful emotions, and they appreciated the concern for their well-being and the allocated time to discuss their feelings at the start and end of each meeting. This highlights the importance of ongoing attention to the emotional well-being of public participants and their sense of psychological safety, which may be particularly relevant to groups who are marginalised, stigmatised, and/or who have experienced trauma.

The issue of group dynamics and researcher positionality was something that they had also considered, although opinions differed. Whereas one Advisor would have preferred the group to lead the meetings themselves, the other shared my concerns about more confident people dominating discussions. This revealed some of the delicacy that may be required when working with public contributors from marginalised populations, such as balancing the need to consider their emotional and psychological safety while also supporting them to lead on their own work. While these issues may never be perfectly resolved, there is value in considering their impact.

In addition to the Ethical Practice Guidelines mentioned earlier (NIHR ARC NENC, 2024), another valuable resource was the Community Engagement Toolkit (NIHR RDS, 2022), which outlined 10 guiding principles for researchers working with diverse communities. The last of these principles mentions feeding back outcomes to the communities involved, and I worked with a community partner who co-facilitated an online dissemination event that was attended by 43 people across the region. During this event, I shared slides from the study, we held several group discussions, and carried out polls and whiteboard exercises. Towards the end of the event, I shared the study's three key findings and recommendations, and attendees were invited to provide feedback anonymously on the relevance of these to their work and/or lived experiences of navigating local health and social care services. Member checking, such as this, aims to find out whether the researcher's interpretation of the data are aligned with participants' experiences, and thus improve the credibility and transferability of qualitative research (Rolfe et al., 2018). Feedback from the dissemination event is being included in the study's plain language report, which will be made available and distributed online, along with the Public Advisors' report. This final stage, therefore, reaped dual rewards: not only improving the study's rigour but also maintaining an ongoing dialogue with the communities who were at its heart.

Conclusion

Dillard (2000) suggested how power relations structure gender, race, and other identities within research, and called instead for a differing metaphor of research that challenges '*unexamined epistemological assumptions that pass as universal truths*' (p. 679). This chapter noted incidents of such assumptions on my part, whose impact would have been reduced had I asked, rather than assumed. This does, however, raise the issue of the complexity found within the process of asking. Lorde (1984) wrote that '*Lesbians and gay men are expected to educate the heterosexual world. The oppressors maintain their position and evade responsibility for their own actions*'. While this sentiment was echoed by one of the Public Advisors who had a strong aversion to being positioned as a fount of knowledge on racism, another was happy to be asked about their experiences as a queer person of colour. This raises issues of representativity and essentialism, and the extent to which we may expect Public Advisors to represent entire populations rather than speaking solely from their own experiences.

The process of thinking critically about my own viewpoints and assumptions, and (most importantly perhaps) holding my hand up to acknowledge these and apologise when I got things wrong, brought rewards both to the study itself and to me personally. The benefits of critical self-awareness are acknowledged here by Shimmin et al. (2017) who suggested that reflexivity '*can help to transform the process of public involvement in health research*'. It is important for researchers to listen carefully to their public contributors and to be genuinely open to learning from them.

This chapter aimed to hold up some examples of public involvement with a marginalised population for the purpose of critical reflection and shared learning. There is of course benefit in discussing best practice, and examples found within this chapter include: a persistent approach to finding the right Public Advisors and the right mix within this group, paying close attention to their emotional well-being, being mindful of different learning styles and any adjustments that may need to be made, keeping a close eye on participant demographics, adopting a reciprocal approach to working with community organisations, feeding back outcomes, reflecting on researcher positionality, and making good use of the invaluable support offered by supervisors, PICE leads, and likeminded and experienced colleagues.

However, genuine involvement with the public can also lead to moments of dissonance and ethical uncertainty. Working with people who have experienced social inequality, marginalisation, disadvantage, and trauma can at times raise complex issues. Reaching across cultural divides may require more than cultural awareness, and may call for 'cultural humility' which has been defined as '*self-awareness of personal and cultural biases as well as awareness and sensitivity to significant cultural issues of others*' (Yeager & Bauer-Wu, 2013). While this may introduce uncertainty for researchers, the engagement developed with the Public Advisors over the course of this PhD brought benefits far greater than anticipated. In highlighting areas of epistemic bias, it made a significant methodological contribution, bringing novel viewpoints on established and perhaps rarely questioned methodologies, methods, and working practices. Public involvement is so much more than consultation, and this troubling of existing processes from an oblique, queer perspective can ultimately lead to more equitable access to research for those on the margins.

References

Adley, M., Alderson, H., Jackson, K., McGovern, W., Spencer, L., Addison, M., & O'Donnell, A. (2024). Ethical and practical considerations for including marginalised groups in quantitative survey research. *International Journal of Social Research Methodology*, 27(5), 559–574.

Ahmed, S. (2006). *Queer phenomenology: Orientations, objects, others*. Duke University Press.

Clandinin, D. J. (2007). *Handbook of narrative inquiry: Mapping a methodology*. SAGE.

Cochran, S. D. (2001). Emerging issues in research on lesbians' and gay men's mental health: Does sexual orientation really matter? *American Psychologist*, 56, 931–947.

Dean, R. J. (2017). Beyond radicalism and resignation: The competing logics for public participation in policy decisions. *Policy & Politics*, 45, 213–230.

Dillard, C. B. (2000). The substance of things hoped for, the evidence of things not seen: Examining an endarkened feminist epistemology in educational research and leadership. *International Journal of Qualitative Studies in Education*, 13, 661–681.

Dinos, S., Tay, N., & Shipsey, F. (2021). *Health and health-related behaviours of lesbian, gay and bisexual adults*. NHS Digital.

England, E., & Turnbull, N. (2024). *2022-23 LGBTQ+ housing and homelessness survey final report*. Cardiff. https://housingevidence.ac.uk/publications/lgbtq-housing-amp-homelessness-survey/

England, E., & Turnbull, N. (2024). LGBTQ+ housing & homelessness survey 2022–23.

Evans, E., & Lépinard, É. (2020). *Intersectionality in feminist and queer movements: Confronting privileges*. Taylor & Francis.

Felner, J. K. (2020). "You get a PhD and we get a few hundred bucks": Mutual benefits in participatory action research? *Health Education & Behavior, 47*, 549–555.

Gillard, S., Simons, L., Turner, K., Lucock, M., & Edwards, C. (2012). Patient and public involvement in the coproduction of knowledge: Reflection on the analysis of qualitative data in a mental health study. *Qualitative Health Research, 22*, 1126–1137.

Henderson, E. R., Goldbach, J. T., & Blosnich, J. R. (2022). Social determinants of sexual and gender minority mental health. *Current Treatment Options in Psychiatry, 9*, 229–245.

Howe, A., Mathie, E., Munday, D., Cowe, M., Goodman, C., Keenan, J., Kendall, S., Poland, F., Staniszewska, S., & Wilson, P. (2017). Learning to work together – Lessons from a reflective analysis of a research project on public involvement. *Research Involvement and Engagement, 3*, 1.

Kok, M., Davies, R., & White, J. (2018). *Developing a practical approach to evaluating public involvement in research*. International perspectives on evaluation of patient and public involvement in research, Newcastle. https://uwe-repository.worktribe.com/output/857063

Kok, M., Davies, R., & White, J. (2018, November). Developing a practical approach to evaluating public involvement in research.

Logie, C. (2021). *Working with excluded populations in HIV: Hard to reach or out of sight?* Springer International Publishing AG.

Lorde, A. (1984). Age, race, class, and sex: Women redefining difference. In J. Rivkin & M. Ryan (Eds.), *Literary theory, an anthology* (pp. 854–860). Blackwell.

Mccarthy, L., & Parr, S. (2022). Is LGBT homelessness different? Reviewing the relationship between LGBT identity and homelessness. *Housing Studies, 40*(7), 1525–1544.

NIHR ARC NENC. (2024). *Ethical practice guidelines for public involvement and community engagement*. https://arc-nenc.nihr.ac.uk/wp-content/uploads/2024/08/Ethical-Practice-Guidelines-FINAL-July-24.pdf

NIHR RDS. (2022). *Community engagement toolkit*. Retrieved November 2, 2023, from https://www.rdsresources.org.uk/ce-toolkit?tags=Toolkit

Pollard, K., Donskoy, A. L., Moule, P., Donald, C., Lima, M., & Rice, C. (2015). Developing and evaluating guidelines for patient and public involvement (PPI) in research. *International Journal of Health Care Quality Assurance, 28*, 141–155.

Rolfe, D. E., Ramsden, V. R., Banner, D., & Graham, I. D. (2018). Using qualitative health research methods to improve patient and public involvement and engagement in research. *Research Involvement and Engagement, 4*, 49.

Sciolla, A. F. (2017). An overview of trauma-informed care. In K. L. Eckstrand & J. Potter (Eds.), *Trauma, resilience, and health promotion in LGBT patients: What every healthcare provider should know* (1st ed., pp. 165–181). Springer International Publishing AG.

Shimmin, C., Wittmeier, K. D. M., Lavoie, J. G., Wicklund, E. D., & Sibley, K. M. (2017). Moving towards a more inclusive patient and public involvement in health research paradigm: The incorporation of a trauma-informed intersectional analysis. *BMC Health Services Research, 17*, 539.

WEAHSN. (2016). *Working together: A toolkit for health professionals on how to involve the public*. West of England Academic Health Science Network.

Wiles, R. (2012). *What are qualitative research ethics?* Bloomsbury Publishing Plc.

Yeager, K. A., & Bauer-Wu, S. (2013). Cultural humility: Essential foundation for clinical researchers. *Applied Nursing Research, 26*, 251–256.

Chapter 13

'Tinkering with Care' in Public Involvement and Community Engagement with People with Experience of Problematic Alcohol and/or Drug Use

Katherine Jackson, Emma-Joy Holland, Elizabeth Titchener and Amy O'Donnell

Population Health Sciences Institute, Faculty of Medical Sciences, Newcastle University, Newcastle upon Tyne, UK

Abstract

Our experiences of public involvement and community engagement (PICE), within and across different studies related to substance use, suggest we continually need to adapt to support people to be involved with research. The term 'tinkering with care' is used to describe a responsive and relational process whereby, through trial and error, we come to find a way of being caring that is best suited to that specific context and population (Mol et al., 2010). If we don't adapt and tinker to find a way of being caring, we run the risk of generating care practices that are unfair and unethical (Mol et al., 2010). In this chapter, we draw on Mol et al.'s concept and three examples from PICE with people with experience of problematic alcohol and/or drug use, to illustrate where we have been attentive and adapted our practice to better support both the public's and the research team's well-being. We also draw on concepts from Feminist Ethics of Care Theory more broadly to illustrate that our capacity to 'tinker' to generate

Public Involvement and Community Engagement in Applied Health and Social Care Research: Critical Perspectives and Innovative Practice, 157–167

good care in different PICE situations is shaped by the social contexts of the research.

Keywords: Substance use; public involvement and community engagement; feminist ethics of care theory; qualitative research; ethics; community advocates

1. Introduction

Involving people with current or previous personal experience of alcohol or drug use (from here referred to as PWUS) in the research process is essential for advancing social justice in substance use research (Cairns & Nicholls, 2018). While PWUS are diverse, many share the experience of significant marginalisation and stigma (Addison et al., 2022). Involving PWUS in the research process can help to ensure that research teams don't reproduce inequality and stigma; it can also help to reduce prejudice and negative assumptions or further stigma and then discrimination towards this population from research audiences (Greer et al., 2018). PWUS may feel they are being listened to in PICE, something they may not often experience in professional settings (Carlin et al., 2020). PICE can be enjoyable and provide an opportunity for PWUS to build authentic relationships with other people with similar experiences and to develop new skills (Cairns & Nicholls, 2018). PICE can also be enjoyable for the researchers, who will learn from the process and may feel more connected to the communities they are researching.

Despite these many positives of PICE with PWUS, there is a growing international literature which critically explores the practical and ethical challenges that researchers have experienced in engaging with marginalised communities and some of the concerns mentioned above (e.g., Foley et al., 2023). Researchers have noted the difficulty of managing the expectations of PWUS about the level of change that research can bring about to existing systems, particularly in a context where they experience significant marginalisation in these systems, and ideally need and want change to happen quickly (Madden et al., 2020). Others have focussed on moral and philosophically driven concerns and these have reported ethical tensions of keeping PWUS safe (Hayashi et al., 2012), or have described how they have needed to re-think the process of engagement during the research process, due to the barriers that they experience in engaging PWUS (Salmon et al., 2010). Overall, many of these critical accounts show that there is a need, as we do, here in this chapter, to be reflexive and adaptable to support the well-being of PWUS alongside the wider research team.

In this chapter, we aim to add to this critical literature by considering ethical and practical challenges we have experienced in PICE with PWUS using examples from three qualitative research studies, conducted since 2021 in the North East of England. The general population of the North East reports similar levels of well-being and satisfaction with life and mental health compared to the rest of the

UK. However, large parts of the region experience poorer health, economic and social outcomes, and higher than average levels of deprivation than other areas of England (Bramley et al., 2020). The region has seen a steep increase in drug overdoses in recent years (Price et al., 2024) and has the highest levels of alcohol-related morbidity and mortality in England (Office for National Statistics, 2024). Trauma is recognised as unequally affecting marginalised populations, including PWUS (Hatch & Dohrenwend, 2007). Trauma can be defined in different ways, but is broadly often used to describe an event or series of events which have '*lasting effects on the individual's functioning and mental, physical, social, emotional, or spiritual wellbeing*' (Substance Abuse and Mental Health Services Administration, 2014, p. 7). Trauma commonly shatters people's perception that they feel safe in their environment and their relationships (Substance Abuse and Mental Health Services Administration, 2014). Recognising the trauma experienced by many people we engage with and the challenging social and political background to our research, our focus is on what we have been able to do to 'care for and support the wellbeing of PWUS and the research team' in these projects. To do this, we draw on concepts from Feminist Ethics of Care Theory, which is discussed below before we move to the examples.

1.1. Concepts from Feminist Ethics of Care to Explore PICE

In terms of positionality, the key underpinning tenet of Feminist Ethics of Care Theory is that it recognises all people as interdependent and relational, and in need of care in all spheres of life, that is, in families, friendships, and in public settings including workplaces where PICE might take place such as community or University settings (Barnes, 2012). Feminist Ethics of Care Theory helps us to understand and theoretically recognise that certain people are positioned to need care in particular contexts, while others can be overlooked (Tronto, 1993). For example, public contributors might be seen to need care, but the research team may not. However, all people need care, and they need to feel supported to care for others as well as possible. Care has been defined broadly by seminal ethics of care theorists as '… *everything that we do to maintain, continue and repair our world so that we can live in it as well as possible*' (Fisher & Tronto, 1990, p. 40). More recently, and drawing back to the title of this chapter, a conceptualisation of 'good care' is as '*Persistent tinkering in a world full of complex ambivalence and shifting tension*' (Mol et al., 2010, p. 10). Mol et al. (2010) and colleagues have helped us to understand that 'good care' involves finding context-based solutions to situations through adapting and responding, and they note that what constitutes good care in one context may not be the same as in others. Importantly, feminist ethics of care scholars argue that the micro process of care, and people's capacity to 'tinker' to enact the best care they can, is shaped by macro processes and structures. In this chapter, we draw on these ideas. We present examples from our work as case studies, and in doing so, we ask YOU, the reader, to consider what we might do to care as well as possible for those involved in PICE with people who use substances.

2. Case Study Examples

2.1. Practical Challenges of Doing Inclusive Intervention Co-design

The first research project we present as a case study explored opportunities to improve care for people experiencing co-occurring heavy alcohol use and depression across the North East region. During the project, we worked with PWUS with co-occurring depression to develop a digital resource to support them. The reflection below concerns the first of three co-design workshops we ran as part of the project.

When planning the workshop, ensuring the 20 workshop attendees would feel comfortable and safe was a priority for us, above and beyond any research activities. We spoke to the project patient and public involvement and engagement (PPIE) group (five PWUS/unpaid carers of PWUS) about what might make people feel comfortable, and they suggested a venue that they felt the attendees would be most familiar with. As a research team, we also drew on our experience of running co-design workshops with people with poor mental health in previous studies, which had highlighted the value of working in small groups to support people to contribute freely, and to have a key contact they could go to with any concerns. We ensured that we had enough helpers so that the public contributors could work in groups of three or four people. We also felt it was important to involve helpers with knowledge of the subject area and who had worked in a formal setting with our study population. At the same time, this offered the helpers the opportunity to use their expertise and to develop skills in PICE. We had pre-workshop meetings with these helpers to ensure they were happy with our plan for the workshop activities. As a group, we discussed what we would do if people were to attend under the influence of substances and agreed that if they were able to contribute without disrupting others, then they could be involved, but if any individual was disruptive, then we may have to ask them to leave. We would recommend pre-workshop meetings to help research teams share ideas and think collectively about issues that could arise.

However, while we were able to prepare for some issues that arose, there were several practical (discussed below around accessibility), but also emotional concerns (not wanting to stigmatise or retraumatise people) that emerged during this workshop. The venue was accessible and familiar to many and seemed to put some people at ease. However, it was also very noisy. Near the beginning of the workshops one attendee approached us and asked if we could reduce the noise because it was making them feel uncomfortable. There was little we could do about this once everyone was there and managing this contingency was proving to be difficult. Sometimes when conducting PICE there will be concerns like these that might not have been previously considered, nevertheless, these types of concerns need to be dealt with swiftly and effectively, so we explained that they could take breaks or leave if they wanted to. Another person arrived with their dog, but the venue didn't allow pets so they couldn't attend. We hadn't prepared for this despite knowing that pets can be very important for some people in recovery from substance use (Kerr-Little et al., 2023). Another issue that emerged was that in the planning we focussed on people's experiences that were relevant to the topic of our project, that is, experiences of heavy alcohol use and depression rather than thinking about people as having a range of identities and experiences that need to be accommodated for workshops to be inclusive. One participant was a wheelchair user, and while fortunately the room was accessible, this was not something we had explicitly considered prior to the event. Taking stock here and reflecting on these concerns with Feminist Ethics of Care Theory, a key learning point was that PWUS, and other marginalised communities are not homogeneous, and it is important to think about and consider the broader range of identities that exist within specific research populations (McGovern et al., 2024) as we plan, develop and deliver research to make it inclusive (Addison et al., 2022) to ensure people feel cared for. In the future workshops for this project, we thought more broadly about inclusion and have used venues that have more breakout spaces to limit the noise and tried to source venues that are pet friendly, although this is not always possible.

2.2. Shaping Engagement to Meet People Where They're at

The second study evaluated a newly developed UK National Health Service based role to support patients who drink heavily and regularly attend Accident and Emergency settings in North East hospitals. At the start of the project, we set out to establish a PPIE group of people with experience of alcohol dependence so they could contribute to a project that could directly affect them, helping to develop research materials and the recruitment strategy, as well as supporting data analysis and project dissemination. We planned for this group to meet in person, face-to-face (rather than online) due to our awareness of digital exclusion potentially experienced by this population.

We were able to draw on existing networks of PPIE individuals and organisations to establish this group, while others were identified through a recovery organisation. Here we would argue that maintaining fieldwork relationships with public contributors is essential to be able to move quickly and respond to funding and fieldwork pressures of involvement. In this sense, we were helping to contribute to building research capacity within these communities, but also continuing to ensure new voices were involved in the project. These prior connections also meant that many individuals were known to each other, and some had worked together in a PPIE role before. The group also consisted of individuals who were often several years into their recovery, and they were able to reflect on their use, their involvement with services, and their recovery needs over time. As such, they appeared able and better prepared to reflect on their own experiences. Arguably, this increased self-understanding and reflexivity among the PPIE group meant that these members were able to give and contribute to critical and in-depth discussions.

It is important to keep in mind that both working in groups and sharing their own traumatic experiences openly can be difficult for PWUS, whatever stage of their recovery or previous experience of PICE (see chapter by Adams and Ramsey in this collection). We also found, as others have reported in this collection, that during the PPIE sessions, a few people told us that they wanted to be involved in the project but did not feel comfortable sharing their thoughts in a public group setting. We made space for these important concerns and then talked with these members individually to ask how we could support them to continue, and agreed to set up one-to-one sessions between them and a member of the research team. Understanding your own positionality, reflexivity, and reflectiveness as a researcher, and in the context of feminist ethics of care theory, making situational adjustments and considering the needs and experiences of all your research PPIE group, is key to inclusive and high-quality research. In the end, this was a relatively straightforward adjustment for the research team, which, although it meant factoring in extra time for receiving PPIE feedback, allowed a more inclusive approach that led to ongoing involvement from PPIE members.

Alongside the group of individuals with direct personal experience of alcohol dependence, during the project we established a PPIE group of unpaid carers who had experience of supporting an individual who drinks heavily. This group said they were happy to meet online via videoconferencing software which widened participation and involvement and allowed members living in rural areas to engage. Despite this widening of access, in relation to Feminist Ethics of Care Theory, this also meant a different approach was needed in managing the emotional group discussions. One carer had recently experienced the bereavement of a loved one who had experienced addiction. The carer openly shared their distressing and traumatic experiences with the group. While listening to their experiences was helpful in setting the complex real-world context of the issue, this was difficult to manage within online PPIE sessions to ensure other members were not upset or had their trauma re-triggered by the topic (Edelman, 2023). On reflection we could have factored in well-being follow-up calls with participants to check-in after the sessions and this is something we would do in future. We noted that face-to-face in-person meetings have allowed the research team to have more informal debriefs with participants, or to follow-up with individuals in a one-to-one conversation. Contingency management and processes which reduce emotional discomfort among PPIE groups will always be welcomed by those we involve in research projects.

The emotional experience of listening to and managing PPIE members share their often-traumatic experiences can also take its toll on the research teams (Williamson et al., 2020). To manage this and support our own well-being, we took time to reflect and discuss the meetings after each session, both immediately after PPIE sessions and the following week. This gave us time to consider any immediate reactions, but also gave us time to process conversations. During the study, we also built in group reflection sessions to share our thoughts about our work more broadly.

2.3. Building on the Skills and Expertise of Local Advocates

The third project aimed to design and evaluate an intervention to improve access to physical health care for PWUS in one region of the North East. At the outset of this study, we had fewer existing relationships with members of the public and relevant community organisations than for the studies mentioned above. We were aware that we would need to spend a significant amount of time building trust and relationships to start the process of PICE. Fortunately, near the start of the project, our project funder introduced us to two individuals who were very active within the recovery community and keen to be involved in the research. We observed the enormous value of these individuals, whom we will refer to as advocates, in helping to drive the research forward, supporting us to connect with PWUS and community organisations we wouldn't have reached as easily without their help, and supporting other members of the community to get involved in the project.

One advocate was working in the recovery community and also had an interest in research. They used their vast network and contacts to connect us to relevant community organisations during the initial phase of data collection. This advocate also became part of our project steering group, and we secured additional funding to support and recognise their expertise and contributions. The other advocate was also closely networked in the recovery community, and their networks and skills were invaluable for helping to establish the study PPIE group and encouraging other PWUS to get involved in it. They acted as a point of contact for some PPIE group members who were not easily contactable via phone or email. They passed on communications, helped with transportation to group meets, and kept our research team updated about these PPIE members' continued involvement in the group. As the project progressed, we noticed how the advocates supported other PPIE members during discussions and observed reciprocal benefits for them in relation to how these PPIE members grew in confidence. The social identity model of recovery (SIMOR) recognises that activities that involve helping others (especially if the outcome is positive) can be beneficial to the identity formation and the recovery of those providing the help or care (McGovern et al., 2021). The advocates also helped us to navigate tricky conversations in co-design workshops, they supported the conversations, and were able to explain the service in a way that was familiar to other PWUS.

Despite the enormous value of the advocates, we had not considered that presenting the project as leading to intervention development in the co-design workshops could mean that our role as researchers could be blurred for some PWUS who attended. In the early workshops attendees would ask us service specific questions such as hiring processes, budgets and service regulations, which we were not able to answer. This misunderstanding meant that focus was drawn away from the planned co-design activities. In response to this, as the project progressed, we invited someone who was involved in the service delivery of the intervention to attend the workshops to limit confusion. Having this person in the workshops meant that queries or concerns could be clarified, and we could focus on the research elements. In these workshops PWUS indicated they could see that they were contributing to a new service that they and their peers might directly benefit from in the immediate future. Overall, our experience demonstrated the value in having advocates and someone involved in service delivery alongside the research team to ensure the foundations of understanding were in place.

3. Discussion

PICE is a relational practice, and ensuring those involved are cared for is essential. Drawing back to the concepts from Feminist Ethics of Care Theory, our examples illustrate just some of the ways we have tried to 'tinker' or adapt to care for people during PICE involving PWUS. For example, we planned for small group work, adapted the ways we engaged with people in response to their requests, for example, by holding individual meetings rather than groups, and involved community advocates and health and social care practitioners to help people feel comfortable and to facilitate their understanding. We have touched on how these care practices were shaped by the wider social contexts of our research, which in these cases were the time/funding that were available to do the research. In this final section, we consider the main issues that our examples suggest are needed to support 'good care' for all the people involved in PICE with PWUS.

Being inclusive and paying attention to diversity is recognised as a fundamental principle of PICE (Imison et al., 2022) and is undoubtedly necessary to ensure people feel cared for. Our examples highlighted the pivotal importance of looking beyond people's identities of the topic under study to consider their broader needs and identities to facilitate inclusion in PICE. We also illustrated that being inclusive involves giving people a choice about how they engage in PICE. This resonates with others who have noted that offering choice about modes of engagement, whether that be in groups or individuals (Hayashi et al., 2012), online or in-person, is pivotal for inclusive PICE with PWUS. We also noted the importance of public contributors having a clear understanding of why they are there and who is involved in the research before any meaningful activities take place. Undoubtedly, these examples show that being inclusive in PICE with PWUS to ensure people are cared for involves making contextual adaptations and responding to need.

A key factor that has supported caring for PWUS in PICE in all these examples has been the relational support from individuals and organisations with specific skills of working with this population. In the co-design workshop, discussed in the first example, we were lucky enough to have helpers who volunteered their time to support the PWUS in smaller group activities. Likewise, having the advocates involved in the third example, who also had professional expertise, gave the team reassurance that if any participants were distressed, we could keep them safe and ensure their well-being. Therefore, having these people involved helped to ensure public contributors were cared for as well as possible. However, and importantly, being able to make adaptations and involve helpers and advocates can take time and use significant resources. In our examples, we were fortunate to have access to additional resources and time, but without these, it might be more difficult to get these foundations right. Many research funders now recognise the need to fund PICE appropriately, and our examples illustrate the need for flexibility within budgets to respond to new issues that emerge during research processes. For example, we were able to source extra funds to pay for the advocates to support the work.

PICE with PWUS can be emotional for all involved, including the research team. A common experience reported by other substance use researchers, that we noted in the second example, is managing the impact of discussing traumatic experience (Clover, 2011). In the first example, we noted that we felt upset when a public contributor couldn't attend the workshop because they had their dog with them. This led to us feeling upset because we felt we hadn't cared for this person appropriately. As noted in the introduction, the emotional impact of PICE work on researchers can be overlooked when trying to provide the best care possible for the public. Overall, we have felt cared for in our work in these projects, but this has been informally organised rather than formally supported within university systems. Undoubtedly, we have benefitted from working in a team who understand and have their own experiences of PICE. We would argue that this work could be more challenging for postgraduate student and researchers working alone and that there should be structures within universities which provide this support.

4. Conclusion

Other researchers have pointed to the value of feminist ethics of care theory for understanding the relational elements of PICE (e.g., Brannelly & Barnes, 2022; Groot et al., 2019). Here, we have contributed to this literature by considering how it can help us to understand some dimensions of PICE with PWUS. It has helped illuminate that the micro-interactions of care and our capacity to be responsive and change our practices are shaped by the social contexts. Good care in PICE work with PWUS needs research teams who are willing to adapt to the different context they find themselves in, and this can only take place in well-resourced environments where everyone is cared for as well as possible.

References

Addison, M., McGovern, W., & McGovern, R. (2022). *Drugs, identity and stigma.* Springer.

Barnes, M. (2012). *Care in everyday life: An ethic of care in practice.* The Polity Press.

Bramley, G., Fitzpatrick, S., & Sosenko, F. (2020). Mapping the "hard edges" of disadvantage in England: Adults involved in homelessness, substance misuse, and offending. *The Geographical Journal, 186,* 390–402.

Brannelly, T., & Barnes, M. (2022). *Researching with care: Applying feminist care ethics to research practice.* Policy Press.

Cairns, J., & Nicholls, J. (2018). Co-production in substance use research. *Drugs and Alcohol Today, 18,* 6–16.

Carlin, E., Nugent, B., & Moulson, R. (2020). *'Stand up and tell me your story' meanings and importance of lived and living experiences for alcohol and drug policy: Findings from a qualitative study.* Scottish Health Action on Alcohol Problems.

Clover, D. (2011). Successes and challenges of feminist arts-based participatory methodologies with homeless/street-involved women in Victoria. *Action Research, 9,* 12–26.

Edelman, N. L. (2023). Trauma and resilience informed research principles and practice: A framework to improve the inclusion and experience of disadvantaged populations in health and social care research. *Journal of Health Services Research & Policy, 28,* 66–75.

Fisher, B., & Tronto, J. (1990). Toward a feminist theory of caring. In E. K. Abel & M. K. Nelson (Eds.), *Circles of care: Work and identity in women's lives* (pp. 35–62). State University of New York Press.

Foley, K., Lunnay, B., Kevin, C., & Ward, P. R. (2023). Developing a women's thought collective methodology for health research: The roles and responsibilities of researchers in the reflexive co-production of knowledge. *Health Expectations, 26,* 1954–1964.

Greer, A. M., Amlani, A., Pauly, B., Burmeister, C., & Buxton, J. A. (2018). Participant, peer and PEEP: considerations and strategies for involving people who have used illicit substances as assistants and advisors in research. *BMC Public Health, 18,* 834.

Groot, B. C., Vink, M., Haveman, A., Huberts, M., Schout, G., & Abma, T. A. (2019). Ethics of care in participatory health research: Mutual responsibility in collaboration with co-researchers. *Educational Action Research, 27,* 286–302.

Hatch, S. L., & Dohrenwend, B. P. (2007). Distribution of traumatic and other stressful life events by race/ethnicity, gender, SES and age: A review of the research. *American Journal of Community Psychology, 40,* 313–332.

Hayashi, K., Fairbairn, N., Suwannawong, P., Kaplan, K., Wood, E., & Kerr, T. (2012). Collective empowerment while creating knowledge: A description of a community-based participatory research project with drug users in Bangkok, Thailand. *Substance Use & Misuse, 47,* 502–510.

Imison, C., Kaur, M., & Dawson, S. (2022). *Supporting equity and tackling inequality: How can NIHR promote inclusion in public partnerships? An agenda for action.* National Institute for Health and Care Research.

Kerr-Little, A., Bramness, J. G., Newberry, R. C., & Biong, S. (2023). Exploring dog ownership in the lives of people with substance use disorder: A qualitative study. *Addiction Science & Clinical Practice, 18,* 57.

Madden, M., Morris, S., Ogden, M., Lewis, D., Stewart, D., & McCambridge, J. (2020). Producing co-production: Reflections on the development of a complex intervention. *Health Expectations, 23,* 659–669.

McGovern, W., Addison, M., & McGovern, R. (2021). An exploration of the psycho-social benefits of providing sponsorship and supporting others in traditional 12 step, self-help groups. *International Journal of Environmental Research and Public Health, 18,* 2208.

McGovern, W., Addison, M., & McGovern, R. (2024). The adoption of a "diseased identity" in traditional 12-step groups: Exploring the implications of these processes for individuals and practitioners in health and social care services. *International Journal of Environmental Research and Public Health, 21,* 1297.

Mol, A., Moser, I., & Pols, J. (2010). Care: Putting practice into theory. In A. Mol, I. Moser, & J. Pols (Eds.), *Care in practice: On tinkering in clinics, homes and farms* (pp. 7–26). Transcript.

Office for National Statistics.(2024). *Alcohol-specific deaths in the UK: Registered in 2022.* Statistical bulletin. ONS Website.

Price, T., McGowan, V., Visram, S., Wildman, J., & Bambra, C. (2024). "They're not mentally ill, their lives are just shit": Stakeholders' understanding of deaths of despair in a deindustrialised community in North East England. *Health & Place, 90,* 103346.

Salmon, A., Browne, A. J., & Pederson, A. (2010). 'Now we call it research': Participatory health research involving marginalized women who use drugs. *Nursing Inquiry, 17*, 336–345.

Substance Abuse and Mental Health Services Administration. (2014). SAMHSA's concept of trauma and guidance for a trauma-informed approach. *HHS publication no. (SMA) 14-4884.* Substance Abuse and Mental Health Services Administration.

Tronto, J. C. (1993). *Moral boundaries: A political argument for an ethic of care.* Routledge.

Williamson, E., Gregory, A., Abrahams, H., Aghtaie, N., Walker, S.-J., & Hester, M. (2020). Secondary trauma: Emotional safety in sensitive research. *Journal of Academic Ethics, 18*, 55–70.

Chapter 14

Co-production in Refugee Research: Navigating Power Dynamics

Fayrouz Al Haj Moussa and Claire Hart

Department of Social Work, Education and Community Wellbeing (SWECW), Northumbria University, UK

Abstract

Refugees are often underrepresented in health and social care research, which in turn can undermine their representation and involvement in the provision of services. Refugee research can be multilayered and complex with challenges that are both explicit and hidden. In order to understand the inherent challenges, we explore the core theme of power and its influence in refugee research. Power imbalances are embedded in many aspects of the lives of refugees, and this can be echoed in the dynamics of research. Power can be experienced through the history, structures, and practice of knowledge production; it can be seen in the exclusion of marginalised voices, and it can be played out in the processes and structures of research partnerships. Within this chapter, researchers are encouraged to challenge the many barriers to inclusion for refugees and address the role of power dynamics in research. Co-produced research, whilst presenting its own difficulties, has enormous potential to create meaningful and situated shared knowledge which enhances the voice and presence of refugees. However, unless researchers challenge their own need for power and address the structural power that surrounds them, they risk exacerbating existing power imbalances.

Keywords: Co-production; refugees; forced migration; power; inequality; meaningful engagement

---

Public Involvement and Community Engagement in Applied Health and Social Care Research: Critical Perspectives and Innovative Practice, 169–180

Introduction

Research promoting public involvement, co-production, and community engagement (PICE) is of growing importance in addressing health and well-being concerns (National Institute for Health and Care Research, 2020). Despite researchers' efforts to engage members of the public, health research continues to minimise the voices of minoritised populations, often due to a lack of researcher awareness, capacity, or funding (Fiske et al., 2019). This has particular importance in health, as services purport to be evidence-based, yet some of the most vulnerable communities, including refugees, are absent from the evidence on which practice is based (Amann & Sleigh, 2021).

In order to design healthcare that is 'fit for purpose', evidence needs to reflect the insights, values, and experiences of diverse populations (Amann & Sleigh, 2021). Public involvement ensures that evidence reflects the real world of those most effected by health inequalities, ensuring their representation (Fiske et al., 2019). Refugees are defined as having a well-founded fear of persecution, leading to their involuntary movement from their home region. They also have complex, often unmet, health needs, and are frequently absent from health research evidence (Harley & Wazefadost, 2023). Research involving refugees includes all the complex linguistic, ethical, methodological and analytical challenges inherent in any cross-cultural study (Van de Vijver & Leung, 2021). However, research can be a particularly high-stakes activity for refugees resulting from power imbalances, legal precarity, and the politicisation of migration (Clark-Kazak, 2017).

Within this chapter we aim to reflect the core issues in refugee research relating to PICE. The breadth of ethical and practical issues inherent in refugee research are beyond the scope of this chapter, and we refer readers to works exploring these in greater detail (Clark-Kazak, 2017; Global Compact on Refugees, 2024; IASFM, 2018). Instead, we introduce the principles of co-production in refugee research, focussing on the influence of power on researchers, partners, and researched populations.

Undertaking Co-produced Research with Refugees

Participatory research methods, such as co-production, are growing in popularity in migration research due to their potential to engage participants, improve the relevance of findings, and enhance academic rigour (Global Compact on Refugees, 2024). The concept of co-production was introduced in the USA in the 1970s and 1980s by academic economist Elinor Ostrom and civil rights lawyer Edgar Cahn. They recognised how engagement between service providers and recipients improved outcomes in their respective fields (Cahn, 2000; Ostrom, 1996).

It has proved difficult to achieve a unified definition of co-production, as the concept is described as 'slippery', 'woolly', and 'muddled' (Oliver et al., 2019). However, all definitions encompass the principles of actively engaging stakeholders throughout the research process in order to work in partnership towards shared discovery (National Institute for Health and Care Research, 2024; Lokot & Wake, 2021).

In health and social care, co-production forms part of a 'participatory zeitgeist', capturing the spirit of service improvement through empowerment

(Palmer et al., 2019). Health research increasingly reflects the principles of power sharing, inclusion, respect, building and maintaining relationships, and reciprocity (National Institute for Health and Care Research, 2024). Support for collaborative research is strong, with multiple gains identified for both researcher and participant. These include interpersonal gains such as enhanced trust, capacity building, and skills development, and improvements to the quality of the research evidence due to increased reflexivity, meaningful and accurate data, and sustainable outcomes (Lokot & Wake, 2021).

Crucially for minoritised populations, like refugees, co-production has the potential to tackle unequal power dynamics and challenge the dominant hierarchies in knowledge production (Pincock & Bakunzi, 2021). Instead of a researcher led enquiry there is an exchange of ideas, through 'dialogical teaching and learning' rather than extraction (Marzi, 2023, p. 4). Findings are therefore meaningfully 'situated' in the context of the participant, so that what is learnt together has greater meaning and potential for application to practice (National Institute for Health Research, 2020).

Power and PICE

Researching refugee lives often centres on issues of power. Power imbalances are embedded in many aspects of the lives of refugees and can be echoed in the dynamics of the research process. Here we explore several key aspects of power in the use of PICE for refugee research, including issues associated with knowledge production, the underlying disempowerment of refugees, the role of 'voice' in research, and the importance of partnership working.

Power and Knowledge Production

Much could be said here about the power dynamics in knowledge and research, which can vary from epistemological values to practical application. Participatory research may be more challenging for researchers than many traditional research methods, as it demands greater awareness of power dynamics, reflection and a willingness to relinquish control (Hernando-Jorge et al., 2024). True partnership working requires researchers to reconsider strongly held epistemological beliefs, challenge systemic and institutional norms and relinquish their power, all of which can be personally and professionally difficult.

The researcher, who may have fought hard to achieve status and an element of control, must surrender this, humble themselves and tolerate the discomfort of 'not knowing' in their work (Albert et al., 2023). Instead, they must desire collective knowledge creation and embrace 'other(ed)' ways of knowing (Thambinathan & Kinsella, 2021). Once they have undertaken this personal shift, they are likely to see the structural challenges inherent in traditional academic settings.

The research context and process contain multiple barriers to co-production driven by imbalances in power. On an epistemological level, there are calls to decolonise research by acknowledging, challenging, and minimising Eurocentric research methods that undermine the knowledge and experiences of marginalised populations (Keikelame & Swartz, 2019). This is a moral imperative, particularly when working with populations oppressed by colonial legacies; however, this can be particularly challenging in a Western/Northern academic context, which is characterised by the control of so many core elements of research, such as ethics, funding and other structural expectations (Thambinathan & Kinsella, 2021). Researchers may be expected to uphold these traditions whilst navigating the need to release control to others, creating a complex interface between the institution, the researcher, and the researched.

On a practical level, the ways in which research is structured and funded in Northern academia directly limits opportunities for co-production and perpetuates existing power imbalances (Freedman et al., 2024). The systems employed to design, fund, conduct, and disseminate research all prioritise academic and institutional gains over equitable collaboration, which places non-academic partners and vulnerable participants/co-researchers at a disadvantage (Freedman et al., 2024). Knowledge production is typically 'top down' with core decisions 'locked in' early in order to secure funding, meaning than non-academic partners are often excluded at crucial points of the process (Shuayb & Brun, 2021).

Whilst the challenges are acknowledged, the role of power imbalances is particularly significant when working with disempowered groups, such as refugees. They are amongst the most underserved and unheard people in any research context (Fiske et al., 2019; Røhnebæk & Bjerck, 2021) and despite 80% of the world's refugees living in the Global South, the vast majority of research into their needs is conducted and published by scholars and organisations in the Global North (Mistry, 2024). This places the voice of refugees in the hands of privileged Northern academics, who decide what to study and fund, how to conduct the research, and how/where to disseminate findings (Mistry, 2024).

PICE has the potential to reduce harm and mitigate power imbalances within entrenched systems of inequality (Alexander et al., 2022; Shivakoti & Milner, 2022). However, if the researcher is to avoid perpetuating paternalistic or neo-colonial behaviour, partnerships need to be approached with sensitivity and care (Keikelame & Swartz, 2019; Thambinathan & Kinsella, 2021). Networks between parties, particularly in Global North and South collaborations, need to have tangible gains for all parties, addressing the additional resources required by researchers in the South, and fostering genuine, lasting solidarity (Shivakoti & Milner, 2022).

A Disempowered Population

Power is a feature of all research, but arguably, refugees and people facing forced migration are amongst the most disempowered populations being researched (Radl-Karimi, 2020). Their experiences before, during, and after flight are characterised by high levels of exclusion, marginalisation, and passivity, which can be echoed within the research process. Power issues arise from the lack of presence of refugees within research and the influence of polarising narratives.

The decision to undertake co-produced research with refugees requires attention to a number of issues affecting participant involvement for authentic partnership working, and the creation of safe and democratic research 'spaces' to promote discourse (IASFM, 2018). Given the potential safety risks for refugee participants, which can include stigma, physical harm and legal issues such as deportation, safety is likely to be a significant barrier to active participation (Amann & Sleigh, 2021).

Creating a safe space can take many forms, but should include environment, pace, and communication to ensure physical, psychological, and cultural safety (Harley & Wazefadost, 2021). Each participant in each study will have unique safety needs, which may be unexpected, hidden, nuanced and may change during the research process (IASFM, 2018; Pincock & Bakunzi, 2021). Ideally, research should be beneficial to all involved parties, yet it is frequently most beneficial to the researcher (IASFM, 2018). Taking time to identify potential gains, such as skill development and financial remuneration is valuable (Freedman et al., 2024), and time taken to understand the motivating factors of potential participants can be an important part of ensuring the research process is meaningful and not exploitative.

The desire to protect research participants can be unwittingly disempowering, and assumptions about the perceived vulnerability of refugees can further rob them of agency, hindering their attempts to take ownership in studies (Amann & Sleigh, 2021). Giving voice to a disempowered population requires us to enable refugees to shape their own dialogue (Røhnebæk & Bjerck, 2021). It can be tempting for researchers to assume that the focus of refugee research should be on narratives of loss, victimhood, and deprivation. Similarly, there is a drive to portray a counter-narrative of resilience and the 'model minority' (Radl-Karimi et al., 2020; Røhnebæk & Bjerck, 2021). Both of these reductionist narratives can shape the direction of research, influencing the formulation of research questions, analysis, and conclusions. Working in co-production enables a more nuanced and varied message based on real lives, real challenges and real capacity, challenging the labels of vulnerability.

It takes time and sensitivity to create a supportive dialogue, and the skills required are not ubiquitous. The researcher needs to show flexibility (Marzi, 2023), leadership (Lokot & Wake, 2021), and emotional intelligence (Hernando-Jorge et al., 2024). Only when a safe space has been constructed is the potential for collaborative knowledge production truly maximised (Albert et al., 2023). We would recommend adopting what Carl Roger's defined as the 'core conditions' of a safe relationship – *empathy, congruence* and *unconditional positive regard* (Rogers, 1950). By taking time to consider the perspective of the participant, at depth, it becomes easier to see the risks and challenges they face, and responding with empathy to their needs makes them feel held and understood. Congruence is a form of honesty, and is fostered through open communication and clearly defined roles and responsibilities. Finally, unconditional regard ensures that all participants are valued and acknowledged as knowledge creators (Harley & Wazefadost, 2023). These three 'states' create conditions in which parties feel understood, well informed, and secure; they are treated with dignity and respect, and can trust the people and the process (Pincock & Bakunzi, 2021).

Power and 'Giving Voice'

If the researcher seeks to widely represent refugees in research, they need to consider the 'voicelessness' of many refugees as a significant power imbalance. Refugees are certainly under-represented, and despite being the most affected by policy decisions, they are the least involved in the policy-making process (Mistry, 2024).

Involvement should include consideration of '*who?*' and '*when?*'. By asking 'who is not here?' on a regular basis, the researcher can ensure their work has greater representation, explicitly reporting gaps and acknowledging the implications of absent groups (Cin et al., 2024; Turnhout et al., 2020). Giving voice to refugee communities is complex, in particular because there is no unified refugee voice (Harley & Wazefadost, 2023) as there is enormous diversity of experience between people with different demographics, such as age, gender, ethnicity, or faith. Additionally, refugees may have other differences related specifically to forced migration, such as legal status, living circumstances, and number of years in exile, which can create major differences in need and experience (Røhnebæ & Bjerck, 2021; Shuayb & Brun, 2021). Inviting the 'right' voices to enrich research requires the researcher to be transparent about their process and navigate the heterogeneity across refugee groups in order to be genuinely inclusive (Radl-Karimi et al., 2020; Røhnebæ & Bjerck, 2021). Within refugees groups, there are people who are 'hard to reach' amongst the 'hard to reach', making it difficult to represent those beyond the more vocal and capable (Cin et al., 2024; National Institute for Health Research, 2020). The most 'available' people are often sought for multiple studies, meaning that their voices could be amplified at the expense of others, with some people experiencing research fatigue and others being excluded and under-researched (Lokot & Zreik, 2024).

In answer to the question '*when?*', it is clear that refugees should be present as active partners throughout the research process, not once the key decisions have been made (Cin et al., 2024; Turnhout et al., 2020). Often co-production is 'retro-fitted' into the project when it should be *designed* into the project to ensure that involvement is an explicit feature of the study (Lokot & Zreik, 2024). Another feature of giving voice to participants lies in language. Language is not a neutral backdrop to research as languages are often afforded a great deal of power (Squires et al., 2020). Undertaking research across language barriers may be an essential part of the access agenda in line with PICE principles, ensuring that research reflects the widening diversity in our communities; however, non-English speakers are often excluded from participating in research (Egilsson et al., 2022). This can be because researchers do not see the relevance of including them, do not feel skilled enough or do not have the funds to support interpreters, or because limited guidance is available (Nikulina et al., 2019). It is impossible to undertake cross-cultural research without attention to linguistic barriers and willingness to address them (Squires et al., 2020). This injects another layer of complexity, planning and cost for the researcher, without which they are automatically excluding large groups of potential participants. Providing interpreters and translated materials is an obvious start. However, this does not automatically solve all linguistic problems, and attention should be paid to conceptual equivalence across dialects, continuity across multiple interpreters, interpreter influence, and the loss of subtle meaning (Egilsson et al., 2022). In addition, researchers need to ensure that invitations reach people who do not speak the dominant language, and undertake robust reflexivity to identify and challenge biases (Squires et al., 2020).

Working in co-production is reliant on the ability to understand and be understood, with language as the primary means of conveying subtle and often abstract messages. The principles of co-production, if applied effectively have the potential to enhance understanding and broaden the researchers' awareness of the multiple linguistic influences that shape the messages they receive (Squires et al., 2020). The aim is to create linguistic equality (Nikulina et al., 2019), which requires both openness to the impact of language and willingness to address the challenges it creates. Arguably, the process of managing language and giving voice is best undertaken in collaboration. By making all relationships explicit and being clear about roles and expectations it is possible to minimise power dynamics and develop the participatory roles of interpreters as co-researchers (Egilsson et al., 2022). Like all relationships in co-production, interpreters inhabit a delicate and complex position; they can be powerful, pressured and vulnerable (Radl-Karimi, 2020; Tiselius, 2019). In co-produced studies the role of the interpreter should be developed, with recognition that they are a valuable asset to the research process (Radl-Karimi, 2020).

Power and Partnership

Co-production is a partnership activity, but the process of engagement is complex. Partner organisations can provide essential cultural brokerage, enabling access to a wide range of people who might otherwise be inaccessible to the researcher. However, the precarious, rapidly changing, underfunded nature of refugee services and organisations; coupled with multiple stakeholders, social/political sensitivities, and entrenched power hierarchies, all place the community partners in a vulnerable place from which to negotiate their needs (Freedman et al., 2024; Lokot & Wake, 2021). Whilst they create valuable points of access, they may also select participants/co-researchers that align with their own perspectives or are not wholly representative of the wider community (Lokot & Zreik, 2024). Agencies and organisations will each have their own agendas, which, if not understood and explored, can shape the power dynamics, creating gatekeeper roles that limit engagement (Gibbes & Skop, 2020).

Despite all the potential benefits of co-production with partner agencies or groups the complexities can make a win-win outcome difficult to achieve and somewhat idealised (Gibbes & Skop, 2020). Instead, co-production partnerships require tentative alliances and considerable compromise (Shivakoti & Milner, 2022). It requires the willingness to recognise and disrupt power hierarchies, accept the messiness of the research process and the unpredictability of outcomes. Practical approaches, such as the avoidance of formal titles, the use of diverse methods (such as small group discussions and limiting the reliance on language through the use of creative approaches), can help to flatten the hierarchy and prioritise input from those without power positions (Lokot & Wake, 2021). In partnerships, it may not always be possible to fully or instantly enact all co-production principles, and researchers should embrace the principles as an ongoing journey rather than a final result (Gibbes & Skop, 2020; Lokot & Wake, 2021).

Partnerships often fail to prioritise the outcomes of the most vulnerable party in order to meet the controls and outcomes favoured by Northern academics (Alexander et al., 2022). In response, Shivakoti and Milner (2022) advocate for a shift from partnerships to supporting localised knowledge production, providing support and funding to institutions and groups in situ, who have contextual knowledge. This is both feasible and beneficial, addressing existing inequalities and broadening perspectives in refugee research (Shivakoti & Milner, 2022).

Recommendations for Co-production in Refugee Research

There are many practical recommendations for conducting co-produced research, including chapters within this text. In addressing co-production within refugee research, we recommend the contributions of the Global Compact on Refugees (2024), Mistry (2024), and Harley and Wazefadost (2023) for their ability to highlight best practices. Our personal recommendations focus on the researcher's development to address the personal and structural challenges ahead through a mixture of humility and courage.

Humility may seem an unexpected suggestion for academic roles that are often steeped in ideas of status and power. Researchers are encouraged to elevate their role and status in research in order to meet the demands of the sector. However, this undermines the heuristic process and thrusts the researcher into the burdensome and impossible role of 'expert' in the lives of others.

The need to be unknowing and inexpert is often uncomfortable, but it is the very essence of discovery, as we must be willing to tolerate the unknown so that we don't only find out what we already know. Phenomenologist Clark Moustakas described this process as akin to the way we locate an empty seat in a dark theatre – the sense of feeling our way and using clues to locate what we need to find (Moustakas, 1990). Disempowering ourselves is a privilege because it is a choice. It is the first step towards solidarity and the acknowledgement of others' expertise and knowledge.

Another personal development that is clearly valued in the literature on co-production lies is positionality and reflexivity. The ability to set aside judgements in research is contentious, but understanding one's influences, biases, and perspectives can be a valuable step. Taking time before, during and after a project supports the development of critical reflection. We would urge you to explore varied ways of engaging in reflexivity, the more creative and exploratory the better. Engaging in any activity designed to turn the attention inward enables the researcher to explore their response to power, enhance their accountability and understand how their identities, preconceptions and motivations may affect the research process and findings (Harley & Wazefadost, 2023; Lenette, 2022).

It takes courage to humble oneself, but here we are asking you to be courageous on behalf of others. We have described many systemic challenges facing the researcher, and having the courage to name the injustices and barriers that impede PICE is crucial. Researchers, especially early career or novice researchers, rarely have real power to effect change, but they have evidence of the value of co-production, and often soft skills to persuade others. Organisations may say 'no' as a matter of course, but when information is presented in a compelling form, and with enough voices, they will frequently find a way to make things happen. Use networks, the power of expert peers and the evidence base to convince others of the validity of PICE, and do not shy away from naming approaches as unjust and discriminatory.

Conclusion

Co-production in research with refugees and people experiencing forced migration is a nuanced and complex process, but one with the potential to reduce the power imbalances inherent in refugee research. It does not, however, guarantee a win–win outcome or the reduction of existing inequalities and power hierarchies (Freedman et al., 2024; Gibbes & Skop, 2020). Pincock and Bakunzi (2021) highlight how power relations are often overlooked in co-produced refugee research, masking underlying power imbalances and leading to symbolic or tokenistic involvement (Freedman et al., 2024).

Through the process of preparing this chapter we have identified multiple strands of power related challenges and explored the potential of co-production as a means of addressing them. There are inherent power challenges in being a refugee, being part of an academic structure, working in partnership and undertaking knowledge production. All of these have the potential to derail attempts at co-production, undermining voices, reducing safety and creating disharmony.

Our key messages hinge of the researchers' abilities in relationship building and reflexivity. Without the capacity to build, manage and maintain respectful, honest and genuinely collaborative connections with partners and co-researchers the research is doomed to fail. Without understanding ones biases, being open to different perspectives and undertaking honest reflexive exploration, the power challenges will remain unaddressed.

The breadth of experiences in the lives of refugees and the socio-political structures in which they live can make it extremely difficult to capture evidence that is meaningful. The researcher bias can cloud their vision, leading the research direction and reducing the opportunity for genuine discovery. Their fears can lead them to employ well-meaning protections against perceived vulnerabilities, which undermine the presence of the co-researching refugee. A desire for control can create a tussle between stakeholders, without recognising that all parties may wish to control the process and achieve their own outcomes.

The answers lie in the foundation principles of co-production: power sharing, inclusion, respect, building and maintaining relationships, and reciprocity (National Institute for Health and Care Research, 2024). The researcher needs to begin by seeing the context from multiple perspectives in order to adopt the role of informed facilitator (Nikulina et al., 2019). The process of partnership requires an understanding of each member organisation or individuals' motivations, navigating the gap between the needs of participants and partners and the demands of academic structures. By investing in core relationship goals through open, trusting and respectful engagement it becomes possible to create the safe and collaborative spaces needed for all parties to be heard and seen (Albert et al., 2023).

References

Albert, A., Islam, S., Haklay, M., & McEachan, R. R. C. (2023). Nothing about us without us: A co-production strategy for communities, researchers and stakeholders to identify ways of improving health and reducing inequalities. *Health Expectations: An International Journal of Public Participation in Health Care and Health Policy, 26*(2), 836–846.

Alexander, H., Baroud, M., Gezahegne, K., Kassak, K., Mourad, Y., Nameh, N., Nyaouro, D., Oucho, L., & Soufan, Z. (2022). *Moments of negotiated independence: Localized knowledge ecosystems on forced migration in East Africa and the Middle East.* LERRN: Local Engagement Refugee Research Network. https://carleton. ca/lerrn/wp-content/uploads/LERRN-Working-Paper-20-Localized-Knowledge-Ecosystems-Alexander-et-al.pdf

Amann, J., & Sleigh, J. (2021). Too vulnerable to involve? Challenges of engaging vulnerable groups in the co-production of public services through research. *International Journal of Public Administration, 44*(9), 715–727.

Cahn, E. S. (2000). *No more throw-away people: The co-production imperative.* Essential Books.

Cin, F. M., Süleymanoğlu-Kürüm, R., Walker, C., Truter, L., Doğan, N., Gunter, A., & Cin, M. M. (2024). The politics of co-production and inclusive deliberation in participatory research. *International Journal of Social Research Methodology, 28*(4), 475–490.

Clark-Kazak, C. (2017). Ethical considerations: Research with people in situations of forced migration. *Refuge, 33*(2), 11–17.

Egilsson, B. R., Dockett, S., & Einarsdóttir, J. (2022). Methodological and ethical challenges in cross-language qualitative research: The role of interpreters. *European Early Childhood Education Research Journal, 30*(4), 638–652.

Fiske, A., Prainsack, B., & Buyx, A. (2019). Meeting the needs of underserved populations: Setting the agenda for more inclusive citizen science of medicine. *Journal of Medical Ethics, 45*(9), 617–622.

Freedman, J., Crankshaw, T. L., Rajah, Y., & Mutambara, V. M. (2024). "But we just need money": (Im)Possibilities of co-producing knowledge with those in vulnerable situations. *Social Inclusion, 12*, Article 8818.

Gibbes, C., & Skop, E. (2020). The messiness of co-produced research with gatekeepers of resettled refugee communities. *Journal of Cultural Geography, 37*(3), 278–295.

Global Compact on Refugees. (2024). Good practices: Building inclusive research practices. Retrieved September 17, 2024, from https://globalcompactrefugees.org/good-practices/building-inclusive-research-practices

Harley, T., & Wazefadost, N. (2023). *Guidelines for co-produced research with refugees and other people with lived experience of displacement.* Kaldor Centre for International Refugee Law, Asia Pacific Network of Refugees and Act for Peace.

Hernando-Jorge, L., Fernández-Mesa, A., Azagra-Caro, J. M., Tur-Porcar, A. M. (2024, August 9). Personality and emotional intelligence of researchers: The importance of affects. *PLoS ONE, 19*(8), e0304905. https://doi.org/10.1371/journal.pone.0304905

IASFM. (2018). *Code of ethics: Critical reflections on research ethics in situations of forced migration.* https://iasfm.org/wp-content/uploads/2018/11/IASFM-Research-Code-of-Ethics-2018.pdf#:~:text=Code%20of%20ethics:%20Critical%20reflections%20on

Keikelame, M. J., & Swartz, L. (2019). Decolonising research methodologies: Lessons from a qualitative research project, Cape Town, South Africa. *Global Health Action, 12*(1), 1561175. https://doi.org/10.1080/16549716.2018.1561175

Lenette, C. (2022). Cultural safety in participatory arts-based research: How can we do better? *Journal of Participatory Research Methods, 3*(1), 1–16.

Lokot, M., & Wake, C. (2021). *The co-production of research between academics, NGOs and communities in humanitarian response: A practice guide.* London School of Hygiene and Tropical Medicine.

Lokot, M., & Zreik, T. (2024). Research co-production within humanitarian health: Reflections on our practice. *International Review of Qualitative Research, 17*(4), 467–492.

Marzi, S. (2023). Participatory video from a distance: Co-producing knowledge during the COVID-19 pandemic using smartphones. *Qualitative Research: QR, 23*(3), 509–525.

Mistry, P. (2024). *Co-production of knowledge in forced migration studies: An interdisciplinary analysis of challenges and the possibilities for the emergence of best practices.* Carleton University. Retrieved October 1, 2024, from https://carleton.ca/lerrn/wp-content/uploads/WorkingPaper_21.pdf

Moustakas, C. E. (1990). *Heuristic research: Design, methodology, and applications.* Sage Publications.

National Institute for Health and Care Research. (2020). Improving inclusion of under-served groups in clinical research: Guidance from the NIHR INCLUDE project, *UK.* Retrieved January 28, 2021, from www.nihr.ac.uk/documents/improving-inclusion-of-under-served-groups-in-clinical-research-guidance-from-include-project/25435

National Institute for Health and Care Research. (2024). *Guidance on co-producing a research project.* https://www.learningforinvolvement.org.uk/content/resource/nihr-guidance-on-co-producing-a-research-project/

Nikulina, V., Larson Lindal, J., Baumann, H., Simon, D., & Ny, H. (2019). Lost in translation: A framework for analysing complexity of co-production settings in relation to epistemic communities, linguistic diversities and culture. *Futures: The Journal of Policy, Planning and Futures Studies, 113*, 102442.

Oliver, K., Kothari, A., & Mays, N. (2019). The dark side of coproduction: Do the costs outweigh the benefits for health research?*Health Research Policy and Systems, 17*(1), 33–43.

Ostrom, E. (1996). Crossing the great divide: Coproduction, synergy, and development. *World Development, 24*(6), 1073–1087.

Palmer, V. J., Weavell, W., Callander, R., Piper, D., Richard, L., Maher, L., Boyd, H., Herrman, H., Furler, J., Gunn, J., Iedema, R., & Robert, G. (2019). The participatory zeitgeist: An explanatory theoretical model of change in an era of coproduction and codesign in healthcare improvement. *Medical Humanities, 45*(3), 247–257.

Pincock, K., & Bakunzi, W. (2021). Power, participation, and 'peer researchers': Addressing gaps in refugee research ethics guidance. *Journal of Refugee Studies, 34*(2), 2333–2348.

Radl-Karimi, C., Nicolaisen, A., Sodemann, M., Batalden, P., & von Plessen, C. (2020). Under what circumstances can immigrant patients and healthcare professionals co-produce health? – An interpretive scoping review. *International Journal of Qualitative Studies on Health and Well-being, 15*(1), 1838052–1838052.

Røhnebæk, M., & Bjerck, M. (2021). Enabling and constraining conditions for co-production with vulnerable users: A case study of refugee services. *International Journal of Public Administration, 44*(9), 741–752.

Shivakoti, R., & Milner, J. (2022). Beyond the partnership debate: Localizing knowledge production in refugee and forced migration studies. *Journal of Refugee Studies, 35*(2), 805–826.

Shuayb, M., & Brun, C. (2021). Carving out space for equitable collaborative research in protracted displacement. *Journal of Refugee Studies, 34*(3), 2539–2553.

Squires, A., Sadarangani, T., & Jones, S. (2020). Strategies for overcoming language barriers in research. *Journal of Advanced Nursing, 76*(2), 706–714.

Thambinathan, V., & Kinsella, E. A. (2021). Decolonizing methodologies in qualitative research: Creating spaces for transformative praxis. *International Journal of Qualitative Methods, 20*. https://doi.org/10.1177/16094069211014766.

Tiselius, E. (2019). The (un-) ethical interpreting researcher: Ethics, voice and discretionary power in interpreting research. *Perspectives, Studies in Translatology, 27*(5), 747–760.

Turnhout, E., Metze, T., Wyborn, C., Klenk, N., & Louder, E. (2020). The politics of co-production: Participation, power, and transformation. *Current Opinion in Environmental Sustainability, 42*, 15–21.

Van de Vijver, F. J., & Leung, K. (2021). *Methods and data analysis for cross-cultural research*. Cambridge University Press.

Warnock, R., Taylor, F. M., & Horton, A. (2022). Should we pay research participants? Feminist political economy for ethical practices in precarious times. *Area (London 1969), 54*(2), 195–202.

Section 4

Parents–Carers–Adolescents and Children's Perspectives of PICE Work

Chapter 15

Involving Children and Young People Who Experience Parental Substance Use in Research

Cassey Muir[a] and Kira Terry[b]

[a]*Population Health Sciences Institute, Newcastle University, Newcastle upon Tyne, United Kingdom*
[b]*Young Person Advisory Group, Newcastle University, Newcastle upon Tyne, United Kingdom*

Abstract

Parental substance use is highly prevalent worldwide, presenting major child safeguarding and public health concerns. Evidence-based interventions aim to reduce risk to the child through primarily focussing on the parent, often overlooking the specific needs of children and young people. Partnership approaches to intervention development, from consultation to co-production with public members, are needed in designing interventions for children and young people who experience parental substance use. Within this chapter, an example of involving children and young people with experience of parental alcohol and/or drug use in research and intervention development will be provided. There will be an acknowledgement of the tension between the importance of active involvement of children and young people in research that concerns their well-being, and the recognition that children and young people may experience additional vulnerabilities or risks. The chapter will conclude with four steps to providing opportunities for enhancing young people's agency in public involvement research. There needs to be a shift from viewing young people as vulnerable or risky due to their experience of adversity or parental substance

Public Involvement and Community Engagement in Applied Health and Social Care Research: Critical Perspectives and Innovative Practice, 183–193

use, to viewing young people as capable of being change agents. This is all whilst acknowledging the real sense that young people may need external support and assistance, but this should be carefully navigated with the young people themselves.

Keywords: Children; young people; parental substance use; intervention development; co-production; public health; public involvement and engagement; agency

Introduction

Prevalence estimates of parental substance use vary globally it is suggested that between 2% and 37% of children live with at least one parent who uses substances problematically (European Monitoring Centre for Drugs and Drug Addiction, 2008; Galligan & Comiskey, 2019). For this chapter, parental substance use includes the problematic use of alcohol and/or illicit drugs, as well as the misuse of prescription drugs by one or both parents or formal caregivers. Many of these children and young people go on to experience a wide range of physical, behavioural, emotional, and social impacts due to parental substance use (McGovern et al., 2018, 2023; Muir, Adams, et al., 2023; Velleman & Templeton, 2016). Systematic reviews exploring the evidence-based interventions to alleviate the impact on children and young people, found that interventions tend to focus on the parent who uses substances, with the aim of reducing risk to the child (McGovern, Newham, et al., 2021, Moreland & McRae-Clark, 2018). Whilst these interventions showed some positive affect on child outcomes, the reviews concluded that child-targeted interventions were also needed to address the lasting impact of substance use. Currently, child and young person-focussed interventions are limited and have mixed and low-evidence of effect (Barrett et al., 2023; McGovern, Smart, et al., 2021). Research has also shown that there are limited interventions that have been co-produced with multiple stakeholders in a power sharing approach, especially involving children and young people with lived and living experience of parental substance use (Barrett et al., 2023).

The Medical Research Council framework for complex interventions recognises intervention development as the first of a series of interconnected steps in the development-evaluation-implementation process (Craig et al., 2008; Skivington et al., 2021), but this framework lacks sufficient detail and specificity to inform intervention development. A recently published taxonomy of approaches to developing interventions outlines eight separate categories for development, inclusive of partnership or population-centred approaches (i.e., active partnership with end-users), evidence and theory-based approaches (i.e., using existing evidence), implementation or efficiency-based approaches (i.e., does it work in the real world), stepped approaches (i.e., taking a systematic process), intervention-specific (purposefully developed for a specific intervention) or combination approaches (i.e., combining existing approaches; O'Cathain, Croot, Sworn, et al., 2019). The partnership approach involves active engagement of stakeholders, including the public, in developing interventions, throughout the whole process from decision making to design, which can facilitate the development of feasible, efficacious, and context-sensitive interventions (Voorberg et al., 2015). Partnership methods can range from consultation to co-design and co-production (O'Cathain, Croot, Duncan, et al., 2019). Throughout our research, we endeavour for active involvement, where we recognise and use the skills, knowledge, and expertise of those with lived and living experience, going beyond developing interventions 'for' to developing interventions 'with' relevant public members (Slay & Stevens, 2013). To ensure that newly developed interventions supporting children and young people whose parents use substances are relevant and acceptable, it is important that their voices are included in the decision-making and priority-setting process, as well as in the later stages of designing and refining the intervention. Within this chapter, an example of involving children and young people with experience of parental substance use in research and intervention development will be provided. There will be an acknowledgement of the tension regarding the involvement of children and young people in research, and we will reflect on our practice of providing opportunities for enhancing young people's agency.

Involving Children and Young People Who Experience Parental Substance Use

Our project was concerned with understanding the experiences of children and young people whose parents use substances and how to support them, from the children and young people's point of view as well as those who provide the support. We started with reviewing worldwide literature, then talking to and involving children and young people who live in England. We aimed to develop resources that would be of most benefit to children and young people who experience parental substance use. Our research was conducted across four stages from January 2019 until January 2024, we (1) reviewed international qualitative studies, (2) interviewed young people and practitioners, (3) ran prioritisation workshops with young people and practitioners, and (4) used co-design workshops, focussed on co-producing interventions for children and young people who experience parental substance use. Throughout each stage of this research, we took a flexible approach and involved different groups of children and young people who had lived or living experience of parental substance use. This approach allowed us to gather increasingly diverse perspectives, whilst also acknowledging a key challenge in researching with young people who experience parental substance use: the temporary nature of accessing services (from which researchers typically recruit) and the issue of ageing out of services. As a result, the same group of young people were not always available or able to be involved continuously in our research. However, young advisors reassured us that this was entirely acceptable.

Firstly, we reviewed the qualitative literature to understand how children and young people experience and are impacted by parental substance use (Muir, Adams, et al., 2023). We involved four young people (aged 11–17 years) who helped us to understand the problem, define key concepts, and make sense of the findings. Secondly, we interviewed young people and practitioners to understand how to support young people who experience parental substance use (Muir, Terry, et al., 2023). We involved four young people (aged 17–24 years) who supported the recruitment, analysis, and dissemination of findings. Thirdly, through workshops, we determined the top three intervention ideas and priorities for support. About 13 young people (aged 12–24 years) were involved in the decision-making and priority-setting workshops alongside health, education, and social care practitioners. Fourthly, we co-produced the top priority intervention with and for children and young people who experience parental substance use. There were seven children (aged 5–13 years) and two young people (18–25 years) involved in the co-production of a social and emotional well-being storybook for children who experience parental substance use, to be used in a school setting.

Children and Young People's Agency

The theoretical assumption underpinning much of public involvement and engagement is that communities of people, however defined, possess agency in the sociological sense, that they have the ability to act and be agents of their own development and care needs. We acknowledge that agency can be bounded by many factors; however, we also recognised that if the starting point is that children are active agents, then as researchers, we needed to have the capacity to make opportunities available to them. However, involving children and young people in research is a widely debated issue, often based on the role of agency in young people's lives. On the one hand, there is an implicit or explicit view that children and young people are vulnerable and in need of protection (Hill et al., 2004). This is especially true for young people who experience family adversities (Kendrick et al., 2008), including parental substance use (Bancroft & Wilson, 2007). It is argued further that, due to this vulnerability, children can be seen as lacking the social or cognitive competence and agency to make informed decisions about their lives, and what care or support would be best for them (Hill et al., 2004). Additionally, Bancroft and Wilson (2007) argued that older children who experience parental substance use may become increasingly seen in policy, practice, and research as having and expressing agency that is problematic and risky. For example, young people may begin engaging in risky behaviours (e.g., drinking or offending) rather than ones that will be supportive of their development. We further argue that some young people move from experiencing associative stigma because they are closely connected with their parents who use alcohol or drugs to experiencing direct stigma and discrimination from peers, practitioners, and researchers connected to their own behaviours due to a negative perception of their character, behaviours, or abilities (Muir et al., 2022). This view implies that young people are not to be trusted to make the right or sensible decisions about their lives or care needs. In a societal context, children and young people who are not seen to be making an active contribution to their own well-being, community, functioning, and furthering of society are often villainised and labelled negatively as trouble (Rose, 1999). Whichever viewpoint, young people's involvement is often governed by the adults in their lives, who make decisions for them instead of with them, either seeing them as vulnerable and in need of protection or as a risk to themselves.

However, there is increasing recognition of the importance of the active participation of children and young people in research that concerns their care. The United Nations Convention on the Rights of the Child states that the views of children and young people should be taken into account in any decision that is likely to affect their well-being (United Nations, 1989). The World Health Organisation also recognises the importance of young people being included as active partners in all health-related activity, from design through to evaluation, especially for interventions impacting their own well-being (Clark et al., 2020). There has also been an increased interest from policy makers in acknowledging and learning from different perspectives, including children and young people with varied lived and living experiences (Involve, 2016). Whilst this is the intended direction for research and practice, a recent qualitative study found that young people who experience family adversity felt like they were not being listened to, valued, or having their needs met within support services (Stafford et al., 2021).

Taking a collaborative approach has shown to improve adaptation and tailoring of interventions and services to be appropriate for a specific context, whilst also identifying the barriers and facilitators critical for success (Leask et al., 2019). Furthermore, interventions are more likely to be acceptable, relevant, and focussed on changes that are most important to the population they seek to benefit (O'Cathain, Croot, Duncan, et al., 2019). Making decisions with, instead of for, young people has also increasingly been applied within research exploring support for families that experience adversities, for example, young people who experience parental domestic violence and abuse (Fellin et al., 2019) or multiple and interacting adversities (Muir et al., 2024). Involving children and young people in research and service design could promote benefits to young people's well-being, including enhancing their agency (Erwin et al., 2016; van Bijleveld et al., 2020).

Creating Opportunities for Agency in Public Involvement

During the research process, agency was identified by our young person advisory groups as a key theme in their experiences of parental substance use and seeking support. The qualitative review further highlighted that children and young people were not passive within their experiences of coping with parental substance use but often reported trying to 'control the situation' at home or within their family (Muir, Adams, et al., 2023). For example, children and young people spoke of ways they enacted agency by taking control of their environment and creating safe spaces for themselves and siblings to escape within an otherwise unsafe home. Within a similar field, Arai et al. (2021) conducted a qualitative systematic review of young people's experiences of domestic violence and abuse and found comparable themes on children's agency and coping, whereby children found creative and meaningful ways to change their situations. Additionally, during the interviews, young people reflected that having their agency acknowledged and built upon by practitioners led to reported increased confidence and self-esteem amongst young people (Muir, Terry, et al., 2023). The social value of increased confidence in children is important for many reasons, and young people wanted to negotiate safety and support alongside practitioners, be offered choices, and be supported to develop their agency. Allowing young people to tailor support to their needs was thought to be a useful approach to empower young people. Likewise, researchers within the field of domestic violence and abuse have argued that interventions should focus on supporting young people by enhancing the strengths they have developed due to living with violence and abuse and to recognise their need for agency (Fellin et al., 2019). We decided that this should also be an important aspect of our public involvement work, to create opportunities for agency amongst the children and young people involved in our research, where their agency may not have been acknowledged or had been problematised before.

The first step was ensuring we were researching what was relevant for children and young people, this was achieved by listening to the voice of children and actively engaging them in the research process. In some of our first young person advisory meetings we developed the research questions together. Young people identified that there was a need to understand what support young people are currently offered and what support they actually wanted. This became one of the main areas of our research, further supported by the qualitative review that identified a lack of access to formal support for young people who experience parental substance use (Muir, Adams, et al., 2023). By incorporating these research questions into our work, we were validating that these were real problems that children and young people faced and wanted effective and relevant solutions for. We also moved beyond listening and were prepared to engage children in difficult subject and topic areas as a way of understanding the lived experience and needs. We asked the question, 'how can we involve young people in the research process', from the initial set-up all the way through to dissemination. We were encouraged by the young advisors to be adaptive and continue asking that question as we went, allowing us to refine and change our approach along the way. It became significant to recognise that researchers need to be prepared to have difficult conversations with children and young people should the opportunity arise to engage in the details about their perspectives.

The second step was to provide flexibility in the opportunities for young people to engage and get involved. This was achieved by asking, listening to, and considering young people's concerns. We took into account how everyone wanted to get involved and provided them with choices and assured them that they could change their mind throughout the process. We were not prepared to simply let young people be 'passengers' or 'prisoners' in this research, being carried by others or being unable to speak their minds and give opinions. For example, we made our research as accessible as possible, and during online meetings with other young people, one young person had their camera off to begin with and asked if they could listen to others first before contributing. This allowed our co-producers to feel more comfortable, and they began actively participating in meetings after the first couple. Equality, diversity, and inclusion were a driving force for us, and all members were encouraged to contribute using their preferred communication style, either by talking aloud, writing in the group chat, or adding notes or images to the interactive resources. Another young person wanted to be involved but did not feel comfortable being in a group setting. They were provided with the notes from the group discussions and could add to this over email or in a one-to-one meeting. The group were also provided with the additional notes from this member. Additionally, all meeting times and frequency were agreed upon with the group, allowing flexibility in when and how often we would meet. Through this process, we acknowledged that young people were able to make decisions, and this validation helped them to act on their decisions by turning up to meetings.

The third step involved young people in specific decision-making about interventions and priority areas. This step recognised young people's ability to contribute to change for other children and young people in similar situations. Intervention ideas had been identified through qualitative interviews with young people and practitioners (Muir, Terry, et al., 2023). The ideas ranged from interventions for children and young people directly (e.g., school well-being lessons, digital applications, or podcasts) to interventions that would have indirect impacts, including support for parents, national stigma campaigns, or specialised training for health, social, and education practitioners. To make sense of these findings, we used co-production workshops and individual consultations to prioritise intervention ideas and understand young people's and practitioners' reasons for prioritisation. Young people's decisions were acknowledged and respected by practitioners and researchers, and one of the top priority ideas (i.e., a social and emotional well-being storybook resource to be used within primary schools) has since been co-designed with children to be tested in real-world settings.

Fourth and finally, we involved and trusted young people in the actual doing of research and co-designing of an intervention. We shared power with young people, where one young person became a co-investigator on the development of the prioritised intervention and other young advisers co-produced the children's storybook. We found creative methods helpful using exploration workshops with young children to come up with the character ideas and storylines, which were supported by a young person who helped facilitate the workshops. Art was used to help children express their thoughts and ideas with different activities including writing, drawing, and structured worksheets. Whilst the sessions were guided, children could choose to spend more time on certain activities if they preferred. The storybook, called 'Twinkle, Twinkle Arti', can be easily embedded into a classroom situation, where the teacher can facilitate age-appropriate discussion about how pupils think the main character is feeling and what might help them to feel better. As the book has been developed by children and young people, it can also help adults to understand the experience of parental substance use from a child's perspective. Storytelling, as an unstructured psychosocial intervention, has been found to be an effective way of delivering messages to younger children in an engaging manner that can encourage the sharing of problems and ideas (Bouchard et al., 2013). Additionally, storybooks can demonstrate positive responses for dealing with a complex problem, by signalling to children what to do if they feel similar to the main character (Bouchard et al., 2013). Storybooks could therefore facilitate conversations between a child and a trusted adult within the school, as well as whole-class discussions around bullying and talking to a safe adult, which could lead to enhanced social resilience (Tillott et al., 2022).

Using Negative Life Experiences for Positive Outcomes

The public involvement throughout this research allowed the children and young people to feel empowered and helped create positive outcomes for themselves and others. Reflecting on their involvement in the research process, a public contributor said:

> It has been an absolute honour to be involved as part of this project. To use my 'negative' life experience and be able to turn it into a positive impact for other children like me in the future: to help speak for those who feel they don't have a voice and aren't seen by people around them in the position they are in. Some children aren't ready, some don't want help, some we won't reach, but to push and be as present for as many children as possible, for as long as possible and to reduce the isolation of the stigma around it is vital.

> Hearing that there was funding to action the findings of the research was absolutely incredible. It was brilliant to be part of the research in the first place, to have my voice heard and really listened to, but to find out that there was then funding to be able to actually create a real life 'product' from the research findings, was the cherry on the top. To take the findings from our lived experience and create something real for families and people beyond the world of research. I gained experience of the process that goes into producing a children's book, which I wouldn't have ever come across otherwise. It has really brought about another positive, rewarding outcome from my hard life experience that still impacts me now. This book is something I would have loved to have been able to give to little me, having something that related to my home situation when I was a child. I feel rewarded to be able to do this for me now, for little me going through all those hard times, and for all the children who will read the book. To be able to show them that they are not alone and there are people around them who are there to give them love and support. To hopefully reach them earlier than I was reached out to. It is incredibly rewarding to have a book that exists, that will last and be passed on to different children who are in a variety of situations for years to come. I am very proud of it. (Female, aged 24)

Conclusion

Researchers, practitioners, and policymakers can either encourage or discourage a young person's sense of agency. Providing opportunities to develop and explore children and young people's own sense of agency, the capacity to act independently and make their own choices, during interactions with adults is vital for children and young people's development. It is important to remember children's involvement is more than just consulting with them for their ideas or views. It is about listening to them, taking them seriously, validating their opinions and views, allowing flexibility, trusting their decision making, and turning their ideas and suggestions into reality. It is also about providing children and young people with the opportunity and ability to influence some of the things that affect them and at the same time helping adults understand children and young people's issues through their lens. Researchers need to be brave and unafraid to have difficult conversations with children and there needs to be an equitable shift from viewing young people as vulnerable or risky due to their experience of adversity or parental substance use, to fairness, inclusion and justice where young people are recognised as capable of being change agents. This is all whilst acknowledging the real sense that young people may need external support and assistance, but this should be carefully navigated with the young people themselves.

References

Arai, L., Shaw, A., Feder, G., Howarth, E., Macmillan, H., Moore, T. H. M., Stanley, N., & Gregory, A. (2021). Hope, agency, and the lived experience of violence: A qualitative systematic review of children's perspectives on domestic violence and abuse. *Trauma, Violence, & Abuse, 22*, 427–438.

Bancroft, A., & Wilson, S. (2007). The 'risk gradient' in policy on children of drug and alcohol users: Framing young people as risky. *Health, Risk and Society, 9*, 311–322.

Barrett, S., Muir, C., Burns, S., Adjei, N., Forman, J., Hackett, S., Hirve, R., Kaner, E., Lynch, R., Taylor-Robinson, D., Wolfe, I., & McGovern, R. (2023). Interventions to reduce parental substance use, domestic violence and mental health problems, and their impacts upon children's well-being: A systematic review of reviews and evidence mapping. *Trauma, Violence, & Abuse, 25*, 393–412.

Bouchard, S., Gervais, J., Gagnier, N., & Loranger, C. (2013). Evaluation of a primary prevention program for anxiety disorders using story books with children aged 9–12 years. *Journal of Primary Prevention, 34*, 345–358.

Clark, H., Coll-Seck, A. M., Banerjee, A., Peterson, S., Dalglish, S. L., Ameratunga, S., Balabanova, D., Bhan, M. K., Bhutta, Z. A., Borrazzo, J., Claeson, M., Doherty, T., El-Jardali, F., George, A. S., Gichaga, A., Gram, L., Hipgrave, D. B., Kwamie, A., Meng, Q., ... Costello, A. (2020). A future for the world's children? A WHO-UNICEF-Lancet Commission. *The Lancet, 395*, 605–658.

Craig, P., Dieppe, P., Macintyre, S., Michie, S., Nazareth, I., & Petticrew, M. (2008). Developing and evaluating complex interventions: The new Medical Research Council guidance. *BMJ, 337*, a1655.

Erwin, E. J., Maude, S. P., Palmer, S. B., Summers, J. A., Brotherson, M. J., Haines, S. J., Stroup-Rentier, V., Zheng, Y., & Peck, N. F. (2016). Fostering the foundations of self-determination in early childhood: A process for enhancing child outcomes across home and school. *Early Childhood Education Journal, 44*, 325–333.

European Monitoring Centre for Drugs and Drug Addiction. (2008). *Drugs and vulnerable groups of young people, Selected issue.* European Union Drugs Agency.

Fellin, L. C., Callaghan, J. E., Alexander, J. H., Harrison-Breed, C., Mavrou, S., & Papathanasiou, M. (2019). Empowering young people who experienced domestic violence and abuse: The development of a group therapy intervention. *Clinical Child Psychology and Psychiatry, 24,* 170–189.

Galligan, K., & Comiskey, C. M. (2019). Hidden harms and the number of children whose parents misuse substances: A stepwise methodological framework for estimating prevalence. *Substance Use and Misuse, 54,* 1429–1437.

Hill, M., Davis, J., Prout, A., & Tisdall, K. (2004). Moving the participation agenda forward. *Children & Society, 18,* 77–96.

Involve, U. (2016). *Involving children and young people in research: Top tips and essential key issues for researchers.* National Institute for Health and Care Research.

Kendrick, A., Steckley, L., & Lerpiniere, J. (2008). Ethical issues, research and vulnerability: Gaining the views of children and young people in residential care. *Children's Geographies, 6,* 79–93.

Leask, C. F., Sandlund, M., Skelton, D. A., Altenburg, T. M., Cardon, G., Chinapaw, M. J. M., De Bourdeaudhuij, I., Verloigne, M., & Chastin, S. F. M. (2019). Framework, principles and recommendations for utilising participatory methodologies in the co-creation and evaluation of public health interventions. *Research Involvement and Engagement, 5,* 2.

McGovern, R., Bogowicz, P., Meader, N., Kaner, E., Alderson, H., Craig, D., Geijer-Simpson, E., Jackson, K., Muir, C., Salonen, D., Smart, D., & Newham, J. J. (2023). The association between maternal and paternal substance use and child substance use, internalizing and externalizing problems: A systematic review and meta-analysis. *Addiction, 118*(5), 804–818.

McGovern, R., Gilvarry, E., Addison, M., Alderson, H., Geijer-Simpson, E., Lingam, R., Smart, D., & Kaner, E. (2018). The association between adverse child health, psychological, educational and social outcomes and non-dependent parental substance: A rapid evidence assessment. *Trauma, Violence & Abuse, 21,* 470–483.

McGovern, R., Newham, J. J., Addison, M., Hickman, M., & Kaner, E. (2021). Effectiveness of psychosocial interventions for reducing parental substance misuse. *Cochrane Database of Systematic Reviews, 3,* CD012823.

McGovern, R., Smart, D., Alderson, H., Araújo-Soares, V., Brown, J., Buykx, P., Evans, V., Fleming, K., Hickman, M., Macleod, J., Meier, P., & Kaner, E. (2021). Psychosocial interventions to improve psychological, social and physical wellbeing in family members affected by an adult relative's substance use: A systematic search and review of the evidence. *International Journal of Environmental Research and Public Health, 18,* 1793.

Moreland, A. D., & McRae-Clark, A. (2018). Parenting outcomes of parenting interventions in integrated substance-use treatment programs: A systematic review. *Journal of Substance Abuse Treatment, 89,* 52–59.

Muir, C., Adams, E. A., Evans, V., Geijer-Simpson, E., Kaner, E., Phillips, S. M., Salonen, D., Smart, D., Winstone, L., & McGovern, R. (2023). A systematic review of qualitative studies exploring lived experiences, perceived impact, and coping strategies of children and young people whose parents use substances. *Trauma, Violence, & Abuse, 24,* 3629–3646.

Muir, C., Kedzior, S. G. E., Barrett, S., McGovern, R., Kaner, E., Wolfe, I., Forman, J. R., & On Behalf of The ORACLE Consortium. (2024). Co-design workshops with families experiencing multiple and interacting adversities including parental mental health, substance use, domestic violence, and poverty: Intervention principles and insights from mothers, fathers, and young people. *Research Involvement and Engagement, 10,* 67.

Muir, C., McGovern, R., & Kaner, E. (2022). Stigma and young people whose parents use substances. In M. Addison, W. McGovern, & R. McGovern (Eds.), *Drugs, identity and stigma* (pp. 173–196).. Palgrave Macmillan.

Muir, C., Terry, K., Kaner, E., & McGovern, R. (2023). OP56 Qualitative study on the support needs of young people who experience parental substance use. *Journal of Epidemiology and Community Health, 77*, A28–A28.

O'Cathain, A., Croot, L., Duncan, E., Rousseau, N., Sworn, K., Turner, K. M., Yardley, L., & Hoddinott, P. (2019). Guidance on how to develop complex interventions to improve health and healthcare. *BMJ Open, 9*, e029954.

O'Cathain, A., Croot, L., Sworn, K., Duncan, E., Rousseau, N., Turner, K., Yardley, L., & Hoddinott, P. (2019). Taxonomy of approaches to developing interventions to improve health: A systematic methods overview. *Pilot Feasibility Studies, 5*, 41.

Rose, N. (1999). *Governing the soul: The shaping of the private self*. Free Association Books.

Skivington, K., Matthews, L., Simpson, S. A., Craig, P., Baird, J., Blazeby, J. M., Boyd, K. A., Craig, N., French, D. P., Mcintosh, E., Petticrew, M., Rycroft-Malone, J., White, M. & Moore, L. (2021). A new framework for developing and evaluating complex interventions: Update of Medical Research Council guidance. *BMJ, 374*, n2061.

Slay, J., & Stevens, L. (2013). *Co-production in mental health: A literature review*. New Economics Foundation.

Stafford, L., Harkin, J.-A., Rolfe, A., Burton, J., & Morley, C. (2021). Why having a voice is important to children who are involved in family support services. *Child Abuse & Neglect, 115*, 104987.

Tillott, S., Weatherby-Fell, N., Pearson, P., & Neumann, M. M. (2022). Using storytelling to unpack resilience theory in accordance with an internationally recognised resilience framework with primary school children. *Journal of Psychologists and Counsellors in Schools, 32*, 134–145.

United Nations. (1989). *The United Nations convention on the rights of the child*. United Nations.

van Bijleveld, G. G., Bunders-Aelen, J. F. G., & Dedding, C. W. M. (2020). Exploring the essence of enabling child participation within child protection services. *Child & Family Social Work, 25*, 286–293.

Velleman, R., & Templeton, L. (2016). Impact of parents' substance misuse on children: An update. *British Journal of Psychiatry Advances, 22*, 108–117.

Voorberg, W., Bekkers, V. J. J. M., & Tummers, L. (2015). A systematic review of co-creation and co-production: Embarking on the social innovation journey. *Public Management Review, 17*, 1333–1357.

Chapter 16

Am I a Carer? Avoiding Research Fatigue and Labelling in Health and Social Care Research

Charlotte Lucy Richardson[a], Matthew Cooper[b] and David Black[a,b]

[a]*School of Pharmacy, Newcastle University, Newcastle upon Tyne, UK*
[b]*Newcastle Patient Safety Research Collaborative, Newcastle University, Newcastle upon Tyne, UK*

Abstract

This chapter examines the challenges of involving informal carers in patient and public involvement and engagement (**PPIE**) in health and social care research, particularly focussing on those who may not identify with the label of 'carer'. A carer usually refers to any individual who provides unpaid care and support to family, friends, or community members. Many individuals will not see themselves as carers and perceive the support they offer as part of a moral duty. The lack of self-identification often makes the recruitment of carers challenging for research. Drawing on the author's experience working with carers across research, we discuss the barriers to engagement with the carer population and how research could adapt to better ensure their meaningful involvement. We discuss the potential ethical dilemma of engaging with carers who may not consider themselves part of the 'carer' group, stressing the importance of recognising carers as individuals, not just as extensions of the patient. We advocate for avoiding imposing the label 'carer' on people who do not self-identify as such and instead use inclusive, experience-based language, thus respecting individuals' journeys towards

Public Involvement and Community Engagement in Applied Health and Social Care Research: Critical Perspectives and Innovative Practice, 195–205

recognising their caregiving roles. We suggest researchers focus on authentic engagement and consider working with the right person, at the right time, for the right purpose. We outline practical strategies for meaningful engagement with carers and call for a shift in culture to better value these carers' unique perspectives and experiences.

Keywords: Caregivers; carers; family; ethics; participation; engagement

Introduction

Part of our nature as social animals is to identify with those who are similar to us, and we seek to connect ourselves with those we feel mirror our own beliefs and values. However, within research, this can conflict with the realities of individualism, a central element of qualitative research. For example, we can use the visualisation of a rugby match where the referee has decided that a play was offside. The home fans and the away fans will have different opinions on whether it was offside or not; their opinion could also be affected by their view of the play from where they are sitting. Additional influences could also come from their knowledge of regulations or the opinions of those sitting nearby. In research, this is known as hermeneutics, and in qualitative work, we can look to ensure the individual voice is captured while grounding experiences about groups. If we consider the rugby match, we will accept that each individual might have a different opinion. However, if we spoke to a representative group of fans, we would find that there are some common experiences that we would interpret as representative of the event. When we are working with populations in research, we need to be comfortable that individuals will have their own beliefs and opinions about their experiences. What we must do as researchers is bring together experiences of the phenomena of enquiry and ensure we can triangulate common themes.

In health and care research, we default to grouping people into categories based on their conditions or experiences. We provide labels to these groups to help define who we are working with and what the population boundaries of our work are. Difficulties can arise when we apply a label that means different things to different people and can isolate those who do not all identify with it at all. Carer is a common term given to both those who provide informal/unpaid support and those who are carers by profession (social care-funded employment). As researchers, we are often interested in the 'other' and within our research, we wanted to speak and engage with the people who do not identify with the label of 'carer'. These 'carers' are a key part of the spectrum of carers and have an important voice that should be heard; however, for the reasons laid out below, they do not necessarily relate to the label, which causes challenges when trying to engage with them as part of PPIE in research. The term carer is used throughout this chapter to refer to informal (unpaid) carers, or:

anyone who looks after a family member, partner or friend who needs help because of their illness, frailty, disability, a mental health problem or an addiction and cannot cope without their support. The care they give is unpaid. (NHS England, 2014)

Readers should be aware that the term 'informal carer' can be misrepresentative, and some carers report it minimises the importance and impact of their role (Wanless, 2006). Alternative terms commonly used can be unpaid carer, family carer, and non-professional carer. For this reason, we have simply used the term 'carer' and by this, we mean carers who provide support to friends, family or community members and are *not* employed as professional carers. We also use the terminology: PPIE, which refers to research which is 'carried out "with" or "by" members of the public rather than "to", "about", or "for" them' (INVOLVE, 2021). PPIE should take place throughout the research and can include contributions to identify a research question, right through to influencing policymakers and aiding in disseminating the results (NIHR Applied Research Collaboration East Midlands, 2019).

As part of a National Institute for Health and Care Research (NIHR), Research for Patient Benefit funded research grant, we set out to consider the involvement of carers in transitions from hospital to home relating to patient medicines use. Specifically, caregivers who are more likely to go unnoticed within the health and social care system. The desire to consider this as a focus for research came, as it does in many different contexts, from the first author's personal experiences, whereby she witnessed her grandmother care for her grandfather as a doting life partner, sometimes to the detriment of her health and wellbeing. Had anyone asked Mrs Dodds if she was a carer for her husband, it would have been likely she would have been confused and responded along the lines of 'it's just what I do'.

Mrs Dodds is not alone; it is estimated that by 2037, there could be as many as 9 million carers in the UK (The Care Provider Alliance, 2020). Carers UK estimated this to be even higher at around one in five people (Carers UK, 2022). Part of the reason for differing estimations of the number of carers is due to the highly personal nature of this role and the inextricable link between caring responsibilities and familial and cultural responsibilities, which can result in carers feeling an obligation to care and thus not identifying with the term (Engster, 2005). Notably, self-identification as a carer is thought to occur over a prolonged period of time, with 51% of carers taking one year and 36% taking over three years to identify with their role as a carer (Carers UK, 2022). Other research has found that carers can be unsure about the norms associated with being a carer and that being a carer can be more obvious in extremes of ill health (Beatie et al., 2021).

When working with carers it is also important to acknowledge and respect the influence of culture within the role. Different cultures and norms will place different emphasis on the role of family and community in supporting individuals. Some may place more emphasis on the use of formal caregiving and some may feel caregiving is not a role but part of their moral duty to support community members. This is where language can be important and to work with the population of carers to understand what beliefs and values systems underpin their perception of caregiving. An example of this is filial piety (traditionally a Chinese cultural value but commonly observed in many cultures), which is the value and respect held for parents, elders and ancestors. This is likely to influence a person's perception of their role as a caregiver and to suggest their role is beyond what they morally should be doing, which could be offensive to some. Researchers should always consider cultural norms and values when working with patients and public members, but particularly when engaging with carers (NIHR School for Social Care Research, 2022).

Carers who do not identify as caregivers are sometimes the ones most in need of support, including for their health and well-being, not least due to the emotional and physical burden that caregiving can cause (Gérain & Zech, 2019). As health and social care professionals and researchers, we need to better understand our own practices and positionality, as well as the implications of labelling, how people perceive themselves and the implications of this and why these carers do not see themselves as carers. Being more reflective and reflexive here, we will argue, will lead to a better understanding and allow us to better design services that these carers require and can access. The challenges of working with carers who do not see themselves as such, can leave a potential ethical dilemma for researchers working in this area when a notable proportion of the people we are trying to engage with do not see themselves as part of that group, and they may ask themselves 'but am I even a carer?'.

In the following chapter, we will reflect on our experiences of working with carers and discuss several key considerations to facilitate more meaningful and authentic engagement with carers. The discussion will touch upon carer identity as complex and multi-faceted, the importance of carefully considering language when engaging with carers, the balance between professional PPIE contributors and those who are research naïve and what they can each bring to a project, and finally, we will hear direct reflections from a carer.

Being a Carer Is Not the Sum of Existence

It is well-established that PPIE is a core element of health and social care research, but in high-level resources, such as the UK Standards for public involvement (UK Public Involvement Standards Development Partnership group, 2019), the 'who', 'why', and 'what' of PPIE can be vague, intended to leave room for flexibility for the individual research project but the risk is that there is confusion on what meaningful PPIE looks like. It is therefore important to first consider the value that including carers in research can offer. This is grounded in the principle of 'research with us not on us' (NHS Health Research Authority, 2023).

Understanding positionality here is key, and recognising that as researchers, we see the world in different ways. We each might have our own experiences of caregiving, for example and will hold our own biases as to how change could be made. By including carers in research from the beginning, we can gain insight into wider views and experiences *via* real-world stories and personal interpretations of caring. As researchers, we can work with people to connect the dots of individual experiences against what is commonly experienced and use this to inform how we design and deliver research.

Carers might be the focus of the research question, like in our grant, and so that value is obvious as carers are central to the research question as opposed to other groups of patients or the broader public; conversely, other topics might warrant more obvious patient involvement, with carer input being secondary. It has been suggested that clarity about 'why' a project needs involvement can consequently direct 'who' to involve (Staley et al., 2021). 'Why' is not the focus of this chapter, and instead, we direct readers to resources that promote reflection as to the purpose and value of PPIE (Graffigna & Barello, 2022). Presuming you have asked yourself 'why' you are conducting PPIE and the answer has led you to recognise that carers are a group who can contribute to fulfilling your 'why', we will now discuss the 'how'.

Carers are routinely involved in health and social care research in a similar way to patients and other people with lived experience relevant to a given research question, and as such, carers are also at risk of experiencing tokenistic PPIE, the same as other contributors (Bowness et al., 2024). From our experiences, however, we suggest that the risks of this tokenism are greater for carers than due to the manner in which they are considered by research teams and then involved. In 2023, the NIHR highlighted a need for more research involving carers and suggested that the benefits included that carers can (i) be a key part of the jigsaw of making services work, (ii) can support the person they care for to be involved to ensure their voice is heard, and (iii) can act as an advocate for those they care for if they are not able to do so themselves (Jarvis & Bowness, 2023). It should be noted that the latter two suggestions are not focussed on the value that the carer themselves can contribute, but are positioned to facilitate better patient input through utilising their carer as a proxy if you pause and imagine this from the perspective of a carer. This carer has its own experiences, thoughts, and opinions. What indication does it give to the carer of the value of their contribution?

In terms of carers' experiences of health services (outside of research), it is acknowledged that carers are individuals and not merely an extension of the patient (Zavagli et al., 2019). Carers' health and well-being are influenced by their caring role. Being a carer has been identified as a social determinant of health, and carers can experience poor physical and mental health and may have unmet care needs (Public Health England, 2020). It is important that carers are viewed as individuals and that the label of carer is not the extent of their identity (Eifert et al., 2015). This has been translated into the research space, whereby the NIHR is publishing a carer-facing and a researcher-facing set of recommendations for research involving carers (NIHR, 2023a, 2023b). These documents acknowledge the value carers can bring to research but fundamentally recognise the importance that researchers *'recognise that carers are people first'*.

Treading Carefully Around Language

Not all carers will see themselves as part of the 'carer' group. Therefore, if we approached people by asking for 'anyone who is a carer to get in touch', we might find ourselves with a certain demographic of carers. Particularly those who are well-established in their identity as a carer are particularly vocal about this and are potentially more aware of research. The concept of 'hidden carers' is documented within the literature and refers to carers who, for various reasons, do not identify as a carer and therefore are less likely to reach out for support; people not identifying as carer and thus being 'hidden' is suggested to be closely linked to cultural and familial roles and responsibilities (Knowles et al., 2016). Our project required a range of carers to contribute, which included hidden carers. Therefore, our reflections on how we approached and involved them are presented below.

Our research topic was broad and considered what works, for whom and in what contexts relating to the involvement of carers in hospital discharge relating to medicines use using a realist methodology (Cooper et al., 2024). In order to identify carers to contribute, we use broad reflective questions in recruitment documents and communication, including 'Do you help someone with their medicines?', 'Have you helped someone during hospital discharge?' and 'Do you support or help a friend or family member with their health?'. The commonality here being – we did not necessarily use the term carer. This was intentional to expose a range of people to the research, people who might have relevant lived experience, even if they do not see themselves as a carer, just like Mrs Dodds. Similar methods have been documented in other projects using groups of participants where the participant identity is not clear-cut (Ibrahim & Sidani, 2014).

Apart from this approach seemingly being suitable to identify the range of people we were interested in working with, we also feel that ethically it is the right thing to do. As researchers, our perspective was that we did not want to engage with this group and, as part of the course of the research, enforce the label of carer upon them without them necessarily going through the personal journey of self-identification as a carer themselves. For this reason, we let the carer lead the use of language – if they described themselves as a carer, then we did too, if they were grainier on the terminology they used to describe themselves and their role, then we were too. This way, we felt we were not unduly accelerating or changing the course of the carer's identity journey as part of the research. This approach is informed by insights from social theorists like Brewer (1991), who have identified that identities will be rejected (people disengage with services or research) if the identities available or imposed upon them are too restrictive.

When Do PPIE Members Become Professionals in Their Contributions?

Some carers, just like patients and other public contributors, are well-versed in contributing to PPIE. This is recognised within the literature, as PPIE contributors can become professionalised in their role (Ives et al., 2013). Ives et al. (2013) summarised that '*the value of PPI[E] lies in the capacity of the agent to be an "outsider" who can reflect and comment, with relative objectivity, on the research process*' and in such a way that it is informed by the person's lived experience of the research topic. For our research, we wanted to avoid research weariness and to engage with a range of carers, including those who were more research naïve to try and ensure that the PPIE was meaningful, to capture the lived experience, and to avoid carers who already had significant research experience contributing in a biased way based on what they expected the researchers to want rather than authentically. Those who choose to use a similar approach to us may find themselves having to ignore traditional approaches and organisations (which may seem counterintuitive) to get to carers who have not been so heavily involved in research in the past.

When planning our research and writing our funding application we identified, through an advert on VOICE-global.org.uk (a PPIE and research support to engaging with members of the public), a carer with a strong sense of identity in their role but with significant previous research experience as both a participant and as a co-applicant, and most notably with connections and relationships with local and national organisations, groups and panels. We took this approach as someone with more certainty in their carer role, and with connections to wider groups and organisations, was what we needed during the planning and running of the research (the involvement). This then allowed us to consider how we could identify carers who don't necessarily see themselves as such for the participation and engagement stages.

On reflection, this seems logical, but for a team of researchers who had never specifically worked with carers in the past, this was more like trial and error, but with a focus on situating authentic PPIE as central to the research project. To adapt an example from the health world where the lead author works as a pharmacist – students are taught to always consider the administration of medicines in terms of: '*the right patient, the right drug, the right time, the right dose, and the right route*' (Grissinger, 2010), is this not the same as considering PPIE in terms of the right person, the relevant lived experience, the right time and the right nature of contribution for the right purpose?

Trying to Be Authentic with Carers

Local and national carer charities and support groups can be a useful starting point but as highlighted previously these will likely only identify people who already identify with the term carer. Awareness of this and the possible bias this brings is needed and we would suggest using a range of approaches from those discussed here, unless your research calls for working with a particular type of carer that is identifiable from only one or two methods. Additional, and more innovative, options could be engaging with other non-carer community and religious groups – any place or group that brings people together where that group could include a carer. It is possible that gatekeepers to communities might be needed to facilitate this, but where this approach is utilised, careful consideration is needed in working with a gatekeeper with who understands the nuances we have reflected on in this chapter regarding the labelling of carers and the varied nature of carers' previous involvement with research.

Other methods we have utilised include more general social media promotion and snowball techniques, and as discussed previously, a careful consideration of language and messaging about what the research is, involves and who it relates to. In this case, a move away from referring to people as carers and instead focussing on the relevant experiences rather than the label. We have also worked with carers to identify their roles and responsibilities, which we have taken to an artist to make into a visual representation of what it means to be a carer. This artwork approach could be used to ask people who identify with an emotion, role, or visual image to take part, leaving the need to use the actual word 'carer' redundant (Fig. 16.1).

Reflections From a Carer by David Black

> I never sought to be a carer. One minute I was getting on with life, the next I was in the world of the carer through looking after my mum. My journey to identifying as a carer started when our GP suggested I apply for Lasting Power of Attorney for my mum. Acting as a carer I started to see at appointments, hospitals, care facilities, and interactions with public bodies the futility of doing what I had always done. Having worked in legal services and healthcare previously I thought that I understood the challenges, but I only really knew part of the story until it became my reality. Starting to navigate systems as a carer brough many new challenges and it changed my outlook on life.

Fig. 16.1.   What Does It Mean to Be a Carer? *Source*: Co-produced with Carers. Cartoons Are Created by Sian McArthur from More Than Minutes, Published with Permission.

I am now a positive disruptor, an advocate for seldom heard voices and most importantly I discovered the role of public involvement in research. Through my research journey as a carer, I have experienced personal growth, fulfilment, and have developed a better understanding of my self-awareness as well as a self-acceptance in my approach to life. My contributions to research are wide ranging and are the most rewarding roles I have ever undertaken. No two research opportunities are alike, and I learn something new with each interaction with the research community. My involvement in research started by commenting on lay summaries, patient information sheets and research proposals at research support groups. It led me into getting involved as a co-applicant on individual research studies and helping to write the patient/public sections of applications. The most satisfying part of my work is being a co-author on several research papers.

A few years ago, I became an informal carer once again to multiple people in my local area. Whilst other people were caring for my mum in a local care home, I was involved in helping others around me. Identifying that in helping others you are a carer is not always apparent; it is more obvious when you have been a carer before. People can help others without really considering being a carer and this creates difficulties when researchers are trying to identify and engage with carers.

In reaching out to carer's it is important that researchers understand that caring activities are wide ranging, can take up a lot of time and are often unpredictable. Flexibility when designing the structure of a research project involving engagement with carers is an important consideration. As a carer the best experiences in engaging with researchers are those with built in flexibility around the needs of the carer. One way to try and focus comments from a carer is to have a clear and concise aim and question for their involvement. It may be necessary to steer the conversations with a carer to keep comments relevant to the research and it is the responsibility of the researcher to focus in on the carer's specific experiences relevant to the research question.

Conclusion

Carers are a heterogenous group and as such flexibility and individualism are needed when engaging with them. Three considerations that appear more unique to carers that were raised as part of our research were as follows. Firstly, carers may need financial support to ensure a continuity of care for the care recipient while the carer contributes to the research, which is in addition to any remuneration. Secondly, carers may need flexibility in the timing and volume of input relative to their caring responsibilities, which can fluctuate and flexibility in the nature of contribution, for example, in person, online, or asynchronously. Thirdly, carers themselves may have health and well-being concerns and may require adjustments in the same way other participants might. Creating a dialogue with carers and getting to know them as individuals can help to establish the need for adjustments to the PPIE to best allow carers to engage, in the same way as we would do for other participant groups.

There is an increasing interest in research focussed on carers, and as such, more research teams will be engaging and working with carers, which can be rewarding and insightful, but requires thoughtfulness to build meaningful relationships. It is important that research teams consider the nuances of the caring role and work towards sharing best practice that involves carers in a way that is of value to them, as well as to the research team, does not label them as something they do not identify with, and that carers are involved throughout the lifecycle of research.

References

Beatie, B. E., Mackenzie, C. S., Funk, L., Davidson, D., Koven, L., & Reynolds, K. A. (2021). Caregiver identity in care partners of persons living with mild cognitive impairment. *Dementia, 20*, 2323–2339.

Bowness, B., Henderson, C., Akhter Khan, S. C., Akiba, M., & Lawrence, V. (2024). Participatory research with carers: A systematic review and narrative synthesis. *Health Expectations, 27*, e13940.

Brewer, B. M. (1991). The social self: On being the same and different at the same time.*Personality and Social Psychology Bulletin, 17*(95), 475–482.

Carers UK. (2022). *State of caring 2022: A snapshot of unpaid care in the UK.* CarkersUK.

Cooper, M., Atkinson, O., Black, D., Lindsey, L., Cooper, C., Nazar, H., Wong, G., Hughes, C., & Richardson, C. L. (2024). Informal carer involvement in the transition of medicines-related care for patients moving from hospital to home: A realist review protocol. *BMJ Open, 14*, e091005.

Eifert, E. K., Adams, R., Dudley, W., & Perko, M. (2015). Family caregiver identity: A literature review. *American Journal of Health Education, 46*, 357–367.

Engster, D. (2005). Rethinking care theory: The practice of caring and the obligation to care. *Hypatia, 20*, 50–74.

Gérain, P., & Zech, E. (2019). Informal caregiver burnout? Development of a theoretical framework to understand the impact of caregiving. *Frontiers in Psychology, 10*, 1748.

Graffigna, G., & Barello, S. (2022). How does patient engagement work in a real-world setting? Recommendations, caveats, and challenges from a psychosocial perspective. *Patient Education and Counseling, 105*, 3567–3573.

Grissinger, M. (2010). The five rights: A destination without a map. *P T, 35*, 542.

Ibrahim, S., & Sidani, S. (2014). Strategies to recruit minority persons: A systematic review. *Journal of Immigrant and Minority Health, 16*, 882–888.

INVOLVE. (2021). *Briefing notes for researchers: Involving the public in NHS, public health and social care research.* [Online]. INVOLVE. Retrieved November 14, 2024, from https://www.nihr.ac.uk/briefing-notes-researchers-public-involvement-nhs-health-and-social-care-research

Ives, J., Damery, S., & Redwod, S. (2013). PPI, paradoxes and Plato: who's sailing the ship? *Journal of Medical Ethics, 39*, 181.

Jarvis, S., & Bowness, B. (2023). *Why is it important to involve unpaid carers in research?* [Online]. NIHR. Retrieved November 14, 2024, from https://www.nihr.ac.uk/blog/why-it-important-involve-unpaid-carers-research#:~:text=All%20researchers%20should%20be%20thinking,by%20giving%20them%20a%20voice

Knowles, S., Combs, R., Kirk, S., Griffiths, M., Patel, N., & Sanders, C. (2016). Hidden caring, hidden carers? Exploring the experience of carers for people with long-term conditions. *Health & Social Care in the Community, 24*, 203–2013.

NHS England. (2014). *NHS England's commitment for carers – Final report.* NHS England.

NHS Health Research Authority. (2023). *Public involvement* [Online].Retrieved December 9, 2024, fromhttps://www.hra.nhs.uk/planning-and-improving-research/best-practice/public-involvement/

NIHR. (2023a). *Tips for carers to get and stay involved in health and care research* [Online]. Retrieved November 14, 2024, from https://www.learningforinvolvement.org.uk/content/resource/tips-for-carers-to-get-and-stay-involved-in-health-and-care-research/

NIHR. (2023b). *Tips for researchers involving unpaid carers in health and care research* [Online]. Retrieved November 14, 2024, from https://www.learningforinvolvement.org.uk/content/resource/tips-for-researchers-involving-carers-health-care-research/

NIHR Applied Research Collaboration East Midlands. (2019). *Our approach to Patient and Public Involvement & Engagement (PPIE) in our funded work.*

NIHR School for Social Care Research. (2022). *Involving and engaging carers in research: Report from a webinar on 6 June 2022* [Online]. https://www.sscr.nihr.ac.uk/reports/involving-and-engaging-carers-in-research/

Public Health England. (2020). *Caring as a social determinant of health findings from a rapid review of reviews and analysis of the GP Patient Survey.*

Staley, K., Elliott, J., Stewart, D., & Wilson, R. (2021). Who should I involve in my research and why? Patients, carers or the public? *Research Involvement and Engagement, 7*, 41.

The Care Provider Alliance. (2020). *Adult social care – market overview* [Online]. Retrieved September 26, 2024, from https://careprovideralliance.org.uk/adult-social-care-market-overview

UK Public Involvement Standards Development Partnership Group. (2019). *UK standards for public involvement in research* [Online]. Retrieved November 14, 2024, from https://sites.google.com/nihr.ac.uk/pi-standards/home

Wanless, D. (2006). Securing good care for older people: Taking a long-term view. In D. Wanless (Ed.), *Wanless social care review* (pp. 137–152). The King's Fund.

Zavagli, V., Raccichini, M., Ercolani, G., Franchini, L., Varani, S., & Pannuti, R. (2019). Care for carers: An investigation on family caregivers' needs, tasks, and experiences. *Translational Medicine @ UniSa, 19*, 54–59.

Chapter 17

Let's Hear It from the Girls: Shining a Light on the Value of PICE in Alternative Educational Provision

Pamela Louise Graham[a] and Melissa Fothergill[b]

[a]*Department of Social Work, Education and Community Wellbeing, Northumbria University, Newcastle upon Tyne, UK*
[b]*Department of Psychology, Northumbria University, Newcastle upon Tyne, UK*

Abstract

The number of young people accessing education outside of mainstream school settings has risen dramatically in recent years. Girls are a minority group within such alternative educational provision, and little is known about their experiences. Drawing on lessons learnt from a project that set out to explore girls' experiences of mental health and well-being support in alternative educational provision, this chapter highlights the value of engaging with girls in these settings. Key considerations relating to relationships, anonymity, power dynamics, and practitioners' ability to engage in sensitive conversations with young people are highlighted and discussed. The chapter concludes with recommendations relating to Public Involvement and Community Engagement (PICE) work, inter-professional working, and ethically informed practice with young people.

Keywords: Alternative provision; exclusion; education; children's rights; power; ethics

Public Involvement and Community Engagement in Applied Health and Social Care Research: Critical Perspectives and Innovative Practice, 207–217

doi:10.1108/978-1-83608-678-920251017

Introduction

This chapter is a reflection on our practice in relation to public involvement and on lessons learnt from a research project that set out to explore girls' experiences of mental health and well-being support in alternative educational provision. In our study, we worked with 13 girls aged 14–16 years from four alternative educational providers based in the North East of England. While the girls were involved in some of the decisions made throughout the project, there were times when it was appropriate for adults to advocate on behalf of the girls. There were also some decisions based on adults' interpretations of what was best for the girls at different points in the research. Managing field work can involve considering personal and professional boundaries, and this chapter discusses some of the tensions in decision-making processes involved in research and PICE activities with young people in educational settings.

Research Context

Alternative provision (AP) in England refers to an arrangement where young people are educated in settings outside of mainstream or special schools for a range of reasons, including school exclusion, illness, and behavioural intervention. APs typically provide academic and vocational training alongside pastoral support and can incorporate a range of settings comprising pupil referral units, colleges, AP academies, and other organisations which can provide support outside of mainstream settings (Malcolm, 2018).

Engagement in AP has increased dramatically in recent years with 15,900 young people of primary and secondary school age attending state-funded AP settings across England in 2023/2024. This figure represented a 20% increase in state-funded AP attendance since 2022/2023 (Department for Education, 2024). Examination of AP statistics shows that particular groups are disproportionately represented in AP including young people with special educational needs and disabilities, those entitled to free school meals and those who have engaged with the criminal justice system (Black, 2022). Boys have also persistently dominated AP settings currently accounting for around two-thirds of state-funded AP places. Historically, this male dominance of AP has been attributed to a greater number of boys receiving disciplinary exclusions (Russell & Thompson, 2011). Indeed, statistics have shown that male pupils have 1.5 times the rate of suspensions and are twice as likely to be excluded than their female counterparts (National Statistics, 2023). Yet, there has been a recent increase in the number of girls experiencing school exclusion and attending AP, but they have received relatively little attention across research and policy compared to boys, resulting in a substantial lack of understanding surrounding girls' experiences of school and their increased engagement in AP (Clarke, 2024; Dance, 2023). This is concerning as research has suggested that girls can experience stereotyping, sexism, isolation, and a lack of engagement in same-sex friendships in male-dominated AP settings (Russell & Thompson, 2011). Friendships are especially important as they play a role in stress-reduction and coping during challenging times

(Hall, 2015). Engagement in secure friendships (i.e., experiencing the continual presence of a supportive and responsive friend) can also support anxiety reduction (Wood et al., 2017).

Motivated by the lack of attention given to girls' experiences in AP, we embarked on a nine-month project to explore girls' experiences of support for mental health and well-being in AP. Initially, we planned to explore girls' perspectives through interviews and then work with the girls in workshop-style groups to prepare written and visual outputs, containing information that they felt was important for other people to know about AP. We also planned to give girls opportunities throughout the project to share information about their experiences of AP through photographs, drawings, written extracts, or any other medium they felt would be suitable. Our intention, which was communicated to the girls from the outset, was to use the interview content as research data to analyse and report on, whereas the arts-based materials could be used in outputs relating to the project, the exact format of which would be decided by the girls. We were keen throughout the project to ensure that the girls' voices were heard, and we hoped to encourage them to take a role in some of the decision making at various points, particularly as young people do not get sufficient opportunities to have their voices heard (Children's Commissioners of Northern Ireland, Scotland and Wales, 2022).

Importance of Young People's Perspectives

Historically, children were viewed as vulnerable, in need of adult supervision and special care (Morrow & Richards, 1996), but it has been increasingly recognised that children are competent social agents capable of expressing their own views and sharing invaluable insights into their own lives and experiences (Tangen, 2008). While adults can reflect retrospectively on their experiences of childhood, children are experts in their own lives now, with current cultural, social, and contextual insights that are not the same as adult recollections. However, children are still not provided with sufficient opportunities to have their views heard. While the importance of children's voices is more widely recognised, implementation remains lacking, especially for typically marginalised groups who are unable to challenge decision-making (Mills et al., 2016). For example, disabled children, children in out-of-home/local authority care and those outside of mainstream education are not provided with sufficient opportunities to share their views on matters that affect them. Where opportunities are provided, these are often tokenistic with mechanisms such as school councils used to evidence participation, but these do not always involve active and inclusive engagement and children often remain uninformed about whether and how their contributions have been used (Children's Commissioners of Northern Ireland, Scotland and Wales, 2022).

In research contexts, there has been a movement to differentiate between 'having' and 'taking' a child's perspective when designing studies, with the latter focussing on the children's voices and providing them with the opportunity to speak for themselves (Nilsson et al., 2015). The incorporation of PICE into research projects can provide a valuable platform for children and young people to have their voices heard. However, it requires a responsible and ongoing ethical approach that demands flexibility to ensure children's voices are listened to and their suggestions acted upon even when these contradict the views of adults who are used to taking the lead in decision-making (Mitchell et al., 2019).

Lessons Learnt from Girls in AP

The girls who contributed to our project provided us with invaluable and privileged insights into their experiences of AP, but also left us reflecting on some important considerations relating to PICE work with young people.

Shifting Power and Flexibility

When we initially approached APs to participate in the project, we received favourable responses from a number of staff who shared our interest in exploring girls' experiences. We arranged meetings with staff to discuss the project in more detail and to make suitable arrangements to meet with girls who had expressed interest in taking part. Staff agreed to share information about the project with girls in their settings to gauge interest and identify any questions or concerns they had before opting to take part.

From this early stage, the importance of involving young people in decision-making became apparent as we found mixed views around engagement with the project. Some girls did not want to participate and exercised their rights not to take part at all. Others expressed an interest in taking part in the arts-based activities (i.e., sharing photographs, drawings, etc.), but did not want to be interviewed as part of the research and had no interest in participating in workshop activities with their peers. These acts of 'informed dissent' are as important as consent and highlight the importance of consent as a process that should be embedded throughout projects. Not something that is simply collated at the start of a project, then assumed throughout (Bourke, 2017, p. 232).

With regards to interviews, we found that while girls initially expressed an interest in being interviewed one-to-one, some decided on the day of their interview that they would prefer to speak to the researcher alongside a peer rather than participating independently. Flexibility and reflexivity are key here, and in some cases, girls also opted to be interviewed on two occasions rather than just one, as initially planned by the project team. In research contexts, the challenge remains 'not to use the power of being an adult and instead to listen to and respect the children's views even if the position as a researcher is defied' (Nilsson et al., 2015, p. 167). The decisions made by the girls prompted us to adapt our plans to incorporate their wishes. This was facilitated by the ongoing communication we had with AP staff and the flexible approach we took to the project, which allowed us to identify and accommodate the girls' requests.

Nevertheless, we cannot say with confidence that our approach represented a shift in the power dynamics (i.e., ability to decide on involvement and ownership) that exist between adults and young people as we relied on AP staff to relay messages from the girls back to the project team as opposed to us hearing from the girls directly. As the project activities were arranged to take place within AP settings with staff acting as gatekeepers, there was no direct line of communication between the girls and the project team between pre-arranged project activities. This approach of adults advocating on behalf of young people is sometimes necessary, but it can be problematic as there is a risk of adults misinterpreting or misrepresenting young people's views (Cunningham et al., 2024). It is also important to recognise that teachers and pupils often revert to their expected roles within the confines of school spaces where well intended promotion of student voice through leadership can often be lost due to teachers being used to being in control (Mitra, 2008). Moreover, while power differentials exist in any research, they are more prominent in projects with young people whereby adults act as gatekeepers (e.g., parents, guardians, and teachers) who can limit their participation (Grover, 2004; Kay, 2019). However, in the context of AP, positive staff-student relationships are frequently cited as a benefit that young people experience within AP settings (Malcolm, 2018). Indeed, the AP staff we worked with acted as important advocates for the girls in their care. They shared information with the girls; facilitated meetings to allow us to discuss the project with the girls; and supported the collection of parent/carer consent, which was required before girls could take part, though the girls had the final decision on whether or not they wanted to participate following parent/carer consent.

Importance of Relationships

There are two elements to our reflections on relationships: the first concerns the inter-professional relationships that informed the initial project plans, and the second concerns the relationships developed between the girls who participated and the project team during the course of the project.

Working to a tight funding deadline with no resources available to support initial PICE work, we were unable to involve girls from AP in the initial planning stages. We therefore planned the project based on the combined research and practice knowledge of the project team. This proved useful as we were able to bring together ideas around research methodologies and consider how these could be applied practically in AP settings. The combination of practice and research experience within the team also prompted us to think more broadly about dissemination in ways that we might not have considered when working independently within our own professional groups.

Despite not involving girls in the planning stages of the project, we were conscious of the need to build positive relationships with girls interested in taking part at the earliest opportunity. Positive relationships are pivotal in educational settings, especially for pupils who struggle emotionally and behaviourally. For pupils in AP, positive relationships have been deemed essential and provide a critical starting point for re-engagement with learning (Knowles et al., 2020; McGrath & Van Bergen, 2019). Therefore, researchers engaging young people in projects within educational settings have a responsibility to establish, maintain, and manage relationships at all stages of the project.

We found that AP staff were crucial to the initial establishment of positive relationships with the girls who took part in our project, but the nature of the project activities facilitated further development of positive relationships. We visited the AP settings and met with the girls on multiple occasions. The use of qualitative approaches also provided us with rich and privileged insights into the girls' past experiences and future aspirations, with discussions sometimes moving towards sensitive topics that we had not initially anticipated. Engaging young people in PICE work requires flexibility, reflexivity, and the ability of the research team to be willing and able to facilitate and manage the discussion of sensitive topics and subject areas effectively. This needs to be done in a way that does not increase vulnerability or act as a detriment to the young people involved (Spencer et al., 2021). The development of trusting relationships is not unusual in qualitative research, but it prompts a need for a clear endpoint to projects, with open communication about what participants should expect following this endpoint. We felt this was especially necessary in the context of AP, as young people who experience disengagement from mainstream education often attribute this to a breakdown of relationships in those settings (Malcolm, 2018).

The girls' participation in the project ended with a celebration lunch, which took place at Northumbria University. On learning that some of the girls had career aspirations that could require degree level qualifications, we invited them to visit the university where they had lunch, a tour of the campus and met some university staff members who had taken non-traditional routes through education. The girls also received a certificate acknowledging their participation in the project, gift vouchers and a printed booklet containing outputs from the project, which were shared online with their permission (www.tinyurl.com/GirlsInAltEd). We made it clear to the girls that the celebration lunch was the end point of their participation in the project, but we did remind them that they could get in touch with us, via their teachers or parents/carers, if they had further questions following their participation. We also contacted AP staff to update them on dissemination activities following conclusion of the project as they had asked the team to let them know of any further developments.

Anonymity

Following the completion of the project, we presented some of the findings at academic conferences and have since been asked whether the girls who took part in the project also contributed to these conferences – they did not. In the initial stages of the project, we obtained university ethical approval for all project activities and stipulated at this point that the girls' anonymity would be upheld throughout the project. We did not offer the opportunity for this anonymity to be waived at any stage of the project unless a safeguarding concern was raised that required intervention from others outside of the project team.

We decided to uphold anonymity as we wanted the girls to feel able to speak openly about their experiences. This is especially important for young people who can have concerns about being critical of adult-led organisations, such as schools, for fear of reprisals resulting from the expression of their views, which are counter to adult authority figures (Graham et al., 2016). Furthermore, young people move from mainstream education to AP for a multitude of reasons, including health, social and educational challenges (Department for Education, 2024). Some of the issues faced by young people can require them to remain as anonymous as possible within the education system for safeguarding purposes (Bessant, 2014). In such cases, it would not be appropriate for young people to engage in activities that revealed their identities and linked them to a particular educational setting or locality within a public space so by upholding anonymity we kept all opportunities for engagement in project activities equal and reduced the burden on schools to support the management of safeguarding in this context.

Additionally, when considering girls' engagement in project activities, we were mindful of the potential permanence of project outputs. The outputs produced by the girls included photographs of a school dog and artwork on the walls of the AP settings, representing some positive aspects of AP. The girls also created mind maps, a painting and written texts detailing their thoughts on what works for them in AP and what could be improved. We offered these creative options in an effort to provide multiple inclusive outlets for the girls' ideas. This proved useful as one girl chose to write her thoughts down but did not want to participate in an interview with a researcher. We encouraged the girls to choose how they would like to participate and did not express a preference for any particular type of output, nor did we stipulate a minimum or maximum amount of content that should be included. The only specific boundaries we set related to anonymity. We advised the girls to avoid taking photographs that included people's faces, and we removed references to the names of people and places that appeared within the outputs.

In discussing the use of photographs in research, Cowie and Khoo (2017) argued for the importance of considering the persistence of images over time and how young people and families might feel about them remaining long into the future. They also highlighted the complexity surrounding the narratives that accompany images and the implications of a context that links young people to a position of vulnerability. In the context of our study, we were aware from previous research that AP is often stigmatised having long been perceived as a place where young people are sent to address poor behaviour (McNulty & Roseboro, 2009). The girls in our project also reflected on these stigmatised perceptions that see them labelled as poorly behaved suggesting that negative societal perceptions of AP persist (Graham, 2023). With this in mind, it was important to consider whether it was appropriate to provide the girls with a public platform to contribute to dissemination activities knowing that this would link them to AP with its stigmatised status. Furthermore, while we hoped that the girls could be proud of the work they produced as part of the project, we could not be sure that the girls would still want to be associated with the project long into the future. Should they have opted to take part in dissemination activities, a lack of anonymity could remove the option for them to separate themselves from the project if they had later changed their minds.

Despite these reservations that led us to uphold anonymity in the context of our project, we would argue that this is an area of PICE that warrants further consideration, especially when working with young people. It has been argued that by taking the decision to protect young people's identities, adults inadvertently de-power and silence them (Cowie & Khoo, 2017). On reflection, had we had the opportunity to engage with young people in the planning stages of the project to outline and discuss our thoughts around anonymity and young people's involvement in dissemination activities, we might have ultimately reached a different decision. Given the chance, the girls in our project might have also provided ideas around how they could contribute to dissemination activities that did not occur to the adult-led team.

A Young Person's Perspective

How does it feel to be asked for your views by adults in a school setting?

> In my take, adults, though some may not say so, believe that children have less rights than they do. For example, adults can create a sense that younger people do not get a say in opposing their ideas or opinions. In my opinion, I don't feel comfortable sharing my criticisms on adults' views due to the lack of support provided. They will always try to change my answer. This has caused me and many other students to be hesitant about displaying their ideas.

> Many adults claim that children still have young and developing minds that have not yet adapted to understand the world today. However, their minds and mindsets are adjusted to know everything that goes on today, thus their opinions are always correct and matter more than ours.

> Personally, I believe that if someone wants a genuine answer out of a child, they should ask them without expressing their opinions first and criticising the child's takes on the topic. They should, once the child's opinion has been given, further question them about their answer and oppose to it, creating a mini debate. This is definitely a better option instead of straight up criticising children for answers that they do not believe in.
>
> Laila, aged 12.

Conclusions

Research funding bids typically require a thorough outline of research approaches at the application stage and increasingly, research funding bodies are requiring these approaches to be informed by public members. However, valuable PICE work requires time and resources, and should include some reimbursement to public partners to recognise their contributions (National Institute for Health and Care Research, 2024). It is therefore essential that funding is made available to support this element of research ideally from initial idea generation through to planning and execution of methods, analysis and dissemination. In the context of our AP research, we were able to accommodate various requests from the girls throughout the project, but on reflection the project would have been much richer if the girls could have been involved right from the start in initial discussions to guide generation of research questions and project activities to ensure we were focussed on issues that really mattered to them. Research has shown that children and young people's active participation can lead to the generation of richer insights and we would argue the provision of resources to support such work could therefore lead to more valuable outcomes that meet the needs of children and young people while recognising their right to have a say in matters that affect them.

The value of taking opportunities to speak to people outside of your own professional group in relation to PICE work cannot be underestimated and these serendipitous conversations with colleagues can spark ideas and provide significant learning opportunities for all involved. Typically, academic publications reporting on research focus positively on the project outcomes with relatively little reflection on what could have been done better. However, much of the learning from our project came from reflecting on things we did not do or had not considered; lessons which could be beneficial to others wishing to carry out similar projects in the future. There is therefore a need for the promotion of spaces that create safe and open opportunities for project teams to share reflections on things that did not work well. Such forums could support more effective and efficient project planning and reduce the possibility that public partners involved in projects will encounter the same challenges or need to repeatedly provide the same feedback across different projects.

Finally, while PICE is not currently governed by the same ethical policies and processes as research, there is a need to ensure that PICE is guided by ethical principles (National Institute for Health and Care Research Applied Research Collaboration North East and North Cumbria, 2024). Throughout our project, we considered issues around consent and anonymity, and adapted our plans to accommodate the girls' wishes as the project progressed. We also worked with an ongoing awareness of the sensitive nature of the challenges that often lead to young people engaging in AP and implemented appropriate plans should safeguarding concerns arise. It is essential that researchers and others wishing to engage in PICE consider their work from an ethical perspective ensuring that participant well-being and inclusion are at the forefront of decision-making ahead of project data and outcomes.

Acknowledgement

The project described in this chapter was funded by the National Institute for Health and Care Research Applied Research Collaboration North East and North Cumbria (ARCNIHR200173).

References

Bessant, C. (2014). Data protection, safeguarding and the protection of children's privacy: Exploring local authority guidance on parental photography at school events. *Information & Communications Technology Law, 23*(3), 256–272.

Black, A. (2022). 'But what do the statistics say?' An overview of permanent school exclusions in England. *Emotional and Behavioural Difficulties, 27*(3), 199–219.

Bourke, R. (2017). The ethics of including and 'standing up' for children and young people in educational research. *International Journal of Inclusive Education, 21*(3), 231–233.

Children's Commissioners of Northern Ireland, Scotland and Wales. (2022). *Report of the Children's Commissioners of Northern Ireland, Scotland and Wales to the United Nations Committee on the Rights of the Child.* Retrieved October 31, 2024, from https://www.cypcs.org.uk/resources/joint-report-crc2022/

Clarke, E. (2024). Voices from the edge: Girls' experiences of being at risk of permanent exclusion. *British Educational Research Journal, 50*(2), 855–875.

Cowie, B., & Khoo, E. (2017). Accountability through access, authenticity and advocacy when researching with young children. *International Journal of Inclusive Education, 21*(3), 234–247.

Cunningham, E., Jamieson-MacKenzie, I.., McMellon, C., McCallin, M., Eltiraifi, M., Smith, L., & Hepburn, K. (2024). "Don't tell me how to tell my story": Exploring young people's perceptions around what it means to 'feel (mis)understood' by adults in supporting roles'. *Children and Youth Services Review, 156*, 107361.

Dance, D. (2023). *Girls and alternative provision – Reframing the narrative.* Retrieved October 17, 2024, from https://www.childrenscommissioner.gov.uk/blog/girls-and-alternative-provision-reframing-the-narrative/

Department for Education. (2024). *Schools, pupils and their characteristics.* Retrieved October 21, 2024, from https://explore-education-statistics.service.gov.uk/find-statistics/school-pupils-and-their-characteristics

Graham, A., Powell, M. A., & Truscott, J. (2016). Exploring the nexus between participatory methods and ethics in early childhood research. *Australasian Journal of Early Childhood, 41*(1), 82–89.

Graham, P. L. (2023). *It's not just for naughty kids' – Project explores girls' experiences of alternative education settings.* Retrieved October 17, 2024, from https://arc-nenc.nihr.ac.uk/news/project-explores-girls-experiences-of-alternative-education/

Grover, S. (2004). Why won't they listen to us? On giving power and voice to children participating in social research. *Childhood, 11*(1), 81–93.

Hall, J. (2015). Same-sex friendships. In C. R. Berger & M. E. Roloff (Eds.), *The international encyclopedia of interpersonal communication* (pp. 1–8). John Wiley and Sons Inc. https://doi.org/10.1002/9781118540190.wbeic138

Kay, L. (2019). Guardians of research: Negotiating the strata of gatekeepers in research with vulnerable participants. *Practice, 1*(1), 37–52.

Knowles, C., Murray, C., Gau, J., & Toste, J. R. (2020). Teacher–student working alliance among students with emotional and behavioral disorders. *Journal of Psychoeducational Assessment, 38*(6), 753–761. https://doi.org/10.1177/0734282919874268

Malcolm, A. (2018). Exclusions and alternative provision: Piecing together the picture. *Emotional and Behavioural Difficulties, 23*(1), 69–80.

McGrath, K. F., & Van Bergen, P. (2019). Attributions and emotional competence: Why some teachers experience close relationships with disruptive students (and others don't). *Teachers and Teaching, Theory and Practice, 25*(3), 334–357. https://doi.org/10.1080/13540602.2019.1569511

McNulty, C. P., and Roseboro, D. L. (2009). "I'm not really that bad": Alternative school students, stigma, and identity politics. *Equity & Excellence in Education, 42*, 412–427.

Mills, M., McGregor, G., Baroutsis, A., Te Riele, K., & Hayes, D. (2016). Alternative education and social justice: Considering issues of affective and contributive justice. *Critical Studies in Education, 57*(1), 100–115.

Mitchell, S. J., Slowther, A. M., Coad, J., Akhtar, S., Hyde, E., Khan, D., & Dale, J. (2019). Ethics and patient and public involvement with children and young people. *Archives of Disease in Childhood: Education and Practice Edition, 104*, 195–200.

Mitra, D. L. (2008). Amplifying student voice. *Educational Leadership, 66*(3), 20–25.

Morrow, V., & Richards, M. (1996). The ethics of social research with children: An overview. *Children & Society, 10*(2), 90–105.

National Institute for Health and Care Research. (2014). *Briefing notes for researchers – public involvement in NHS, health and social care research.* Retrieved October 17, 2024, from https://www.nihr.ac.uk/briefing-notes-researchers-public-involvement-nhs-health-and-social-care-research

National Institute for Health and Care Research Applied Research Collaboration North East and North Cumbria. (2024). *Ethical practice guidelines for public involvement and community engagement.* Retrieved October 31, 2024, from https://arc-nenc.nihr.ac.uk/wp-content/uploads/2024/08/Ethical-Practice-Guidelines-FINAL-July-24-1.pdf

National Statistics. (2023). *Permanent exclusions and suspensions in England, autumn term 2022/23.* Retrieved October 31, 2024, from https://explore-education-statistics.service.gov.uk/find-statistics/suspensions-and-permanent-exclusions-in-england

Nilsson, S., Björkman, B., Almqvist, A. L., Almqvist, L., Björk-Willén, P., Donohue, D., Enskär, K., Granlund, M., Huus, K., & Hvit, S. (2015). Children's voices – Differentiating a child perspective from a child's perspective. *Developmental Neurorehabilitation, 18*(3), 162–168.

Russell, L., & Thomson, P. (2011). Girls and gender in alternative education provision. *Ethnography and Education, 6*(3), 293–308.

Spencer, L. P., Addison, M., Alderson, H., McGovern, W., McGovern, R., Kaner, E., & O'Donnell, A. (2021). 'The drugs did for me what I couldn't do for myself': A qualitative exploration of the relationship between mental health and amphetamine-type stimulant (ATS) use. *Substance Abuse: Research and Treatment, 15*, 1–8. https://doi.org/10.1177/11782218211060852

Tangen, R. (2008). Listening to children's voices in educational research: Some theoretical and methodological problems. *European Journal of Special Needs Education, 23*, 157–166.

Wood, M. A., Bukowski, W. M., & Santo, J. B. (2017). Friendship security, but not friendship intimacy, moderates the stability of anxiety during preadolescence. *Journal of Clinical Child and Adolescent Psychology, 46*(6), 798–809.

Chapter 18

The Young Dads Collective: Sustaining PICE Through a Qualitative Longitudinal and Participatory Research Programme

Anna Tarrant[a], Linzi Ladlow[a] and Laura Way[b]

[a]*University of Lincoln, UK*
[b]*University of Roehampton, UK*

Abstract

This chapter introduces the Young Dads Collective (YDC) as a Public Involvement and Community Engagement (PICE) model that has evolved and been reformed through the various funded phases of a qualitative, longitudinal, and participatory research programme called Following Young Fathers Further (FYFF). Supporting young fathers, aged 25 and under, to advocate for father-inclusive support, the model engages young fathers to share their insights about fatherhood and navigating complex health and social care systems as 'experts by experience' while simultaneously addressing training gaps for professionals about 'what works' in more effectively supporting men as-fathers. The chapter highlights the significance of the PICE model in fostering trust, ownership, and agency among young fathers who are often underrepresented or overlooked in traditional research, practice, and policy frameworks, demonstrating how they can be effectively supported to become not only subjects of study but active agents of change within their communities. The power of collaborations and relational dialogues between fathers, researchers, multi-agency professionals, and policymakers are also explored. In particular, the potentials

Public Involvement and Community Engagement in Applied Health and Social Care Research: Critical Perspectives and Innovative Practice, 219–230

and challenges of bringing together diverse communities around a shared set of interests in father-inclusion are exemplified and considered.

Keywords: Experts by experience; father-inclusion; health and social care practice; PICE; young fathers

Introduction

Young fathers, aged 25 and under when they first become a parent or conceive a pregnancy, represent a cohort who are often underserved and misrepresented in the context of the wider public health and social welfare systems that are designed to serve the needs of families and alleviate social distress. Evidence suggests that they are often overlooked and marginalised in parenting support, public health, and social welfare contexts more generally. Often problematically assumed to be a risk to their children rather than a resource to their families, they report numerous challenges in navigating the variety of services and systems that are ostensibly designed to support them as fathers (Neale & Tarrant, 2024).

Responding to these challenges, this chapter presents on one aspect of a programme of participatory, inclusive, and collaborative research and innovation work, that has been sustained through three funded phases of qualitative longitudinal research exploring the parenting journeys and support needs of a cohort of young fathers, aged 25 and under. Together, these phases of research comprise the Following Young Fathers Further (*FYFF*) research programme (see Neale & Tarrant, 2024; Tarrant et al., 2024). The instigation of two place-based initiatives, built around a model of best practice called the Young Dads Collective (YDC), later referred to as the YDC North (2016–2017) and the Grimsby Dads Collective (2020–2024), have both been funded by and facilitated through this extended research and innovation programme. Utilising qualitative longitudinal and participatory methodologies and approaches and fostering a collective commitment to father-inclusive practice and policy (Tarrant, 2025a), these linked and connected studies and initiatives have been innovative both in facilitating sustained collaborative relationships and dialogues between young fathers and multi-agency professionals for the purposes of driving whole systems change and transformation.

The *YDC* is introduced here as a novel PICE initiative that has evolved throughout the FYFF programme of research to engage communities of young fathers and multi-agency professionals more directly in dialogues built around influencing more inclusive service design and delivery. Central to this chapter is an exploration of how the FYFF programme has supported the evolution of the YDC model over time while simultaneously capturing the impacts of what we have come to call *longitudinal co-creation* (Tarrant, 2025a, 2025b) on the key communities involved.

While conducted by a team of largely sociological researchers, the interdisciplinary relevance and applications of the FYFF programme and the YDC model reported here have had a significant influence and impact on health and social care practice through advocacy and promotion of father-inclusive practice and policy.

Background: The Marginalisation of Young Fathers in Contexts of Service Support

The evolution of the YDC model through the FYFF study reflects a responsiveness to extended, real-time research findings generated with young fathers and multi-agency youth and family support professionals about 'what works' (and doesn't) in ensuring young fathers receive the support they need to better fulfil their ambitions to be there for their children (Davies & Neale, 2015; Neale & Tarrant, 2024). Two key findings prompted the instigation of new versions of the model in Leeds and Grimsby in subsequent funded phases of the studies. Firstly, in tracing the parenting journeys and support of young fathers over time, it became clear that they were keen to 'be there' for their children and to remain so over time but they encountered a complex set of challenges in doing so (Neale & Tarrant, 2024). The increasingly insecure labour market, welfare conditionality, the housing crisis, and complex relationships with co-parents and wider family members, including (grand)parents, combine to either support or hinder young men in sustaining their relationships with their children.

Secondly, given that the support needs of young fathers are often amplified, as parents but also as young people navigating challenging social and political contexts, they often need and come into contact with numerous services and support providers across their parenting journeys. This can range from universal public health services, social care, and child welfare services, to specialist support services that are designed to engage young fathers through strengths-based approaches (Neale & Tarrant, 2024; Tarrant et al., 2024). In terms of universal and mainstream service engagements, young fathers often encounter services that under-serve fathers or, as noted, assume them to be a potential risk to their families. Indeed, there is a growing body of interdisciplinary evidence, developed and applied across numerous fields of research and practice, including social work, public health, and criminal justice, that is centred around the concept of *father engagement*, that draws attention to low levels engagement of fathers in parenting interventions, housing, and child and family welfare and child protection systems (Ladlow et al., 2024; Panter-Brick et al., 2014; Philip et al., 2018; Perez-Vaisvidovsky et al., 2023; Scourfield et al., 2024; Tarrant, 2025a).

Much of this research in synthesis confirms why there are cross-sector and persistent systemic challenges in engaging men as fathers, highlighting numerous societal, organisational, interpersonal, cultural, and systemic factors (Bateson et al., 2017; Darwin et al., 2017; Phillip et al., 2018; Tarrant, 2021, see Tarrant (2025a) for a review). Evidence also suggests that cultures and practices within family and child services often contribute to the exclusion of men from caregiving roles (Pfitzner et al., 2020). This exclusion is reinforced by policies and practices centred on mothers and a care landscape shaped by deeply gendered ideologies about parenting roles (Pfitzner et al., 2020; Philip et al., 2018). Fuelled by the neoliberal logics of services and policies, as well as years of austerity, increased pressure on financial resources and time limitations also means that professionals often lack access to training on gender sensitivity, inclusivity, and cultural diversity, hindering the development of strategies that support diverse father participation.

In the UK, specialised services for fathers are fragmented and difficult to access, due to a lack of adequate funding and long-term support. While there are examples of effective, community-based initiatives offering social support for young fathers (e.g., Hanna, 2018), their availability is uneven, creating a 'postcode lottery' (Tarrant & Neale, 2017). This colloquial concept in the UK refers to a situation where there is a geographically unequal provision of services, such as healthcare, medical treatment, or education, meaning that access is determined by where people live rather than the extent of need.

The interpersonal relationships between young fathers and professionals are also key here. Young fathers report how often interchangeable practices of *support*, *sidelining*, and *surveillance* (Neale & Tarrant, 2024) variably influence their abilities to access the resources they need to support their families and/or sustain their relationships with their children and co-parents.

This complex and dynamic picture means that changing service delivery models and resource constraints for the purposes of becoming more father-inclusive (see Tarrant, 2025) often contributes to the perception that there is something immutable about engaging men as fathers (Bateson et al., 2017). Across the FYFF research programme, the YDC has been identified as relatively unique in this space, offering a feasible and adaptable model of education and training delivered by and for young fathers and as an effective way of addressing regional training gaps around father-inclusion for professional audiences.

The Evolution of the Young Dads Collective as an Innovative PICE Initiative

The first funded phase of the FYFF programme, Following Young Fathers (2012-15, Neale & Tarrant, 2024), identified several specialist models of practice in the third sector that were working effectively to transform systems from within, not only by highlighting the historical exclusion of young fathers from health and social care sectors but by providing opportunities for young fathers themselves to promote father-inclusion (Tarrant & Neale, 2017). Specialist models of support including the North East Young Dads and Lads (Gateshead), DadsRock (Edinburgh) and the YDC, work nationally to advocate for more father-friendly support and service cultures and greater inclusion for men as caregivers in parenting services, healthcare, and social policy, and ensuring that young fathers are supported and valued (see also Hanna, 2018). However, the YDC was noted at the time for the effectiveness of its participatory design and its capacity to involve young fathers directly in the process of influencing practice and policy through sharing insights about their lives and what works in engagements with services (Tarrant & Neale, 2017).

For brief context, the YDC model was originally developed by a national charity with a remit to improve social conditions for British families through a focus on childcare and the early years. First established in 2010 and running until 2013 as a digital and social media platform called 'Young Dads TV' (Colfer et al., 2015), the initiative was created to represent a more 'authentic' voice of young fathers in a context where their experiences, perceptions, and voices were seldom heard. As an offer, it was therefore novel in responding to an observation that young fathers lacked a forum for their own voices and experiences, where discourses about young fatherhood were dominated by professionals, researchers, and policymakers (Colfer et al., 2015).

The model evolved into an education and training programme whereby young fathers are supported to share their experiences of parenting and service support with multi-agency professionals. A unique strategy employed by YDC is training and recognising young fathers as 'experts by experience' (Neale & Tarrant, 2024; Tarrant & Neale, 2017). The organisation initially recruited a small team of young fathers based in London and provided them with training, mentorship, and opportunities to share their insights with practitioners, service providers, and policymakers. The training, referred to as train the trainer, provided support to young fathers around how to present their experiences of their parenting and support engagements, as well as insights about the wider exclusion of fathers from services and the value of advocating for father-inclusive practices and services. In so doing, the model was designed to influence changes in policy and practice while offering individual and peer support to the young men involved.

The YDC model evolved to involving young fathers in co-designing and delivering a wide range of flexible interventions, such as consultations, staff training, workshops, action research, outreach, advocacy, and mentoring. Via these engagements, it began to support new dialogues between young fathers as a community and between professionals from different services and sectors, in a way that proactively and productively addressed gaps in communications between professionals and their beneficiaries.

For professionals, the model works as a training opportunity, enabling them to communicate the lived experiences of young fathers in their own service contexts and to advocate for practice and policy improvements. Through these initiatives, YDC strives to improve the quality and scope of services available to young fathers and to enhance the ways professionals engage, communicate with, and support them. An overview of the core tenets of the model and its theory of change are outlined next.

The YDC Theory of Change

In its current iteration the YDC model empowers young fathers (aged 25 and under) by involving them directly in educating professionals about father-inclusion as a mechanism for shaping the services and policies that affect their lives. It operates on three key pillars:

1. *A Peer-Led Approach:* Young fathers with lived experience are trained to become ambassadors, sharing their insights and advocating for better support for young dads. The fathers involved also benefit from peer support and learning.
2. *Workshops and Consultations with Multi-agency Professionals:* Training sessions led by young fathers are run with audiences of cross-sector professionals, helping them to understand the challenges young fathers face and providing a space for exploration of how to improve engagement.

3. *Policy Influence and Advocacy:* With the support of professional staff, young fathers are supported to collaborate with policymakers to raise awareness about the needs of young fathers, aiming to create systemic changes that promote inclusive services.

Co-creating Place-based Models of the YDC

Through various funded phases of the FYFF programme of research, what started out as a London-centric digital and social media platform for advocacy and campaigning has since evolved into a place- and evidence-based model of support. These models have been developed to provide a voice and a platform for young fathers in new areas of England by engaging them in the process of influencing service design and delivery through the education and training of multi-agency professionals about father-inclusive practice (Tarrant & Neale, 2017; Tarrant et al., 2024). In these ways, it reflects the public involvement and community engagement approach.

The scale-up of the YDC model was enabled by the participatory ethos of the FYFF study and the qualitative longitudinal methodology underpinning each study phase (Tarrant, 2023). The co-creation of two additional place-based offers: the YDC North in Leeds (Tarrant & Neale, 2017) and the Grimsby Dads Collective (Way & Tarrant, 2023) also responded to regionally identified challenges in delivering young father inclusive support. Engagement with professionals from these areas confirmed the baseline findings from the FYF study, that there is a need for young fathers to be understood and acknowledged in new ways (Neale & Davies, 2015). A key barrier to their engagement with services is the widespread perception that they are 'hard to reach', a problematic language that contributes to their silencing and marginalisation (Davies & Neale, 2015; Neale & Davies, 2015; Neale et al., 2015). As we note elsewhere (Tarrant et al., 2024), the language has been used in health and social care spheres and discourse to describe 'community groups that are difficult to involve, engage or achieve participation in research or health delivery programmes' (Islam & Small, 2020, p. 7). Critiques of the language suggest that as a concept that connotates a deficit located within certain marginalised and/or minoritised communities, onus and blame is placed on those who are under-represented in health and social systems, meaning that opportunities for productive engagement with those communities, as well as how services might be made 'easier to access', are overlooked.

The study emphasised the importance of recognising young fathers as 'experts by experience' – allowing them to speak for themselves, offer peer support, participate in professional training, and act as ambassadors for young fathers more broadly. This approach not only empowers young fathers but also aims to shift professional attitudes towards them. Achieving this cultural change, however, requires ongoing professional support and training for the young fathers involved, including for those residing outside of London. Expanding the YDC to new regions in the UK was therefore identified as a critical next step in extending this lived experience and practitioner-led effort.

Both the co-creation process and the delivery of the new models have involved local communities of young fathers in the design and delivery of the models. Local and national champions of father-inclusive practice have also engaged in the co-design process of these transformative projects, both iteratively designed to respond to the needs of local communities and ensure a place-based and context-responsive version of the intervention. As community-driven models, both shared the core aim of fostering engagement, support, and positive outcomes for young fathers, as well as evidence and lived-experience-driven approaches to professional education and training.

Opportunities and Challenges in Co-creating the Young Dad Collective

Underpinned by the participatory ethos of the FYFF study, public involvement and community engagement principles were embedded throughout the co-creation process. Both place-based models were built on the evidence that those with lived experience – young fathers – are best positioned to inform and improve service provision for families. Their insights are critical to understanding the unique challenges and opportunities young fathers face, and their participation ensures that solutions including those developed and delivered via the YDC models, are grounded in real-world experiences rather than assumptions or stereotypes.

Recruitment and Training of Young Fathers as 'Experts by Experience'

One of the key elements of the model was the training of young fathers in a way that enables their recognition as 'experts by experience' but also the crafting and telling of these experiences in a way that is influential for a multi-agency, cross-sector professional audience. This process, which involved active partnership working with the dads and professionals from the core services involved in co-creating the YDC models, began with a targeted recruitment effort and working closely with local community organisations youth services, and social care providers to identify young fathers who had the potential to act as advocates and educators. Recruitment was aimed at those with lived experience of young fatherhood, a commitment to engaged fatherhood, willingness and capability to share personal experiences, and an interest in influencing health and social care policies and practices.

The training programme involved a process of supporting young fathers to tell their narratives and share research findings about the support needs and service experiences of young fathers in health and social care and wider social welfare services. This process was designed not only to empower the young fathers but also to ensure that they could engage meaningfully with health and social care professionals, equipping them with the tools to advocate for father-inclusion in service delivery. Interviews with the young fathers who benefited from the training in each model confirmed that they felt valued, heard, and supported:

> I was really nervous before I had to present, because of it being a big crowd. It helped with me courage. I felt valued by the people

in the room, people who came over and talked to me and said well done, which really give me a boost. Made me feel confident to do it again. (YDC North member)

Buzzing, love being listened to. It's not just the work with the professionals it's about meeting up with other dads when we do the planning. We all want other dads to have a better experience. (YDC North member)

In a context where young fathers often feel overlooked and sidelined the YDC model provides a space for dialogue, communication, and empowerment for those it supports. Our interviews with the young fathers confirmed that their engagement contributed to a growing sense of self-worth and self-perception, which was linked to being included, listened to, making an active contribution, and participating in aspects of activism and motivation.

As a PICE model, the YDC also involved the young fathers in wider and participatory processes of impact, as a form of participatory impact. As reported elsewhere (Tarrant, 2023; Tarrant & Neale, 2017), YDC North supported five young dads to develop new skills and grow in confidence as they observed the reactions of professionals from varied health and social care agencies, education, and the statutory and voluntary sectors. All three versions of the model have also prompted local changes to regional policy, creating new opportunities for the political participation of the young men. One of the young fathers in Leeds was consulted on a new draft action policy plan aimed to support teenage parents and joined a regional board as a user representative, enabling him to influence local decision making (Tarrant, 2023; Tarrant & Neale, 2017). In Grimsby, there have been strategic and operational changes to policy and practice, as one local manager reflected (see also, Way & Tarrant, 2023):

The training for professionals, and the process of promoting and championing the project, have contributed to improvements in the strategic and operational environment in Grimsby that have had a positive impact on families' lives.

Despite the varying benefits to the young fathers who engaged with each YDC initiative, a key challenge was the continued recruitment of young men to the model and sustaining their involvement over time. This was especially the case in Grimsby, where the impacts of deprivation and limited travel options made the model much less accessible for some than others. Varying degrees of confidence and skill also reflected inequalities between the young dads, meaning that the most eloquent and capable young fathers were selected initially to deliver the training. This sat in tension with our principles around democratisation and participation, so efforts were made to explore the inclusion of those with higher support needs. In London, for example, the more established model, a young father with learning difficulties was supported to film a video to play in case he felt unable to deliver on the day, but he felt confident enough to present at the training.

Through a process of concerted reflexivity that was built in throughout the co-creation process, all efforts were made to ensure that inclusive language and imagery was used in communications and outreach, to offer digital delivery of the training, and to generate data and evidence about diverse experiences and perceptions of the model experiences of the model to ensure a responsive, flexible and inclusive approach that would be accessible to all young fathers, regardless of circumstance. The messiness and iterative character of the co-creation process, however, meant that the teams involved in co-creating each place-based model often had to make trade-offs to ensure they functioned effectively while also providing a space for the transformative dialogues necessary to instigate a culture change across the wider health and care system that would have wider benefits for all fathers.

A key function of the longitudinal co-creation process, albeit one that also provided essential insights for further analytic consideration of the contexts through which young fatherhood and service design and engagements are shaped, was the need for all partners to engage in a process of constant reflexivity the process to support the facilitation of the young father's involvement in real time and in ways that were attuned to their diverse needs, experiences and capabilities.

Educating Health and Social Care Professionals: Impacts on Learning and Professional Development

The training had a profound impact on many of the professionals who participated in it. Confirming the broad appeal of the training and its need, attendees at the workshops are those representing the education sector; youth, family, and parenthood provisions; social work; housing; employment; and health and social care. The structure and constraints many professionals experience in their professional contexts mean they often have limited opportunities for reflexive practice. Because of this, and combined with the wider cultural, organisational, and relational barriers they navigate, they report struggles around identifying and implementing father-inclusive practice (see Tarrant, 2023). The training uniquely creates an opportunity for communication and dialogue between multi-agency professionals and young fathers that do not currently exist.

Hearing directly from the young fathers was one of the most powerful and reported aspects of the training, as it provided real-world insights that could not be captured through textbooks or traditional training methods. Moreover, the training was reported to be transformational not only because it equipped professionals with practical tools and strategies that they could realistically implement in their practice but it also provided a transformative or 'sacred learning experience' (Mezirow, 1997; Tisdell, 2008) where professionals experienced revelation moments and shifts in mindset where they said they would consider dads in ways they had not before. This included changes to how they communicated with fathers, as well as adjustments to the way services were structured and delivered to ensure that they were more inclusive of fathers.

To capture potential for changes in mindset and practice following the training, professionals are asked to provide qualitative feedback and 'pledges to practice', confirming their key learning and plans for adapting their practice in the future. Delegates have said:

> '*I'll think more about how to help young fathers. I will think beyond mums.*'

Professional feedback after YDC North training

> '*I believe that services will make changes after listening to the dads*'

Professional feedback after Grimsby Dads Collective training

The extent to which professionals were able to instigate change within their organisations in the longer term has been less straightforward to capture. Despite sending out surveys three months post-training to attendees, responses were thin. Nevertheless, professionals were keen to share their experience of making changes with the team, as the following quote by a health worker exemplifies:

> Thank you for your delivery yesterday, it was extremely useful to our organisation. On returning to the office following this I had a case discussion with one of my team. We discussed the worries that mum has and difficulties in the case. We mapped our worries and then I asked what dads' thoughts were and how does he support the family, are there any family members on his side of the family. The reply from the [health organisation] was that dad is not really in the picture and doesn't really have much involvement. I asked if dad had been spoken to and the reply was 'no' as I don't think mum wants him involved. I reminded the [health organisation professional] what training she had just attended and she had a penny drop moment and said that her first task was to contact dad and discuss the case with him and explore the wider family network.

Key here is that the mutual creation of these novel dialogic contexts for public involvement and community engagement meant that the workshops themselves, and the new space for dialogues they engendered, were vital in the reconstruction of deficit views of young fathers. As an additional form of evidence, the feedback confirms the transformative potential of establishing unique, curated spaces for engagement between young fathers and professionals. In encouraging support and the avoidance of sidelining and surveillance, young fathers influence constructions of young fatherhood, and practice change is actively encouraged.

Conclusion

As a PICE initiative that has been co-created through multiple phases of funded research through the *FYFF* study, the YDC is a powerful model of professional training and engagement that empowers fathers who are marginalised in health and social care contexts. A commitment to public involvement and community engagement is central to the effectiveness of the model, which is designed to engender processes of transformation and systems change in ways that respond to the voices and experiences of young fathers and the training needs of professionals.

Indeed, the delivery of young father-led training and education provides a space for productive dialogue and transformation for diverse communities in ways that are not presently provided within existing systems of support and highlights both the value and challenges of public involvement and community engagement in engaging 'experts by experience' to address social and health inequalities; in this case through the promotion of father-inclusion as a connective language for promoting father-inclusive practice.

By involving young fathers in this way, the co-creative process not only worked to improve the inclusivity of health and social care services but also empowered select young fathers to advocate for changes that would improve service experiences for them and for those who follow behind them. As a participatory approach, the model exemplifies how marginalised groups can be involved in professional training and service change in meaningful and empowering ways, while also ensuring that their voices are heard and have influence on the policies and practices that affect their lives and shape their parenting journeys. Furthermore, the involvement and support of researchers enabled transformations to occur at the dynamic interface of research, practice and policy (Neale, 2021), ensuring that the exchange of knowledge is aligned closely with the evidence-base about what matters to fathers and what works for professionals in the provision of inclusive support offers and cultures. Ultimately, this model of PICE demonstrates the importance of recognising communities as essential partners in the process of establishing more inclusive, equitable, and responsive systems of care and provides an approach that may also work with other marginalised and seldom heard communities.

References

Bateson, K., Darwin, Z., Galdas, P., & Rosan, C. (2017). Engaging father: Acknowledging the barriers. *Journal of Health Visiting, 5*(3), 126–132.

Colfer, S., Turner-Uaandja, H., & Johnson, L. (2015). Young Dads TV: Digital voices of young fathers. *Families, Relationships and Societies, 4*(2), 339–345.

Darwin, Z., Galdas, P., Hinchliff, S., Littlewood, E., McMillan, D., McGowan, L., & Gilbody, S. (2017). Fathers' views and experiences of their own mental health during pregnancy and the first postnatal year: A qualitative interview study of men participating in the UK Born and Bred in Yorkshire (BaBY) cohort. *BMC Pregnancy Childbirth, 17*(1), 1–15.

Davies, L., & Neale, B. (2015). Supporting young fathers: The promise, potential and perils of statutory service provision. *Families, Relationships and Societies, 4*(2), 331–338.

Hanna, E. (2018). *Supporting young men as fathers: Gendered understandings of group-based community provisions.* Palgrave MacMillan.

Islam, S., & Small, N. (2020). An annotated and critical glossary of the terminology of inclusion in healthcare and health research. *Research Involvement and Engagement, 6*, 14.

Ladlow, L., Neale, B., & Tarrant, A. (2024). Finding a place to parent. In B. Neale & A. Tarrant (Eds.), *The dynamics of young fatherhood: Understanding the parenting journeys and support needs of young fathers* (pp. 157–176). Policy Press.

Mezirow, J. (1997). Transformative learning: Theory to practice. *New Directions for Adult and Continuing Education, 74*, 5–12.

Neale, B. (2021). Fluid enquiry, complex causality, policy processes: Making a difference with qualitative longitudinal research. *Social Policy and Society, 20*(4), 653–669.

Neale, B., & Davies, L. (2015). Seeing young fathers in a different way: Editorial. *Families, Relationships and Societies, 4*(2), 309–314.

Neale, B., Lau Clayton, C., Davies, L., & Ladlow, L. (2015). *Researching the lives of young fathers: The Following Young Fathers study and dataset.* Briefing Paper no. 8. University of Leeds.

Neale, B., & Tarrant, A. (2024). *The dynamics of young fatherhood: Understanding the parenting journeys and support needs of young fathers.* Policy Press.

Panter-Brick, C., Burgess, A., Eggerman, M., McAllister, F., Pruett, K., & Leckman, J. F. (2014). Practitioner review: Engaging fathers – Recommendations for a game change in parenting interventions based on a systematic review of the global evidence. *The Journal of Child Psychology and Psychiatry, 55*(11), 1187–1212.

Perez-Vaisvidovsky, N., Halpern, A., Mizrahi, R., & Atalla, Z. (2023). "Fathers are very important, but they aren't our contact persons": The primary contact person assumption and the absence of fathers in social work interventions. *Families in Society, 104*(3), 292–305.

Pfitzner, N., Humphreys, C., & Hegarty, K. (2020). Bringing men in from the margins: Father-inclusive practices for the delivery of parenting interventions. *Child & Family Social Work, 25*(1), 198–206.

Phillip, G., Clifton, J., & Brandon, M. (2018). The trouble with fathers: The impact of time and gendered-thinking on working relationships between fathers and social workers in child protection practice in England. *Journal of Family Issues, 40*(16), 2288–2309.

Scourfield, J., Davies, J., Jones, K., & Maxwell, N. (2024). Improving children's services engagement of fathers in child protection: Logic model for an organisational development and staff training intervention. *International Journal on Child Maltreatment, 7*, 607–614.

Tarrant, A. (2021). *Fathering and poverty: Uncovering men's participation in low-income family life.* Policy Press.

Tarrant, A. (2025a). Father-inclusion: A sensitising concept and framing strategy for addressing the systemic exclusion of men as-fathers across services. *Families, Relationships and Societies.* https://doi.org/10.1332/20467435Y2025D000000061

Tarrant, A. (2025b). Instigating father-inclusive practice interventions with young fathers and multi-agency professionals: The transformative potential of qualitative longitudinal and co-creative methodologies. *Families, Relationships and Societies, 14*(2), 158–176.

Tarrant, A., & Neale, B. (Eds.). (2017). *Learning to support young dads, responding to young fathers in a different way.* University of Leeds.

Tarrant, A., Way, L., & Ladlow, L. (2024). Increasing father engagement among minoritised fathers through proactive service support and outreach: Insights from a participatory pilot study. *Community, Work & Family*, 1–18. https://doi.org/10.1080/13668803.2023.2299248

Tisdell, E. (2008). Spirituality and adult learning. In S. Merriam (Ed.), *Third update on adult learning theory: New directions for adult and continuing education, No. 119* (pp. 27–36). Jossey-Bass.

Way, L., & Tarrant, A. (2023). *Co-creating a father-inclusive practice intervention: Insights for policy and practice from the process of instigating the Grimsby Dads Collective, FYFF findings and innovation series 2020–24, report 5.* University of Lincoln. https://fyff.co.uk files/7d0ea445d79f2cdfb6d450ef9914314317fb653a.pdf

Chapter 19

Co-producing Research with Care Experienced Young Adults and Social Work Professionals

Emily R. Munro[a], Seana Friel[a], Amy Lynch[b] and CJ Hamilton[a]

[a]*Tilda Goldberg Centre for Social Work and Social Care, University of Bedfordshire, UK*
[b]*Warwick Business School, University of Warwick, UK*

Abstract

Drawing on the National Institute for Health and Care Research (NIHR) principles of co-production, the chapter reflects on and critiques the approaches adopted in two leaving care studies. The first employed care-experienced young adults as peer researchers in a study that aimed to advance understanding of the 'ingredients' to implement and sustain innovations. In the second study, a Networked Learning Community (NLC) was established, bringing together care-experienced young people, frontline practitioners, and managers to develop accessible tools and resources to support social work practice. The findings highlight the need for attentiveness to relational safety, capacity-building, and reflective practices. They also demonstrate the role that values play in building authentic relationships, and disrupting traditional power hierarchies. However, practical considerations, including training, adequate time and resources, and the use of a range of communications channels, are also important. The chapter concludes with a call for further formal evaluation of co-production models, particularly the NLC model, and their

Public Involvement and Community Engagement in Applied Health and Social Care Research: Critical Perspectives and Innovative Practice, 231–245

long-term effects on both research outcomes and the development of participants' skills and confidence.

Keywords: Care leavers; co-production; Networked Learning Community; participatory; research; peer research; knowledge animation

Introduction

Over the last two decades, there has been considerable expansion in the field of care-leaving research to understand the needs and experiences of young people negotiating the transition from care to adulthood. Article 12 of the United Nations Convention on the Rights of the Child (the right to be heard and taken seriously) has also provided impetus for the rise in participatory research approaches (United Nations, 2009). It has been noted that a range of activities have been hung under the 'participatory' umbrella. These include: simply being invited to participate in studies designed and directed by academics using traditional methods; projects using 'child-centred' forms of communication (e.g., art, photography, or drama); involving children and young people in research about aspects of their own lives and encouraging participants to have some impact on aspects of the process, such as research design, analysis or dissemination; formal training in social research methods to carry out research into other people's lives on topics relevant to them (Holland et al., 2010). Mannay et al. (2019) highlight that 'giving voice' to marginalised groups using participatory approaches is not the same as these voices being *heard* and *acted upon*. Consideration also needs to be given to disseminating messages in accessible ways to engender changes in practice (Mannay et al., 2019).

Peer research, that is, research which is steered, conducted, and implemented with individuals who share lived experiences with the study's participant group (Lushey, 2017), has been employed in care-leaving studies both nationally and internationally (Kelly, van Breda, et al., 2020; Munro & Kelly, 2025). Levels of participation across the research cycle vary, but the approach seeks to democratise the research process with the aim 'to empower both the respondents and the peer researchers and to maximise the scope for deeper insight into issues through a common experience or understanding' (Dixon et al., 2018, p. 10). Bridging the gap between researchers and participants has the potential to facilitate access to 'harder to reach' members of the community by mitigating traditional power imbalances (Yang & Dibb, 2020). This can create space for more honest and open dialogue, overall involvement, and thus offers the potential for the generation of richer data. However, these benefits are not automatic. Sharing power with peer researchers may be perceived as a threat to 'objectivity' and the validity of findings may be questioned by the academic community and/or policy makers (Lushey & Munro, 2015).

The literature on peer research in care-leaving research in the UK suggests that whilst there are variations in how this approach is operationalised, studies employing peer research have had a policy impact. For example, findings from the Staying Put evaluation (Munro et al., 2012) were used to lobby for legislative reforms, which were subsequently enacted. In Northern Ireland, the You Only Leave Once study (Kelly et al., 2016) led to changes in mandatory data collection regarding young people's disability status. However, concerns have been raised that legal rights and policy developments do not always translate into practice and that there are multiple barriers to implementation in practice (Munro et al., 2024).

Chapter Focus

This chapter provides reflections on the application of co-production principles in two leaving-care research studies. The studies differed in terms of design, resourcing, duration, and focus. The Exploring Innovation in Transitions (EXIT) study employed care-experienced peer researchers over a three-year period in a study that aimed to advance understanding of 'ingredients' to implement and sustain innovations. In the care leavers, COVID-19 and Transitions from Care (CCTC) study, care leavers were not involved in shaping the research design or in data collection. Instead, a NLC was established, bringing together care leavers and social work professionals, who over an eight-month period, engaged in collaborative learning and offered their expertise to assist with data interpretation, develop recommendations, and create accessible tools for practice.

It is recognised that although co-production has gained prominence, definitional ambiguities persist (Bandola-Gill et al., 2023). The NIHR five principles of co-production (sharing power, including all perspectives and skills, respecting and valuing all knowledge, reciprocity, and building and maintaining relationships) were used as a guiding framework to reflect on and critique the approaches adopted in the two studies.

Overview of the Studies

EXIT (2020–2024) was funded by the Economic and Social Research Council (ESRC) and brought together an academic research team from organisational science, public health, social care, and participation experts to develop understanding of how to sustain, scale, and spread innovations designed to improve young people's transition from care (Currie et al., 2025). Five care-experienced young adults were recruited as peer researchers and contributed to empirical case study research, including designing consent materials, shadowing and conducting interviews, attending meetings with case study sites and sharing findings. Due to the social distancing regulations imposed as a response to COVID-19, research activities mostly took place in virtual online spaces. In parallel to the case study research, an internally focussed nested action research study (Reason & Bradbury, 2008) was co-designed and undertaken to obtain everyone in the team's perspectives upon strengths and limitations of the peer research approach, including through a series of focus groups (Lynch et al., 2024).

CCTC (2020–2022) was also funded by ESRC, as part of UK Research and Innovation's rapid response to COVID-19. It explored the impact of COVID-19 on young people's experiences and transitions, examining where they went, the services and support they received, and how they fared (Munro et al., 2022). In CCTC, an NLC was established, which brought together seven care-experienced young adults, six leaving care personal advisors or team managers, and five operational managers from six of the participating local authorities. NLC activity predominantly took the form of community workshops, and a total of six workshops lasting between 1.5 and 4.5 hours were convened. All but one of the workshops were held online, as participants were geographically spread and had competing demands on their time. Outside of allocated workshop time, participants were invited to share views and ideas on topics that had been discussed in the group.

Reflections on the Application of NIHR's Principles of Co-production in EXIT and CCTC

Sharing Power

Providing *opportunities to be involved throughout the research* has been identified as a principle for 'good' involvement in research, although it has been recognised that levels of involvement might fluctuate at different points in the research cycle (Liabo et al., 2020). Traditionally, academics and funders have determined research priorities based on their assessment of gaps in the evidence base and perspectives on what is important. There have been calls to pay more attention to service users' and providers' perspectives on *what* should be researched, to produce findings that are relevant and responsive to their needs (Liabo & Roberts, 2019). Williams et al. (2020) emphasise the importance of service users making 'meaningful contributions to agenda setting, not merely being "involved" once these important decisions have been made by those who traditionally hold power in research settings' (p. 4). It has also been suggested that there may be a reluctance on the part of researchers to share power during the analysis and write-up stages of the research cycle (Hopkins et al., 2024). In parallel, however, it has been noted that 'power without responsibility and responsibility without power are problematic' (Liabo & Roberts, 2019). An equal partnership may not be realistic; roles and responsibilities will vary, but attention should be given to valuing everyone's ideas and providing opportunities for meaningful involvement in the research process, as well as recognising the contributions that people bring (MacLachlan et al., 2024).

The EXIT proposal was submitted in response to a funder call for research to address a gap in the evidence base, rather than responding to service-user defined topics of enquiry. A care-leaver led charity were involved in discussions surrounding the development of the proposal and in the research partnership throughout, but the peer researchers were not partners in the initial phases of the study. Once the peer researchers were recruited, efforts were made to build relationships within the team, including through the induction training which brought together all the peer researchers and offered a safe space to become familiar with the aims and objectives of the study. Each peer researcher was allocated to a university and case study site with a dedicated Research Fellow as a main point of contact. Weekly meetings were held to discuss the status of the study, and to explore and reflect on opportunities to participate using a novel framework developed in the study. The 'Peer Researcher: Ability-Motivation-Opportunity' (PR: A-M-O) framework integrated elements of the human resource management theory 'Ability-Motivation-Opportunity' (A-M-O) (Applebaum et al., 2000) to guide Peer Researchers and Research Fellows' review and reflection on study opportunities (O) available to the peer researchers that they considered to be motivating and of interest (M) and that fitted with their existing or developing skills and abilities (A) (Lynch et al., 2024). Using the PR: A-M-O framework enabled consideration of roles and contributions in respect of skills, interests and peer researcher's capacity to be involved. As one of the peer researchers reflected:

> I've certainly felt like an equal partner in those meetings with the Research Fellows ... I have had opportunity to, to influence ... we have an opportunity to, you know speak and add to, to the conversation and, and influence the study.
>
> Peer Researcher Focus Group

Quarterly meetings involving the Research Fellow, peer researcher, and the co-investigator were convened as a forum to reflect upon the role and resolve any issues. Opportunities to bring together the whole research team via team meetings were another opportunity to 'share power'. This was particularly true in EXIT, as the inter-disciplinary nature of the study meant that knowledge gaps existed across the team regardless of academic grade; that is, each team member was confronted with new concepts, and whole team meetings provided an opportunity for cross-team learning.

The CCTC proposal was submitted in response to a rapid response call to address urgent issues raised by the COVID-19 crisis. Again, service users were not involved at the proposal stage, but the research questions were responsive to concerns being raised by leaving care advocacy organisations. Throughout the recruitment process, local authorities and young people provided informal feedback, which suggested that the research questions were still seen to be timely and relevant to the leaving care community and practitioners. Whilst the purpose of the NLC was set by the researchers, buy-in was high, and the networked learning approach aimed to draw upon and respect the different knowledge and expertise everyone had to bring.

Including All Perspectives and Skills

Concerns have been raised that recruitment challenges in research with care-leavers mean that samples of participants may not be representative, and that those who are 'disengaged' from services may be less likely to hear about opportunities to take part and/or may be disinclined to do so (Purtell, 2024). One of the potential benefits of peer research is that it may encourage young people whose voices are seldom heard to participate and express views that they may not be confident sharing with an academic researcher (Dixon et al., 2018; Kelly, Friel, et al., 2020). However, Lushey and Munro (2015) also reflect that:

> It is important that the desire to be 'inclusive' does not take precedence over the selection of peer researchers who have the skill and capability (with appropriate support and training) to contribute to the process and interview young people ... Poor recruitment and selection denies participants optimum conditions to tell their story. Proactive management of this part of the process is also important because otherwise there is a danger that peer researchers are 'set up to fail', which is contrary to the aim of empowering and equipping them with transferrable skills. (p. 525)

In the EXIT study peer researchers were recruited via university widening participation teams, reflecting a desire for inclusivity, but also recognising that undergraduate educational experience might be advantageous to facilitate meaningful engagement in a complex interdisciplinary study. By virtue of the recruitment strategy, the 5 peer researchers were all care-experienced undergraduates aged between 18 and 25 years. One young person, who was not a student, but was interested in the opportunity, ultimately decided not to pursue this because the employment contract and pay rate would affect their welfare payments (Lynch et al., 2024).

The ability of all the peer researchers to contribute to the study was also influenced by formal and informal training. None of the peer researchers had prior experience in research roles, and so skill and capacity development were prioritised. All the peer researchers attended a virtual 10-week induction programme which introduced the study, ethics, methodology, and methods. Peer researchers reported that they welcomed this formal induction phase as an important capacity-building process but questioned the relevance of a health-focussed ethics session and disliked the virtual format (Lynch et al., 2024). Training in analytical methods delivered later in the research cycle was designed to address these concerns. It included interview transcripts from the EXIT study as training materials and was delivered in person at a mutually convenient location.

MacLachlan et al. (2024) have drawn attention to the fact that young people may not fully recognise their abilities or perceive themselves to be 'qualified' enough. In this context, support from a researcher who can recognise their strengths and suggest appropriate roles and opportunities can be useful. In addition to formal training, the peer researchers in EXIT emphasised the valuable role that informal training and support from Research Fellows played in enhancing their ability to contribute. Furthermore, using the A-M-O framework to attend to both peer researchers' skills and interests and mentoring to support them in contributing to the study in ways that built upon their existing skills and enabled them to develop new ones was welcomed (Lynch et al., 2024). Rather than prescribing the activities that peer researchers 'could or should' contribute to, a flexible, relational approach was adopted, which was responsive to peer researchers' unique skills, interests, and availability. As a result, the peer researchers contributed to the study at different points in the research cycle, to different extents, and in varying ways (Lynch et al., 2024).

In the CCTC study, the opportunity to participate in the NLC was open to all care leavers from the participating local authorities, and the research team did not set prescriptive inclusion criteria, in respect of qualifications or prior work experience, in keeping with the principle of inclusivity, irrespective of background and abilities. The desire to include young people with diverse care histories and in different living arrangements was emphasised. Leaving care workers approached young people on behalf of the research team, which contributed to successful recruitment; however, the research team noted that there was limited information about the number or backgrounds of young people who were originally approached to participate. Most of the young people who participated in the NLC were already engaged in advocacy groups. However, pre-existing knowledge and skills were not assumed, and a variety of platforms were used to share material and seek feedback, for example, presentation of findings, breakout rooms, open floor discussions, whiteboards, and interactive polls to create space for everyone to contribute their ideas and share their views.

Respecting and Valuing the Knowledge of All Those Working Together on the Research

In the EXIT study, the research team were explicit that members would bring different knowledge and skills, reflecting their different experiences, roles, training and disciplinary backgrounds. The importance of peer researchers' lived experience of care-leaving was emphasised from the outset and roles and potential contributions were openly discussed. Over the course of the study, the distinction between the peer researchers and the academic team blurred, as the peer researchers' technical and academic experience grew and they took on additional responsibilities (see also, MacLachlan et al., 2024). Peer researchers developed interview skills through a gradual process of piloting interviews within the research team, observing a Research Fellow over time, and steadily building experience of inviting potential interviewees to participate. Towards the end of this process, two peer researchers skilfully led interviews with professionals and care-experienced young people. Research Fellows supported the peer researchers at this latter stage by attending interviews and being available to assist if necessary, and facilitating immediate de-brief sessions, reflecting responsibility and accountability in respect of safeguarding and broader ethical issues. The de-brief sessions provided the opportunity to reflect on any negative impact of the interviewing experience on peer researchers' well-being and their application and development of interviewing skills. Outside of the de-brief sessions, no safeguarding or ethical concerns were raised. Two peer researchers also designed and delivered a presentation at an academic conference with minimal input from Research Fellows, although they offered support and attended the presentations.

The NLC aimed to:

- Foster relational connections and adopt '*knowledge animation*' strategies to support learning within and between local authorities, drawing upon the expertise and experiences of those with different lenses on the system (care-experienced, frontline practitioners, operational managers, and researchers).

- To utilise the 'new knowledge' created through the collaboration to develop accessible tools and resources to support social work practice.

Stoll (2009) defines '*knowledge animation*' as:

> a social process by which practitioners and policy makers make learning connections when engaging with research findings. Knowledge animation is about helping people to learn and use ideas generated elsewhere and through this process create their own knowledge. (p. 1)

In this model, what practitioners and service users know from their own experiences and in their own contexts (tacit knowledge) is of equal importance to what is known from research and theory (explicit knowledge) (Stoll, 2009).

In CCTC, it was acknowledged that '*everyone in the learning community will have different but equally valued experience and perspectives to bring to the study*'. This ethos was communicated via written materials and at each workshop. A range of educational processes were employed to facilitate reflection, collaboration, learning, and action. The sessions were also designed to provide opportunities: to make links between research and practice ('research-practice' bridging); explore similarities and differences in perspectives and learning within local authority teams (care experienced/frontline/managerial); cross-context learning and resource development drawing on collective insights. The NLC community and research team co-developed outputs, including: a resource for social workers and leaving care personal advisors to assist them to consider the implications of the findings in their own local context and recommendations for policy and practice (Munro et al., 2022). During NLC sessions, time was spent discussing language, key terms and phrases, and what should be included in the research outputs. For example, the original proposal for the study specified the aim to explore 'transition pathways' from care whereas later discussions with the NLC led to a change of this term to 'pathways out of care' in final outputs because there was consensus that this felt less technical or 'academic' as a term, and more reflective of real-life experience. Specific recommendations surrounding outcomes data were also shaped by the NLC and encouraged movement away from deficit-oriented measures towards a more balanced narrative, recognising that many of the data items collected are negative, for example, 'substance use', or a number of criminal convictions. New items that were recommended included information about how young people feel they are doing, satisfaction with services received, and the degree to which young people feel involved in pathway planning.

Reciprocity

There is a danger that co-production is experienced as extractive or tokenistic if the experience is not meaningful or beneficial for those with lived experience and/ or practitioners. In EXIT, as part of the action research study, the peer researchers reflected on an important intrinsic motivation to participate by virtue of the study's potential to make a difference to the lives of care leavers in the future. Additional extrinsic factors related to individual benefits associated with capacity-building, including development of more general transferable skills ahead of seeking employment, such as teamwork, and specific research skills in pursuit of post-graduate study (Lynch et al., 2024).

The costs associated with recompensing peer researchers for their time and to facilitate their meaningful participation were built into the EXIT budget. The level of pay was identified as an important motivating factor by peer researchers. A budget was also allocated for travel and subsistence costs to facilitate peer researchers' attendance at in-person meetings and participation in conferences.

In CCTC, young people were provided with vouchers to recognise their time and contributions. Travel and subsistence costs were also covered for all participants. Young people and professionals articulated a range of reasons for participating in the NLC, including: contributing to improvements in leaving care services and practice; learning from other local authorities; listening to young people's views; learning more about the research cycle; and maximising the study's impact. Members of the NLC presented at a conference bringing together care-experienced young people, health and social care professionals, and advocacy organisations to disseminate the findings and the co-developed resources. One of the 'experts by experience' also took part in a radio interview to discuss the research findings and share their views. Identified benefits included: meeting new people, increased confidence, gaining knowledge, and increased hope that the system will change.

Building and Maintaining Relationships

The impact of experiences of abuse and neglect, and discontinuities in placements and relationships in the care system, needs to be considered in the design and delivery of research projects. As others have noted, here and in this wider collection of work, attentiveness to 'care' in research relationships (Farragher et al., 2024) and building trust and promoting relational safety (Bovarnick & Cody, 2021) are important.

In the EXIT study, the budget provided for a participation expert with lived experience from a care leaver-led charity to provide pastoral support for the duration of the study, and this was highly valued by the peer researchers. This allowed space and time to build trust and develop relationships. Each peer researcher was also allocated to work alongside a Research Fellow, aligned to a specific case study site. Preferred frequency and methods of communication were agreed and revisited (in recognition of changes in the nature and extent of the peer researcher's involvement in different aspects of the research and fluctuations in their availability). This consistency, joint working overtime, including in-person fieldwork and a supportive ethos, was valued by the peer researchers, as one reflected:

> Working with [the Research Fellows] that's allowed me to enjoy every week of the project ... they've been very helpful, very supportive, you know they've provided us with lots of opportunities and when we've had problems they've been there to help us,

certainly if that wasn't there, if that whole network was not there, definitely my involvement in this project would not be as enjoyable as it is now. (Peer Researcher Focus Group)

With the benefit of hindsight, arguably, more time and resource should have been allocated to the Research Fellows to support peer researchers' engagement and to provide them with skills and training to fulfil the central role they ultimately played in ensuring participation was a positive experience for the peer researchers (in addition to the dedicated pastoral support provided by the participation expert) (Lynch et al., 2024). This reflects a tendency to under-estimate the time, inter-personal skills, and emotional labour involved in facilitating meaningful co-production in care-leaving research (Kelly, Friel, et al., 2020).

In CCTC, young people attended workshops with workers with whom they had already established relationships. In the initial sessions, relationship-building amongst participants was also prioritised and facilitated through the co-development of a set of principles and values for the group, outlining how everyone should work together in a way that appreciated each person's experiences and views. Additionally, all young people were offered 1-1 discussions with the care-experienced researcher on the project prior to and after the workshop sessions. Consistent communication through newsletters and regular meetings was also established with the aim of fostering trust and engagement.

Peer Researcher's Reflections

For all my adult life since leaving care, I have been motivated to improve social interventions targeted at young people at risk of harm or in contact with children's social care services. This interest has been most profoundly informed by my own journey as a young person navigating the child protection and out-of-home care system. During this time, I was affected by the differences between disjointed care and personalised, trauma-informed intervention grounded in evidence. This underlying motivation has led to commitments to build a strong case for high-quality children's social care nationally, underpinned by effective social policy and upscale. Consistent with these commitments were the aims of the EXIT study and CCTC study, and I felt very positive about putting myself forward to offer my passions and talents to their efforts.

From 2016 to 2021, I was a founding member of the Young Researchers' Advisory Panel (YRAP), a group of young people consulted to support the work of the Safer Young Lives Research Centre (SYLRC) at the University of Bedfordshire. This role offered many opportunities to influence the Centre's work on childhood sexual violence.

As I was ageing out of YRAP, I felt that being offered the opportunity to gain employment and continue to support the work of the Institute through a partner-led project was extremely valuable to me. Up until this point, I had only supported research by SYLRC, primarily on Child Sexual Exploitation (CSE). Being afforded the opportunity to research transitions from care, another element of lived experience for me, was exciting because it gave me an opportunity to expand the skills I had gained in YRAP and utilise them in new research contexts and topic areas. The greater data collection, analysis, and dissemination responsibilities attached to the role helped me gain new skills relevant to the development of my career in academia and my goals of completing doctoral and postdoctoral research.

Activities I engaged in included: undertaking semi-structured interviews, focus group facilitation, audio transcription, thematic analysis, literature reviewing, dissemination through conference presentations, building rapport with case study site participants and stakeholders, improved accessibility of data collection for participants, collaborating with other team members, use of coding and video conferencing software for data collection and analysis.

I was most heavily involved in the case study of a group-based intervention which aims to develop independence skills and enhance the social capital of care leavers at risk of social exclusion, delivered by a leading national children's charity. Throughout the study I contributed to the design and ongoing refinement of research protocols, tools and disseminations processes, both demonstrating my commitment to the authentically experiential learning-informed collection and expression of research data as well as supporting that of the study. I later took a leading role applying many of these principles to a separate strand of the study related to innovations targeted at the mental health of care leavers.

As the role progressed, I took increased responsibility and independence as a researcher, having facilitated semi-structured interviews, transcribed focus group discussion recordings, engaged in thematic analysis, and collaborated extensively with colleagues and project partners to achieve impactful dissemination. I took a leading role in the development of a peer-reviewed journal article and delivered an international conference presentation that critically examined the EXIT study's peer-reviewed research design.

With increased exposure to various research samples, case study settings, and innovations in intervention design and implementation, I have developed a critical insight into and understanding of children's social care far beyond my personal experience, thoroughly informed by both user diversity and the complexity of different practice and policy contexts. Led by my supervisor, I gained valuable experience in collaboration with young research participants in our assigned case study before commencing semi-structured interviews. Changes made as a result of my input were felt to have improved accessibility, aided discussion, and uncovered richer context to the data collected, serving as a useful lesson and one of many examples of the mentorship I benefitted from during my time supporting the study. This personal growth particularly accelerated towards the end of the study, at the beginning of the mental health innovations work.

During my tenure as a peer researcher supporting the EXIT Study, there were times when I needed to step back or reduce my workload from the study, either at times when my education needed to be prioritised or because of poor health. The door was always open for people to come back and contribute in ways that were meaningful and useful to both the study and peer researchers. The design of the peer research role, as well as the supportive nature of academic staff, meant that this could be done without having too much of an adverse impact on the study and afforded much flexibility to me and others in the role.

Key points:

• *Building and maintaining relationships.*
    Building relationships takes time, but it is important to establish trust and facilitate open communication. Allocation of a named and consistent contact within the research team (in addition to access to experts from specialist support services where needed) provides scaffolding that facilitates open communication and young people's meaningful participation. Adequate training and support are needed to equip them with soft skills to fulfil this role. Sufficient time and resources also need to be allocated to 'mentors' so they can invest time in building trusting relationships and in supporting the peer researchers' development.

• *Reflective practice.*
    In EXIT, the A-M-O framework (Applebaum et al., 2000) was adapted to guide reflective conversations with peer researchers and inform planning and review. Regular reflective conversations facilitated identification of skills that had been acquired through participation, as well as exploration of the availability of future opportunities and their alignment to skills that peer researchers wanted to develop (Lynch et al., 2024).

• *Flexibility and adaptability.*
    It is not uncommon to design studies and recruit peer researchers or experts by experience to undertake a pre-defined set of activities. Although opportunities to participate at each stage of the research cycle are desirable, it is important to be flexible and adaptable, recognising individual skills, strengths, and interests, as well as changes in circumstances and fluctuating availability.

• *Networked learning.*
    From the authors' perspectives, the NLC generated rich insights to support the development of accessible resources to increase the likelihood of knowledge utilisation. Bringing together care-experienced young people, frontline practitioners, and managers offered diverse expertise and different insights into system challenges. Although participation was over a relatively short timeframe, towards the end of the study, feedback suggested that engagement had supported relationship-building, learning, and skills development. A more formal evaluation is needed to understand more about the strengths and weaknesses of this approach.

Conclusion

There is no 'one size' fits all guide to co-production or a single formula for co-producing research (NIHR, 2024). Whilst the approaches adopted in the two care-leaving studies differed, applying the NIHR principles of co-production to reflect on learning from both provided a valuable unifying framework. It clearly demonstrated the role that values play in building authentic relationships and disrupting traditional power hierarchies. This includes transparency about the purpose of involvement and the opportunities that may (or may not) be available, as well as valuing different kinds of knowledge (Liabo et al., 2020). Consistent with other accounts, practical considerations, including training and capacity building, adequate and timely support, and the use of a range of communication channels, are also important (Dixon et al., 2018; Kelly, Friel, et al., 2020; Lushey & Munro, 2015).

References

Applebaum, E., Bailey, T., Berg, P., & Kalleberg, A. L. (2000). *Manufacturing advantage: Why high performance work systems pay off.* ILR Press.

Bandola-Gill, J., Arthur, M., & Leng, R. I. (2023). What is co-production? Conceptualising and understanding co-production of knowledge and policy across different theoretical perspectives. *Evidence & Policy, 19*(2), 275–298. https://doi.org/10.1332/1744264 21X16420955772641

Bovarnick, S., & Cody, C. (2021). Putting risk into perspective: Lessons for children and youth services from a participatory advocacy project with survivors of sexual violence in Albania, Moldova and Serbia. *Children and Youth Services Review, 126,* 106003. https://doi.org/10.1016/j.childyouth.2021.106003

Currie, G., Lynch, A., Swan, J., Alderson, H., Friel, S., Harrop, C., Johnson, R. E., Kerridge, G., McGovern, R., & Munro, E. (2025). How to extend pilot innovation in public services: A case of children's social care innovation. *Public Administration, 103*(2), 357–373. https://doi.org/10.1111/padm.13028

Dixon, J., Ward, J., & Blower, S. (2018). "They sat and actually listened to what we think about the care system": The use of participation, consultation, peer research and co-production to raise the voices of young people in and leaving care in England. *Child Care in Practice, 25*(1), 6–21. https://doi.org/10.1080/13575279.2018.1521380

Farragher, R., Göbbels-Koch, P., Horn, J. P., & Smith, A. (2024). Care foundations: Making care central in research with care-experienced people. In S. Keller, I. Oterholm, V. Paulsen, & A. D. van Breda (Eds.), *Living on the edge: Innovative research on leaving care and transitions to adulthood* (pp. 148–168). Policy Press.

Holland, S., Renold, E., Ross, N. J., & Hillman, A. (2010). Power, agency and participatory agendas: A critical exploration of young people's engagement in participative qualitative research. *Childhood, 17*(3), 360–375. https://doi.org/10.1177/0907568210369310

Hopkins, I., Verlander, M., Clarkson, L., & Jacobsen, P. (2024). What do we know about sharing power in co-production in mental health research? A systematic review and thematic synthesis. *Health Expectations, 27*(5), e70014. https://doi.org/10.1111/hex.70014

Kelly, B., Friel, S., McShane, T., Pinkerton, J., & Gilligan, E. (2020). "I haven't read it, I've lived it!" The benefits and challenges of peer research with young people leaving care. *Qualitative Social Work, 19*(1), 108–124. https://doi.org/10.1177/1473325018800370

Kelly, B., McShane, T., Davidson, G., Pinkerton, J., Gilligan, E., & Webb, P. (2016). *Transitions and outcomes for care leavers with mental health and/or intellectual disabilities: Final report.* QUB. https://research.hscni.net/sites/default/files/YOLO%20Final%20Report.pdf

Kelly, B., van Breda, A. D., Santin, O., Bekoe, J., Bukuluki, P., Chereni, A., Frimpong-Manso, K., Jacobs, D., Luwangula, R., Maanyi, M., Makadho, B., Muchiendza, T., Pinkerton, J., & Ringson, J. (2020). *Building positive futures: Exploring a peer research approach to study leaving care in Africa.* Queen's University Belfast.

Liabo, K., Boddy, K., Bortoli, S., Irvine, J., Boult, H., Fredlund, M., Joseph, N., Bjornstad, G., & Morris, C. (2020). Public involvement in health research: What does 'good' look like in practice? *Research Involvement and Engagement, 6*, 1–12. https://doi.org/10.1186/s40900-020-0183-x

Liabo, K., & Roberts, H. (2019). Coproduction and coproducing research with children and their parents. *Archives of Disease in Childhood, 104*(12), 1134–137. https://doi.org/10.1136/archdischild-2018-316387

Lushey, C. (2017). *SAGE research methods cases part 2.* SAGE Publications Ltd. https://methods.sagepub.com/case/peer-research-methodology-challenges-and-solutions

Lushey, C. J., & Munro, E. R. (2015). Participatory peer research methodology: An effective method for obtaining young people's perspectives on transitions from care to adulthood? *Qualitative Social Work, 14*(4), 522–537. https://doi.org/10.1177/1473325014559282

Lynch, A., Friel, S., Munro, E. R., Sultana, M., Hamilton, C.J., Kerridge, G., Oswick, R., Mitchell, T. P., Alderson, H., Harrop, C., McGovern, R., Mohamoud, J., Smart, D., & Currie, G. (2024). Developing care experienced young peoples' participation as peer researchers in an inter-disciplinary study: Applying the 'Ability-Motivation-Opportunity' framework. *European Journal of Social Work*, 1–16. https://doi.org/10.1080/13691457.2024.2424980

MacLachlan, A., Pemmasani, P., Jamieson-Mackenzie, I., McMellon, C., Cunningham, E., Lewis, R., & Tisdall, E. K. M. (2024). Applying co-production principles in research: Reflections from young people and academics. *Childhood, 31*(3), 309–328. https://doi.org/10.1177/09075682241269692

Mannay, D., Staples, E., Hallett, S., Roberts, L., Rees, A., Evans, R., & Andrews, D. (2019). Enabling talk and reframing messages: Working creatively with care experienced children and young people to recount and re-represent their everyday experiences. *Child Care in Practice, 25*(1), 51–63. https://doi.org/10.1080/13575279.2018.1521375

Munro, E. R., Friel, S., Baker, C., Lynch, A., Walker, K., Williams, J., Cook, E., & Chater, A. (2022). *Care leavers' transitions to adulthood in the context of COVID-19: Understanding pathways, experiences and outcomes to improve policy and practice.* University of Bedfordshire.

Munro, E. R., Kelly, B., Mannay, D., & McGhee, K. (2024). Comparing leaving-care policy and practice across the four nations of the United Kingdom: Exploring similarities, differences, and implementation gaps. *Journal of Comparative Policy Analysis: Research and Practice, 26*(2), 178–195. https://doi.org/10.1080/13876988.2024.2317234

Munro, E. R., Lushey, C., National Care Advisory Service, Maskell-Graham, D., Ward, H., & Holmes, L. (2012). *Evaluation of the staying put: 18+ family placement programme pilot: Final report. Research report DFERR191.* Department for Education.

Munro, E. R., & Kelly, B. (2025). United Kingdom. In T. Rafaeli & V. Mann-Feder (Eds.), *Leaving care around the world: Twenty years of the international network on transitions to adulthood from care* (pp. XX-XX). Oxford University Press.

National Institute for Health and Care Research (NIHR). (2024). *Guidance on co-producing a research project.* NIHR. https://www.learningforinvolvement.org.uk/content/resource/nihr-guidance-on-co-producing-a-research-project/

Purtell, J. (2024). Trauma-informed research with young people transitioning from care: Balancing methodological rigour with participatory and empowering practice. In S. Keller, I. Oterholm, V. Paulsen, & A. D. van Breda (Eds.), *Living on the edge: Innovative research on leaving care and transitions to adulthood* (pp. 129–147). Policy Press. https://doi.org/10.51952/9781447366317.ch007

Reason, P., & Bradbury, H. (Eds.) (2008). *The SAGE handbook of action research*. SAGE Publications Ltd.

Stoll, L. (2009). Knowledge animation in policy and practice: Making connections [Paper presented]. *The annual meeting of the American Educational Research Association*, San Diego, 13–17.

United Nations. (2009). *UN Committee on the rights of the child. General comment No. 12: The right of the child to be heard*. United Nations. https://www2.ohchr.org/english/bodies/crc/docs/AdvanceVersions/CRC-C-GC-12.pdf

Williams, O., Sarre, S., Papoulias, S.C., Knowles, S., Robert, G., Beresford, P., Rose, D., Carr, S., Kaur, M., & Palmer, V. J. (2020). Lost in the shadows: Reflections on the dark side of co-production. *Health Research Policy and Systems*, *18*, 43. https://doi.org/10.1186/s12961-020-00558-0

Yang, C., & Dibb, Z. (2020). Peer research in the UK. *Working Paper. Institute for Community Studies*. The Young Foundation. http://pub344.jb4-2.eprints-hosting.org/id/ep

Index